Born in Adelaide, Shane Mensforth w[...]
mad family. He played Under 17s and[...]
Woodville in the SANFL before training as a teacher with the
South Australian Department of Education and ultimately being
sent to Whyalla. His schoolteaching days were short-lived,
however, and after just a few years in the classroom, he left the
Education Department to pursue a career in journalism.

Always keen on the outdoors and sports of any kind, he began
contributing to several national fishing and boating magazines,
and was soon a regular feature writer and columnist for some of
the bestselling titles in the country. In 1985 he bought a 50 per
cent share in *South Australian Angler* magazine, which he owns
outright today. As well as organising his own publication, he is
editor of the national quarterly *Sportfishing Marine and Trailer
Boats* and is also a weekly columnist for *The Advertiser* newspaper
in Adelaide.

Shane is married to Merrilyn and has three 'grown-up'
children.

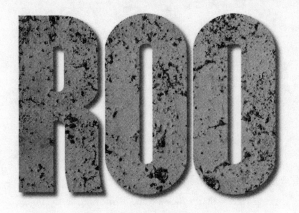

ROO

MARK RICCIUTO
and Shane Mensforth

MACMILLAN
Pan Macmillan Australia

First published 2007 in Macmillan by Pan Macmillan Australia Pty Limited
1 Market Street, Sydney

National Library of Australia
Cataloguing-in-Publication data:

Mensforth, Shane.
Roo.

ISBN 978 1 4050 3825 6 (pbk.).

1. Ricciuto, Mark. 2. Australian football players – South
Australia – Biography. 3. Australian football – South
Australia. I. Title.

796.336092

Typeset in 12/16pt Janson by Midland Typesetters, Australia
Printed in Australia by McPherson's Printing Group

CONTENTS

FOREWORD BY NEIL KERLEY

I felt very honoured when asked to write a foreword for this book. Mark Ricciuto has undoubtedly become one of South Australia's greatest ever footballers and sporting personalities.

His name first came to my notice in 1991 while I was Football Manager for the Adelaide Crows. Although Mark was only sixteen at that stage, there were some big wraps on this kid from Waikerie, where he was playing as an A Grade footballer. I rang his dad, Murray, who arranged to hold a car-parking space on the oval fence for me.

We sat there, chatting with Mark's older brother, Craig, who had suffered a serious knee injury. Mark had been playing at centre half back and I was keen to see how someone so young would handle that position against bigger, stronger men. I was naturally disappointed that the Waikerie coach had decided to play the boy out of a forward pocket that afternoon, but as the game wore on, my disappointment evaporated. He ended up kicking ten goals in a great display, and I knew there and then that we had to get this kid for the Crows.

After a few beers with his mum and dad, and some reflecting during the two-hour return drive to Adelaide, I knew this boy's future lay in the Big Smoke.

Little did I realise at that time that I would be his coach at West Adelaide during the following season and a half. Mark proved an absolute joy to coach, and it was obvious he wouldn't be wearing red and black for long.

Not only has Mark Ricciuto gone on to be a great player for the Crows, he is also a great leader of men. He will be remembered as a true champion of the game and an inspirational captain.

Well done, Mark. You are a credit to yourself, your family, and to our great game of Australian Rules Football.

INTRODUCTION

The term 'champion' is one that is used both liberally and indiscriminately, especially when it comes to elite, high-level sport. By simple definition, a champion is someone who is clearly ahead of the rest; someone who is the first or best of all competitors. Seemingly, each time you open the sports section of a newspaper or watch a TV news sports report, there will be a focus on at least one 'champion' from one field or another. It's a term that has been thrust at us on a regular basis for as long as sporting commentators have had our ears.

In reality, there are few true sporting champions – certainly far fewer than the media would have us believe. When it comes to Australian Rules Football, there may be a handful in a given era who fulfil the criteria and wear the tag well. Names like Bob Skilton, Robert Harvey, Leigh Matthews, Gary Ablett, Malcolm Blight, Tony Lockett and Wayne Carey spring to mind as genuine champions of the game; they have all won the consistent acclaim of critics, received countless high-profile awards, represented their home states on numerous occasions and displayed outstanding longevity in the sport.

In its relatively short history, the Adelaide Football Club has bred an elite band of top-level players. Rehn, McLeod, Hart, Smart, Goodwin, Edwards and Modra are part of the AFC elite, but only one individual can, in the strictest sense of the word, be called a true champion.

Mark Ricciuto came to the Adelaide Crows as a pimply-faced teenager after playing just a handful of games in the South Australian National Football League. Born and raised in the Riverland, he showed outstanding sporting prowess as a junior and it didn't take long for those at the highest level to notice his youthful achievements and recognise his obvious talent. It was South Australia's 'Mr Football', Neil Kerley, who played the key role in getting Mark to West Adelaide and, ultimately, to the Crows.

The Ricciuto family, and particularly parents Carolyn and Murray, were the driving force behind Mark's early entry into elite sport. Both made huge sacrifices to ensure their son had every opportunity to succeed in the 'Big League', with Murray driving back and forth between Waikerie and Adelaide several times a week to enable Mark to train and, ultimately, play in West Adelaide's senior team. They also provided him with a traditional country upbringing, where love, advice, warmth and a keen work ethic were all key components of his development.

Mark's achievements at the highest level in the country's most revered team sport have been well documented: a Brownlow Medal, Premiership medallion, three Club Champion awards, six State of Origin selections, eight All-Australian selections, dual All-Australian captaincy . . . the list is indeed an impressive one. However, his life achievements are equally impressive, and this is what elevates Mark Ricciuto above many of his elite sporting counterparts.

I first met Mark at four o'clock on an uncomfortably warm

summer morning in 1995. He was sitting on the front fence at the home of fellow Crows player Andrew Jarman awaiting collection for a hastily organised pre-dawn fishing excursion to Victor Harbor. Being the affable gent he is, Jarman had taken Mark under his wing at the club and, as he knew of the young lad's penchant for fishing, phoned me to arrange an offshore trip.

We had a great time that morning, catching plenty of fish and enjoying the trademark Jarman antics. Obvious from the outset was Ricciuto's love of the fresh air, the water, and the camaraderie that develops from spending time with mates in the great outdoors – traits instilled in him by his Riverland upbringing. He appealed to me immediately; as a fanatical Crows supporter, I knew of his football ability and potential in the game, but there was obviously a lot more to this country boy than just the talent and tenacity we had all seen on the footy field.

Mark Ricciuto's distinguished football career is now drawing towards its inevitable conclusion. Unlike some before him, he's not the sort of guy who will play beyond his use-by date. He knows when enough is enough and has long been planning for life after footy. His investments, business interests and, above all, a new family will consume Mark's time when he ultimately hangs up his boots.

His on-field presence will be missed by the Adelaide Crows; team leadership will pass on and a handful of teenagers will pull on the club tri-colours for the first time in Mark's final season. One or two of them will make it in the Big League and maybe – just maybe – there will be a potential club captain among them.

Undoubtedly, the biggest obstacle I have had to overcome while extracting information for this book was getting past Mark's humility. He had been keen to record his life in football for some time, but had resisted the temptation because talking about himself is definitely not a Ricciuto trait. His insistence on keeping his achievements tempered and handing out credit to those around him was always evident during our interview sessions. There are a couple of chapters for which Mark provided the information exclusively on a digital voice recorder. These dealt with segments of his life he preferred to talk about in private, as he knew emotion would intervene if we spoke face to face.

At his Brownlow Medal acceptance speech in September 2003, Mark opened by saying the three most important things in his life were football, family and friends. He gave no indication as to the order in which the three components fitted, but I'm certain it will become obvious as you read on.

I'm sure I can safely say that, in the strictest definition of the term, Mark Ricciuto is a champion; not just a champion AFL footballer, but a champion human being. I've enjoyed recording his life story immensely and I hope all football devotees, regardless of team allegiance, will enjoy what follows.

1

THE EARLY YEARS

On 8 June 1975, Mark Anthony Ricciuto was born, and spent most of his formative years, on a 40-acre (sixteen-hectare) fruit block near the South Australian Riverland town of Waikerie. A 'backyard' of this size was every young boy's idea of paradise, providing unlimited opportunities to do what most kids in the city can only ever dream about. Trail bike riding, fishing, yabby-ing, catching lizards and chasing rabbits were part of an average day for the Ricciuto youngsters, Lisa, Craig and Mark. They all learned to water-ski at an early age and generally revelled in the lifestyle the Riverland offered.

In the 1970s and 1980s, Waikerie was a friendly, progressive town, with everything needed for a comfortable existence. The schools were good, the facilities were first class, and there were unlimited opportunities for any youngster with a keen interest in competitive sport. It was very much an agricultural community, with wine grapes, fruits and vegetables responsible for much of the region's employment. Forty-acre fruit blocks were commonplace, and most were owned and farmed by family businesses. There were plenty of growers of European origin throughout the Riverland, most of whom toiled hard to make a living from stone and citrus fruits, and assorted vegetables. Many were second- and third-generation farmers and, as is the case in most walks of life, some succeeded while others fell by the wayside.

The Ricciuto 'block' was typical of most on the outskirts of Waikerie. Mark's parents, Carolyn and Murray, worked long days to ensure a good crop, occasionally employing outside help during the busy times, but generally carrying the load themselves. Mark and his brother and sister became important team members as well, often working after school and on weekends to help out. Although they understood that working on the block was vital to the wellbeing of the family business, the Ricciuto youngsters were often frustrated at having to pick fruit and tend to the vegetables while many of their schoolmates were out catching yabbies or kicking a football. But making sacrifices was always part of the Riverland fruit block culture and something most families of immigrants took for granted.

Grapes, stone fruit and citrus fruit were the mainstays of the Ricciuto block in the 1980s, with tomatoes, zucchinis, button squash, pumpkin and olives handy supplements. Most of the vegetable crops ripened in the summer months, when Riverland temperatures regularly pushed beyond 40 degrees. The work was also hard on the back, but the family operated as a team and got by, while many others struggled. This grounding in teamwork, and the strong work ethic instilled in him as a young lad, would go a long way towards helping Mark achieve success later in life.

None of the Ricciuto clan has ever been afraid to get dirt on their hands. In 1927, at the age of eighteen, Mark's 'Nonno' (grandfather), Nicola, left his young wife and his home town of Fragneto Monforte, in Benevento Province, Italy, equipped with little more than a change of clothes, an English phrase book and a keen sense of adventure. His initial ambition was to settle in America, where there was already a strong Italian community and the employment opportunities seemed lucrative. However, the emigration authorities intervened and he ultimately found himself on a ship bound for Australia. Accompanying him was a long-time friend, Joe DeVito, who was also seeking in a foreign country the life opportunities that simply didn't exist at that time in Italy.

The lads' first job in their new country was picking peas and clearing wattlebark trees at Noarlunga, south of Adelaide. They then moved to the cane fields in Queensland, where they took on the excruciating job of cutting sugar cane by hand. Racism was rife during that era, and both Ricciuto and DeVito were targets of abuse from the locals. From Queensland, the pair travelled back to Adelaide. Clearing mallee trees in the Adelaide Hills for farmland got them by for a while, but with high expectations and a little cash, they made their way to Melbourne and opened a small fruit stall in the Queen Victoria Market. This venture prospered temporarily, but the polio epidemic that swept through the country, and particularly Victoria, in the 1930s hit all businesses hard and soon they were forced to return to South Australia, where work was easier to find.

Picking fruit was something the two young immigrants knew well, and they soon found themselves in the Riverland, working for several of the long-established growers. The lifestyle suited them and, as there were already quite a few other Italians working in the region, they decided to settle there. Nicola eventually earned enough to buy a parcel of land at Ramco, on the Murray, where he built a small but comfortable house and began cultivating his own fruit and vegetables. Joe DeVito did the same a little closer to Waikerie, and the pair decided that this was where they would stay.

In 1936, after becoming established, Nicola and Joe returned to Italy to collect their wives, Carmelina and Lolanda, who were sisters. Nicola made sure he secured just a six-month re-entry permit to his native country to avoid being conscripted into the army. The two couples then made the journey together back to Australia, where they began a totally new life.

Ultimately, the Ricciutos raised six children on their Ramco property, including Mark's father, Mario, who is better known around the Riverland these days as Murray.

Murray and Carolyn, Mark's mother, met at Waikerie High School. Carolyn's family had moved to the Riverland from Blackwood, in the Adelaide Hills and, although she wasn't enthusiastic about the move at first, she soon settled into rural life. She was charmed by Murray's strong Italian heritage.

Life wasn't easy for any of the Italian immigrants, and most existed on what they could grow or raise on the land. Keeping chickens was commonplace, both for meat and eggs, as was growing fruit and vegetables, butchering their own stock, and making their own pasta and pasta sauce.

Growing tomatoes was always significant to the Italian community, and making pasta sauce became an important family tradition. When the tomatoes were sufficiently ripe, some of the children were given the job of crushing the fruit, while others poured the puree into bottles, added mint, secured the caps and wrapped the bottles in newspaper. Each was then carefully stacked in a 44-gallon drum, under which a fire was lit. The puree would then be left to simmer for several hours. This process would produce enough traditional Italian pasta sauce to last the family for the entire year. Years later, the annual ritual of helping to bottle the sauce was a firmly entrenched family tradition, and one Mark, his brother Craig and sister Lisa and their cousins eagerly looked forward to. There may well be a Mark Ricciuto brand of pasta sauce some day!

Wine making was another family tradition. Nicola Ricciuto and his family loved rich Italian wines, and Mark remembers fondly the hours he and Craig spent in their grandfather's wine vat, crushing grapes with their bare feet. Olive oil, meat and the other foodstuffs produced on the property were all shared among the extended family. The children made their own sausages from sheep's intestines, and their first 'football' had been a sheep's bladder. These were memorable times that strengthened the family bond and instilled a deep sense of tradition in all the Ricciuto offspring.

Both Mark and Craig were sports mad at an early age. In fact, Mark remembers wondering what else there would be to do in life if there were no sport. They played cricket, golf and tennis during the summer, then football as soon as the weather cooled down. Mark was a huge fan of the West Indies cricket team, which was at the peak of its fame in the 1980s. He bowled hundreds of overs in the backyard at Craig, calling himself 'Big Bird' after the Caribbean fast bowler, Joel Garner. So taken was Mark with Garner, he asked his mother to make him a West Indies uniform and even tried to darken his skin.

Mark and Craig shared a bedroom, the walls of which were covered in football, cricket and car posters. Craig would hear Mark talking in his sleep about the number of fish he had caught, goals he had kicked or wickets he had taken. Being the youngest of three, Mark regularly got away with things Craig and Lisa couldn't and he became the master of 'skipping out' when there was work to be done.

Football was always number one on the brothers' list of sporting priorities, and if they weren't kicking a football out in the street, they were watching the game on television or reading about it in the newspapers. Neither could keep still for more than a few moments and drove Carolyn to distraction with the games played indoors. The Mike Brady song 'Up There Cazaly' became their anthem. The boys would pile all the lounge suite cushions on the floor, turn up the volume on the record player, then throw a football in the air and jump up to take spectacular marks. Ornaments and furniture were occasionally broken – but fortunately, the boys' bones were spared.

The local Italian Club was always a popular venue with the Waikerie/Ramco crowd. The first Sunday of every month saw practically all the local Italian families gather for food, wine and games. As had been the tradition for generations, the women would congregate in the kitchen, preparing a pasta feast, while their husbands played bocce or gambled at cards. Quite a few dollars changed hands around the card table, and it was here that Mark learned a comprehensive repertoire of Italian swear words, which would come in handy in later years during exchanges with umpires and opposing players. The swearing that went on around the card table was all in good fun. The Italian Club gatherings were significant in promoting a sense of togetherness and community spirit among the immigrants who had made their homes in the district. They also enabled ideas on farming practices to be discussed and shared. Successful growers regularly passed on hints to those who weren't enjoying such good yields, making the whole local industry much stronger and more stable.

This practice of sticking together and providing assistance whenever needed became very important in the mid-1980s, when Riverland orange growers were hit hard by the government's decision to allow cheaper Brazilian-grown orange concentrate to be brought into Australia. This knocked the stuffing out of the local industry. With prices for Riverland fruit plummeting to below cost, many growers went to the wall. Times were tough for the Ricciutos, DeVitos and others with a big investment in orange groves, and they became even tougher when Turkish apricots arrived on the market as well. Although they lacked the taste of the home-grown fruit, they sold well in local markets. That was the thing about being a primary producer, the Riverland market gardeners complained: you could do everything right, grow top-quality fruit and still never be guaranteed of selling it in the right quantities or at the right price. Overseas imports aside, there would always be seasonal fluctuations to contend with and a traditionally unstable market, which made the whole business unpredictable.

Somehow the Ricciutos pushed through all this adversity, with Mark, Craig and Lisa being taught plenty of valuable life lessons along the way. They quickly learned that things are often beyond one's control, and all three of Murray and Carolyn's children discovered that building contingency plans is an important survival skill. In fact, having to deal with hardship, and ultimately coming through it as a better person, is the significant life lesson that Mark has taken from his teenage years.

Few of the Riverland growers of that era made a good living from their fruit blocks, so looking after the money they earned was of paramount importance. In fact, this was one of the Ricciuto family's 'golden rules'. Mark learned early in life to accumulate what he could while he could, then to save or invest it wisely – an axiom that he would take into both his football career and his later life in general.

The strong work ethic that had always been encouraged during Mark's childhood came to the fore in his early teenage years, and particularly so when he began thinking about buying his first car. He had always been impressed by good-looking automobiles and was aware that the only way he would ever own one was to save hard and buy it himself. His parents certainly weren't well enough off to contribute. Mark knew how hard they worked to put food on the table and he expected little in the way of handouts from them. All three children knew that if they wanted something badly enough, they would have to work for it.

Mark initiated a plan that would enable him to afford a car by the time he was old enough to have a driver's licence. Along with the work required of him by his parents on the home property, there was often more to be had on the fruit blocks of neighbours. Mark resolved to earn at least $1000 during the summer holidays each year. He would put the money away and not touch it until there was enough to buy the car he wanted. It's the sort of plan many teenagers come up with as a way to purchase their first car, but few of them ever follow through with it.

Cutting apricots was far from an enjoyable way to earn extra cash, but it was readily available work and Mark embraced it during most summer holidays with surprising determination. The going rate was around a dollar a tray. If the fruit was a good size and he worked flat out, Mark could cut four trays an hour, or around 30 trays for an eight-hour day. This meant 33 days' work to achieve his goal of saving $1000 in a given holiday period. Always looking to maximise his return for effort, and to gain an edge over others doing the same job, Mark devised a plan with Craig and a couple of mates, who were picking the apricots he was cutting. As larger fruit made it easier to fill the trays, he got Craig to three-quarters fill his crates with large apricots, then top them up with a few very small ones. Mark's fellow cutters would ignore the crates with the small 'decoy' apricots on top, and he would then choose those and get to work, wearing a grin from ear to ear.

Eventually, Mark also began to pick the apricots, and the $1000 he saved each summer soon became $2000. By the time he was seventeen, he had accumulated close to $10,000 and could comfortably afford to buy a VH series Holden Commodore V8.

2

LEARNING THE BASICS

Mark's earliest recollections of football go back to the Waikerie Under 10s, where his brother had been playing for a couple of years and his father was coach. Mark had always been impressed with the gear footballers wore and, although he didn't understand much of the game at age five, he had declared then he wanted to play. Murray and Carolyn weren't too sure about this, as Mark was about half the size of the others in the team, but they admired his courage and eventually relented. They bought him a pair of boots, socks and shorts, which he put on in front of an old three-element radiator while watching his favourite cartoons on TV. This was where his fighting spirit first showed itself, as he declared that if *he* were the coyote, the Road Runner would have been caught long ago. It appeared that the football career of Mark Ricciuto was about to take off.

Finding a jumper small enough to fit Mark was the Ricciutos' first dilemma. Waikerie had two Under 10 teams in those days, the Magpies and the Tigers, and before going down to the ground to organise the lads for the first match of the season, Murray sorted through the guernseys and eventually found one that didn't look ridiculous on his younger son. All kitted out and full of enthusiasm, Mark sat down in the change-rooms with the rest of the squad to listen to his father's pre-game address. Around the country there were probably many other potential League footballers doing the same thing at the same time.

However, just when all seemed in readiness for Mark Ricciuto's first game, he announced that he wanted out. He had spent much of the pre-match time looking around at the rest of the boys in the team, most of whom were aged between eight and ten, before suddenly deciding that discretion may indeed be the better part of valour. In tears, he told his dad that it might be better if he waited a while before making his debut. The coach was more than a little relieved to have his son on the sidelines watching the game, instead of getting knocked around by boys twice his size – at least for a year or so.

The following season, Mark overcame his jitters and took to the field for the first time. With his dad at the helm and his big brother out there to look after him, he enjoyed the Saturday morning games on Waikerie Primary School's top oval. It seemed a huge arena at the time, but when he looks at the ground these days, he wonders how 36 kids and an umpire could fit on it. It's just one decent AFL kick from end to end!

Mark played several seasons in the Waikerie Under 10s, learning the basics of the game from his father and becoming a profic- ient junior footballer by the time he was ready to move on to the next age class. Football was beginning to become an obsession with both Ricciuto boys by this stage; in fact, they would play in the Waikerie Junior competition on Saturday mornings, then ride their bikes to nearby Ramco and play a second game in another league. As they didn't have the correct socks or shorts for the afternoon matches, they usually just threw on a guernsey and played in their jeans and sneakers. They were never sure if this was within the rules, but rules meant little to Mark or his mates, Troy and Jason Lehmann, who were equally passionate about the game.

In 1987 Mark was selected in the state primary school team, which travelled to Canberra for a national carnival. His first representative venture didn't start well when he discovered he was to be billeted by a girl, while the rest of the squad were to stay with boys. After copping a bit of stick from the other boys in the team over the billeting arrangements, Mark phoned his parents, who travelled to Canberra to sort out the mess. Fortunately, they had a friend who had moved to the capital from Waikerie. Mark stayed with the family, salvaging his pride and saving him from exposure to what he termed 'girls' germs', which he had feared would infect him and rule him out of playing.

Other future AFL players involved in the event included Scott Camporeale, who would go on to play many high-quality games for Carlton and, later, Essendon.

On his father's advice, Mark always played outside of his age group in the Waikerie competition. Murray knew that his son had plenty of potential and that the challenge of competing against older lads would serve the dual purpose of toughening him up and refining his skills. Mark enjoyed playing in the same side as Craig, who was three years older and also showed signs of progressing to the top level. They played in the Waikerie Under 16s together in 1988, where Mark more than held his own as a thirteen-year-old.

Further state representation came at the Under 15 level in 1990, when he again played in the national carnival and was chosen as best player overall. This earned him his first All-Australian jumper, and he backed up the following year with a Teal Cup Championship in Darwin and a second All-Australian spot.

Craig Ricciuto graduated from age-level football in 1989 and went on to play in the Senior team, while Mark stayed back to be an integral part of an Under 16 Premiership. West Adelaide had been keeping a close eye on the progress of both brothers and made their first official overtures to Mark in 1990 when he had turned fifteen. Westies' president Doug Thomas made his club's intentions clear: they wanted Mark to move to Adelaide. They offered to pay for private school education, and cheques kept arriving in the mail as sign-on incentives, one of which was for $3000 – an amount that it would take Mark nearly two summers spent cutting apricots to earn – but he resisted the temptation to accept. His heart was very much in the Riverland, and while he was still being challenged in the local league, he saw no real advantage in shifting to the Big Smoke.

In 1991, after winning the Colts' medal for the best player in the Under 16 competition, Mark decided he was ready to play in Waikerie's A grade team. He was certainly well skilled by that stage, and although he was aware that his opponents would be bigger and the hits would be harder, he was prepared for the challenge. There would be no tears or pulling out this time. He was ready to go.

The Riverland A Grade competition during that era was right up there with the best regional leagues in South Australia. Most of the players worked on the land, so they were tough and uncompromising and few were impressed by the prospect of being taken on by a fifteen-year-old upstart. Mark was still a scrawny lad and was grateful that his older brother would be there to look after him. Craig was physically bigger than Mark and didn't take kindly to rough treatment from the opposition. Mark recalls being 'king hit' at Waikerie Oval in a match early that season; when he came to, he could see Craig with the opposition offender in a headlock and throwing him around like a rag doll.

While he took a few games to adjust to the tempo of Senior football, Mark soon found his feet and made a quick impression on everyone around him. So successful was this transition from Juniors to Seniors, in fact, he won the club's Best and Fairest award in his inaugural season and was suddenly big news in his home town. Local commentators remarked that, like Muhammad Ali, he could 'float like a butterfly, but sting like a bee'. Waikerie Football Club had been in the doldrums for some time; they hadn't won an A Grade Premiership for seventeen years – since before Mark was born. They had reached the Grand Final on a couple of occasions, but hadn't been able to take the ultimate step. The newly formed Adelaide Crows' (Adelaide Football Club) most famous full forward, Tony Modra, kicked the winning goal after the siren to pinch the 1990 Premiership for Renmark, and Waikerie desperately needed a flag to restore confidence and enthusiasm.

There was plenty of buzz and hype at both West Adelaide (in the South Australian National Football League) and Adelaide (now in the Australian Football League) about Mark's achievements. The season had been a good one for the youngster – so good, in fact, that Neil ('Knuckles') Kerley, Football Operations Manager for the Crows and coach of West Adelaide, travelled to Waikerie to watch him play in the last minor-round game. Mark had little warning that Kerley would be in the crowd. Just fifteen minutes before the first bounce, his good mate Matt Western alerted him: 'Hey, Roo. "Knuckles" is here to see you play, so you'd better make sure you get a kick. He's probably got his chequebook in his pocket.'

Kerley had long since attained legend status in South Australian football circles, and young Ricciuto was nervous at the thought of being under his scrutiny. 'Knuckles' was well known for his intimidating manner. The match would be Mark's first taste of real pressure.

Kerley had arranged with Murray Ricciuto to make the lightning visit, and the pair sat together in the outer, from where they would watch the game while having a few beers.

'Where's the boy going to play?' Kerley asked Murray.

'We're down a goal kicker, so I reckon they're going to start him up in the forward pocket,' Murray replied.

'I didn't drive all this way to watch him play in a pocket!' Kerley snapped. He wanted to see the youngster start in the centre, where he thought his skills would be better showcased. However, Kerley left the ground more than satisfied after Mark had kicked his tenth goal and was clearly best on the field. Neil Kerley's report to the Adelaide Football Club, dated 17 August 1991, makes for interesting reading:

Mark has been playing centre half back in the A Grade for the last six weeks, but on Saturday played permanent forward pocket, where he kicked 10 goals. Mark has a good football brain, reads the play well, and shows good team work. Very strong in the air (and will get better) with good hands. Leads well and hits the ball hard, with his body staying on line.

His ground work is sound, but I feel needs some attention. His kicking action is good, but does have a habit of waving the ball about as he comes in to kick. (Needs attention)

He attacks the ball well for one so young in senior company.

Has a good attitude and works very well to improve himself. Summing up – A very good prospect for an AFL career. Mum and dad are very keen, when he completes his schooling, for that to happen.

* * *

It's not often a sixteen-year-old gets to win a Senior Best and Fairest award and to play in a Grand Final in his first year, but that's where Mark found himself in September 1991. Even at that age he recognised the significance of what he had achieved. If Waikerie could eclipse Loxton North on the Barmera Oval that day, it would certainly provide a dream start to his career in Senior football. The inaugural Adelaide Crows ruckman, Mark Mickan, and the much-respected Michael Taylor would be there on the day to watch him play, but for Mark the prospect of being part of a Premiership side pushed from his mind any thoughts of performing for the 'heavies' from Adelaide.

Mark recalls that match as being one of the most memorable in his 25 years in the game. The teams were locked together at five goals apiece at quarter-time; it was 11 goals each at half time and 18 to 17 at the last break. Waikerie ended on top after a tense last quarter, winning the match with 23 goals 12 to Loxton North's 22 goals 6. It was a top-class affair, with some of the best passages of play ever seen in the Riverland competition. Mark was rated second best on the ground and was elated at both the result and his own form. The Waikerie doldrums were instantly a thing of the past, and Mark Ricciuto had played an integral role in securing the win.

During Mark's days as a junior player, end-of-season football trips had been tame, well-organised affairs. That was all about to change. Following the A Grade Premiership, the team travelled to Port Pirie, where the still under-age Mark celebrated with his team-mates their club's long-overdue Grand Final win by consuming copious amounts of alcohol. But it was both a happy and a sad time for Mark, who knew that his Riverland football days had come to an end. From running around in an oversized jumper as a six-year-old, to starring in the Waikerie Seniors less than a decade later, the road had been both challenging and exciting. His biggest challenge, however, lay just around the corner.

Like most who are keen to play football at the elite level, Mark would have to prove himself first in the SANFL. This was where he would gain valuable experience and prepare himself physically for the ultimate challenge ahead. Adelaide's local competition is highly regarded within national football circles and a season with West Adelaide was exactly what Mark needed before taking the next step.

3

A PLAYER OF PROMISE

West Adelaide's overtures to Mark as a sixteen-year-old reached a new level after the 1991 Riverland Grand Final. The club stepped up its efforts to woo him to the city, offering to pay for a place at Sacred Heart College where he could complete Year 12. Mark was flattered by all the attention from an SANFL club, but his ties with Waikerie and his family were still very strong. While he wanted to take the next step in football, he wasn't yet ready to leave home. He signed for both the West Adelaide Seniors side and the Adelaide Crows, who were also acutely aware of the youngster's talent.

Adelaide Football Club's Bill Sanders and Neil Kerley drove to the Riverland's Waikerie Hotel to secure Mark's signature. The deal was sealed with a drink after the paperwork had been completed – beers all around for everyone except Mark, who was still two years away from his first legal taste of alcohol. If he snuck in a celebratory drink when he got home, he could probably be forgiven.

Mark's first official correspondence from the Adelaide Football Club was dated 22 October 1991 and read as follows:

Dear Mark,

An invitation is extended to you to attend pre-season training with the Adelaide Football Club.

The training programme and other details will be given at the first session, which commences on 28th October at 5.00pm.

Please report to change room Number 1 at Football Park, where you will be met by our Football Manager, Mr. Neil Kerley. Track shoes will be required for this session.

Yours sincerely,
Adelaide Football Club Ltd.
W.B. Sanders,
General Manager.

The alternative to relocating to Adelaide involved a tedious amount of travel. In 1992, Mark began Year 12 at Waikerie High. As soon as school got out on Tuesday afternoons, Mark would jump in the family's VL Commodore with Murray and make the 400-kilometre return journey to Adelaide's Richmond Oval. So as not to fall behind with his studies, Mark would work on his homework assignments by torchlight in the passenger's seat.

After training, they would get back in the car and on to the Sturt Highway again, bound for home. Quite often the pair would stop for a bucket of fried chicken or other take-away food on the return leg – something that as a top-level footballer he would later steer clear of. The trip was repeated on Saturdays, when Mark would line up for West Adelaide in the afternoon and be back in Waikerie that evening in time for a late dinner.

After completing his first summer training campaign at SANFL level, Mark was picked to play in a pre-season game at Laura, in the state's mid-north. It was a stinking-hot day, and many of the players on the bus became desperately thirsty during the long road trip. Coach Neil Kerley, however, refused their request to stop for a drink. The players argued that, given the conditions in which they would have to play, it might be wise to drink lots of water in the lead-up to the game. Kerley disagreed. He reminded the squad that camels could go for days without taking a drink, and said that anyone in his side who couldn't do likewise was just weak. No one was game enough to point out to Kerley that camels don't play football; they just stand around.

Despite being just sixteen years of age, Mark's debut at SANFL level was an auspicious one. He kicked three goals from centre wing in that pre-season encounter and earned praise from several astute critics. He went on to play in every league match for which he was available that season, missing just a couple with an ankle injury and another when called upon for the Teal Cup team.

Such was his enthusiasm for competitive sport in general, Mark also immersed himself in school athletics while playing Seniors for West Adelaide. Sports Day was always a big event at Waikerie High, and although he knew it wouldn't go down well with Westies' administration – and Neil Kerley, in particular – if they found out about it, Mark decided to tackle the complete program of school sports events. He ran the 1500 metres, 800 metres, 400 metres and 100 metres, as well as competing in the long jump, high jump, hurdles, discus, javelin and shot put – hardly the ideal preparation for his fourth Senior SANFL game, which was to be played under lights at Football Park that evening. He stood Redleg tough man Garry MacIntosh, who was at the peak of his career, and did well enough to avoid any backlash about the toll the day's physical efforts may have taken. In his bag were five gold medals.

As was to be expected, however, Mark's school workload, and a travelling schedule that involved two trips a week to the city to train and play for West Adelaide, then a third to train on Sunday mornings for the Teal Cup side, eventually caught up with him. He recalls lying on the lounge-room floor at Waikerie one Sunday morning and flatly refusing to make the road trip to Adelaide. He had simply had enough. He had already played Teal Cup under Russell Ebert the year before and couldn't see the value in going through it all again. It took Murray Ricciuto quite a bit of fancy talking to get his son back on track, but eventually he convinced Mark that captaining the state at the Under 17 level was an honour not to be sneezed at. The lad ultimately came around and loaded his well-worn footy gear into the car. Mark would later be very grateful for his father's advice.

Mark captained the Teal Cup side that year at the Melbourne carnival, gained All-Australian selection once more, and narrowly missed out on bringing home the Premiers' trophy. It had been an incredible year, considering he had been playing Senior Colts for Waikerie just two years earlier.

Neil Kerley threw Mark around a bit in his first season at League level, starting him most games on the wing, but also asking him to fill in at half back, where he had spent a bit of time in the Waikerie Seniors. He acquitted himself well in both positions, and at the end of the season it was obvious his future lay beyond the local league. Finishing Year 12 in Waikerie became Mark's top priority after the SANFL season had finished and with this eventually out of the way, he took a short break and then headed to Football Park to try out for the Crows.

Kerley had played a significant role in Mark's football development to that point. Not only was 'Knuckles' instrumental in getting him to play in Adelaide, he had also taught Mark a lot about hardness in football. He is pretty much the same in real life as he comes across in the media. He is uncompromising when it comes to elite competitive sport, but also very astute and a good teacher of the game. Aggression at the ball was always Kerley's bottom-line instruction to his team, and although he never directly promoted physical aggression at the player, Mark knew that his coach didn't mind a bit of tough stuff if the opposition was looking for it.

There was no complicated game plan when Mark was at West Adelaide. Winning the ball at all costs dominated the way Kerley approached each match, and as long as Mark showed 100 per cent commitment, he was given a free rein to play the way he wished. There had been a strong connection between Kerley and the Ricciuto family since his first visit to the Riverland to watch Mark play in the Waikerie Seniors. Having come down from the country to play league football at a young age himself, Kerley was aware of the hardships Mark was going through and the bond between them was obvious. It's likely that Kerley could see a bit of himself in young Mark and they have remained good friends ever since. Kerley lives on the Murray River at Walker Flat these days, and the two men occasionally catch some fish together or have a beer when the opportunity arises. Kerley is exceptionally good at netting yabbies, but Mark always remembers to bring a calculator when he goes yabbying with Kerley to keep tabs on the catch.

Mark's form during his one and only full season at West Adelaide had been exceptional. Unlike most lads who ultimately worked their way into a SANFL Senior side, Mark hadn't played in the SANFL Under 17s, Under 19s or Seconds. He went from the Waikerie team in the Riverland Grand Final in 1991 straight into the West Adelaide league side for 1992, with virtually no transition period at all – probably the first time in SANFL history this had been done. He ended the season strongly, polling well in the Westies' Best and Fairest award, and received a cheque for $3000. He played one league game that season with his brother, Craig, who also showed plenty of potential. However, Craig seriously injured his back and ultimately retired before his career had a chance to take off.

Neil Kerley saw Mark's physical strength as one of his greatest attributes when he arrived at West Adelaide as a sixteen-year-old. The coach had come across very few lads of that age who could bench press the sort of weight Mark could handle, and he attributes much of this natural ability to Mark's helping out on his parents' fruit block and his enormous appetite for training and competitive sport. Most of the 'city kids' coming through the West Adelaide ranks at that time had undeveloped physiques, and Mark's advantage in this area enabled him to match it with more seasoned opponents from day one in the SANFL.

Kerley monitored Mark's progress closely during his time at West Adelaide and knew the lad was destined for great things. It was his versatility that made him, as Kerley puts it, 'a coach's dream' and he gave the club great drive from either the wing or half back. Shaun Rehn and Tony Modra were playing for West Adelaide at the same time, and Kerley knew that the trio wouldn't be there for long.

Compared with country football, Mark had found his pre-season with West Adelaide tough, but summer training at the AFL level at the end of 1992 proved to be something else again.

Graham Cornes had been a top-class SANFL player who had crossed the border towards the end of his career to have a late crack at the VFL. He had played in a Premiership side for Glenelg, represented South Australia on 21 occasions in State of Origin, been All-Australian coach, and coached both South Adelaide and

Glenelg before snagging the top job at the Crows. When the Adelaide Football Club was born in 1990, his appointment had surprised no one.

Mark remembers his first pre-season training campaign under Cornes as being the toughest, both physically and mentally, he had ever experienced. By applying himself, watching what he ate and drank (no more fried chicken), and making a conscious lift in overall effort, Mark got through the first two weeks pretty well. Cornes was big on competitive drills at training. Sessions weren't as numerous or regular as they are these days, but they were longer and generally more arduous. There were times when Mark thought he simply couldn't do the sorts of things seasoned players like McDermott, Maynard and Lee could manage; after all, these guys had spent a lot of time in the SANFL and their bodies were far stronger and better prepared than his. However, Mark soldiered on and was feeling pretty good about his progress until 23 December – the last day of pre-season training before the Christmas break.

As something to remember over the holiday period, Cornes instructed the entire Crows squad to complete 110 x 100-metre sprints. He gave them 17 seconds to finish each run and 43 seconds to recover before fronting up for the next leg. The Carlton squad had recently completed a highly publicised set of 100 sprints, and Cornes was determined his squad would outperform the Victorians not just by one run, but by ten. Regardless of fitness level, endurance profile and mental toughness, eleven kilometres of sprinting in 110 minutes was a big ask.

Mark had completed 30 sprints before he started to feel the pinch. His stomach began to churn, his legs felt like lead, and the thought of having to complete 80 more against the stopwatch was almost too much to consider. Never before in his life had he been confronted with such a difficult challenge, but being one of the new kids on the block and unwilling to show any signs of weakness, he pushed through the pain barrier and ultimately completed all 110 sprints. Quite a few of his team-mates didn't go the distance that day. Mark concedes that it was a considerable milestone in his development as an AFL player and did a lot to elevate him in the eyes of his new coach.

Since his youthful days on the Waikerie fruit block, it had been drilled into Mark that achieving goals required hard work and determination. It was an attitude and a work ethic that he would need if he were to succeed at football's elite level.

After Christmas, Mark returned to training with the Crows with a considerably different outlook. His successful completion of the big sprint session had given him a level of confidence he'd never known before. He had always been aware that sportspeople who make it at the elite level are special people – people who can push through extraordinary pain barriers on a regular basis. He understood that the way an athlete handles adversity, and extreme physical and mental challenges, separates the great from the good, and he was determined to make it into the former category – and to stay there.

As hard as pre-season training may have been at the Crows, however, it wasn't as tough for Mark as was living away from home. He shared a house in Lillian Street, Prospect, with Craig, who had also moved to town to play football with West Adelaide, and two other lads. According to Craig, the place could best be described as a 'male drop-in house'. At its worst, it looked like a cyclone had been through the place. It was 'Burgy', 'Robbo' and the 'Roo boys' who paid the rent, but there were usually a dozen or more others in various states of residence.

As is often the case when teenage lads share a house, furniture was at a premium. One item they really couldn't do without was a dining table, so they drove Burgy's old Holden to a furniture shop to buy one, but with no real idea of how to get it home. The car had no roof rack and the boys weren't keen to pay an extra delivery charge, so they sat the table on the car roof and hung on to it with one arm each until they reached home.

Despite having his brother close by and a large number of mates in Adelaide, overwhelming homesickness regularly drove Mark to tears. As much as he tried, he simply couldn't break his ties with the Riverland. At every opportunity he would jump in the car and head for Waikerie, dreading the time when he would have to return to Adelaide. Homesickness is something that affects most at some stage or another, and with the current level of interstate exchange in AFL football, it's an issue many young players have to face.

Mark worked hard to overcome his dislike of city life. He picked up a part-time job at the Central Market with an affable fruiterer, Jim Mitris. He would often start the day at 6 am with his Riverland mate, Jason Lehmann, stacking watermelons and carting fruit. The job brought back memories of visiting the market as a child with an uncle, Ralph Pope, who owned the local Mini-mart in Waikerie, to collect fruit and other produce for the store. Mark had always been intrigued and excited by all he saw and heard there, and being able to join in the bustle of activity in the pre-dawn made him feel a little more at home.

As pre-season training progressed, Mark began to test himself against the other players. It wasn't all bump, slug and long-distance running under Graham Cornes. There was also plenty of skills work, which most of the players enjoyed. Cornes was a stickler for getting things right on the training track; he demanded perfection, and let the players know in no uncertain terms if they failed to achieve it.

Whether it was a one-on-one marking contest, tackling exercise or some other competitive drill, Mark always went at it full tilt and made mental notes of how he'd fared against his opponents. Just sharing the training track with names like McDermott, McGuinness and Jarman – players he had idolised from afar not so long before – was mind-blowing enough, but coming up against them in competitive work was something else again. These were his team-mates, but they would also be rivals when it came to breaking into the side.

Mark's first official game in the big league was a trial against North Melbourne at Football Park. He was playing pretty well, grabbing his share of the ball and making a fair contribution, when renowned Kangaroos defender Mick Martyn lined him up and barrelled him on the grandstand half forward flank. Mark recalls flying through the air for several metres and struggling for a few seconds to regain his feet, but there was no real damage done. Although he knew he would be sore after the event, he managed to run out the game and finished off well.

Despite his encouraging trial game form, however, the Ricciuto name didn't appear on the team sheet after the side was picked for the opening round of home-and-away matches that year. This was the first occasion in his life that Mark had missed out on top-level selection for a football side. He went back to play for West Adelaide, feeling a little disappointed, but determined to show such good form in the local competition that the Crows selectors wouldn't overlook him in future. Adelaide defeated Richmond at the Melbourne Cricket Ground in round one by an imposing 94 points, and Mark knew he would have to pull out all stops to earn a position in the team.

Four consecutive best-on-ground performances with West Adelaide, however, elicited the selection response he had been hoping for, and Mark was eventually chosen to play against

Hawthorn at Football Park in round six. At that stage the Crows were sitting on a record four wins and one loss, but the might of Hawthorn at full strength would provide the ultimate test. Pulling on the Crows jumper for the first time in a contest of this significance was enough to get the butterflies well and truly fluttering, and Mark was understandably nervous in the lead-up to the game. A full house was a certainty and, with the likes of Ayres, Platten, Brereton, Langford and Dunstall on the opposing side, he knew he was in for a baptism of fire.

It proved a tough, see-sawing affair all night, with Hawthorn ultimately prevailing by 17 points, but the Adelaide players could hold their heads high as they left the arena. Mark had finished with one goal and 15-odd possessions, well and truly justifying his selection and setting him up for the remainder of the season. His most vivid recollection from the game was of running in off the line after a centre bounce and copping a whack from the rugged Gary Ayres. At that time, Ayres' 'mullet' hairstyle was enough to knock players out! The collision badly corked Mark's thigh and he hobbled around for a while, but he refused to let the early contact rob him of his long-awaited game time. He would suffer from that knock for much of the following week, but he wasn't going to let it stop him from playing game number two.

After the noise had subsided, the crowd had filtered away, and the post-match meetings were concluded, Mark sat back in the locker room to reflect on what he had achieved in his first game of top-level football. He had shared the arena with at least a dozen legends of the game, and while this thought might have been daunting as the ball was bounced for the first time, he quickly felt comfortable out in the middle and confident that he could hold his own with them. Given time and some much-needed experience, Mark knew that he would establish himself in the Crows lineup.

Collingwood was Adelaide's next opponent, and this would be Mark's first trip interstate. Graham Cornes liked to study the opposition side prior to a match, and would prepare a two-page dossier on each of the opposing players for his players to examine, usually on the plane if they were travelling to an interstate venue. Cornes would quiz the squad at the team dinner the evening before the game to make sure they had read and digested his reports. Much of the information was statistical, but he would also describe the opposing players' personalities and idiosyncrasies. 'Golden boy' Mark Bickley usually won the Cherry Ripe that went to the player who got the most correct answers.

Victoria Park was an intimidating venue, with 25,000 wildly parochial supporters filling the outer and the likes of Gavin Brown, Craig Kelly, Tony Shaw and Damian Monkhorst to contend with out in the middle. Mark started up forward and was quickly into the game, but after being 'clothes-lined' by Kelly in the first quarter and having his hand deliberately stomped on by Monkhorst a few minutes later, he knew it was going to be a big afternoon. Mark recalls looking up at the 200-centimetre-tall Monkhorst while trying to extricate his hand from beneath his size-14 boot and momentarily considering retaliation. However, on seeing the 'I'm gonna kill ya' look on 'Monkey's' face, Mark thought again and retreated to a safer place on the field. There wouldn't be many occasions when he would retreat over the next fourteen years.

When Magpie small man Brad Rowe began to cause a few problems around goal, Graham Cornes shifted Mark into defence. Curbing Rowe's influence became his top priority, and he did the job well. Adelaide lost that game by four goals, but played pretty well on the least friendly of all foreign soil and was still in the mix at mid-season.

Mark's demonstrated ability as a defender found him on the half back flank for much of the remainder of 1993. Another youngster, Mark Viska, played on the opposite flank, and the two were soon well established as competent defenders. Both were hard at the ball and enjoyed the straight running approach that comes with playing across half back.

By this stage, Mark had settled well into the Adelaide Football Club. He had developed close friendships with Simon Tregenza and Sean Tasker, both of whom were experienced campaigners and provided him with advice and support. Mark was slowly overcoming the homesickness that had plagued him early in the year and began to revel in the atmosphere of football as played at its top level. He loved the crowds, he loved travelling around the country to play and, of course, he loved being paid to play. Still a teenager, he was earning around $1000 a game – money that was well earned given the prospect of being stood on by Damian Monkhorst. At West Adelaide, the year before, he had been paid $3000 for playing the full season. The hard work Mark was putting into training was literally paying off.

Chris McDermott quickly became the team-mate Mark most respected at Adelaide. Chris helped him in a variety of ways, including providing support when Mark battled with home-sickness, and he led the club as Mark considered a great skipper should. He was the perfect role model for a young footballer. It was at the Players Bar, a venue in Grenfell Street owned by McDermott, that Mark had his first taste of working in the hospitality industry – an experience that would play an important role in his life a few years down the track. A lot of Mark's later decisions and directions as captain were based on the way McDermott did things, and there can be no doubt that he was a significant influence on Mark.

As the 1993 home-and-away season drew to a close, excitement levels around Adelaide rose to fever pitch. The Crows needed to defeat Collingwood at Football Park in round 22 to qualify for their first finals campaign and, before a feverish crowd of 48,000, they did so by 24 points. Mark would play major-round football in his first season, and he could scarcely believe it. He had gone from Waikerie's Senior Colts in 1990 to an AFL final in 1993. He had turned eighteen mid-season and had played just sixteen games leading up to the major round, but his body was in good shape and he felt ready for the challenge that lay ahead.

Mark lined up on a half back flank for the first final against experienced campaigners Hawthorn at the MCG. Expatriate South Australian Tony Hall was his opponent. To this day, Mark says Hall is one of the most difficult forwards he has ever had to stop. His work rate and skill level were dazzling, and Mark recalls being almost spent after the Crows' 15-point victory. Some 55,000 people watched that game, including many who had travelled from Adelaide to support their team.

Elation took hold in the City of Churches after the Crows' historic first final win. Mark remembers flying back to Adelaide that night to a welcome usually reserved for royalty and rock stars. More than 5000 delirious fans packed the airport terminal. Before the players were allowed to leave the plane, a police officer came on board to inform the club officials of the situation and to ask the players to make their way as quickly as possible through the crowd. Police were concerned that younger fans might be injured in the crush. It was a reception that none in the playing party will ever forget. Mark recalls they felt like The Beatles!

The second Semi-final against Carlton the following week provided a stark contrast. It was one of the most frustrating games Mark can ever recall playing. Adelaide played the better football most of the afternoon, but kicked inaccurately and this cost them dearly in the end. Despite having seven more scoring shots, the Crows went down by 18 points and would have to face Essendon to earn a spot in the Grand Final.

If the Carlton loss had been a frustrating one for all at the Adelaide Football Club, the Preliminary Final match the following week would turn out to be a nightmare. Up by over 40 points at half time and cruising towards victory, the Crows suddenly lost their way in the third quarter and found themselves behind at the last change. Mark recalls the three-quarter-time huddle, when Cornes was livid at the 30 minutes of football his side had just played. The Crows went down to the Bombers by 11 points, allowing a Grand Final appearance to slip through their fingers. It was a game all concerned would like to forget. It wasn't until four years later, after Adelaide had won the first of its back-to-back flags, that Mark Bickley eventually owned up to his three-quarter-time flatulence on the MCG during the loss to Essendon – something he will never live down!

The result of that match was shattering for the Adelaide Football Club, and although Mark was disappointed over the loss, he felt worse for the more senior members of the side such as Chris McDermott, Tony McGuinness, Andrew Jarman, Greg Anderson and Wayne Weideman. These players had enjoyed distinguished careers and were the backbone of the club, and to lose an opportunity of that magnitude cut them to the quick. When they flew back to Adelaide there was no one at the airport to greet them. This time they felt more like Milli Vanilli.

Mark had played an excellent first season with the Crows. Once he had broken into the side in round six, his form was steady enough to warrant consistent selection and, despite not playing a full year, he finished seventh in the Club Champion award. His family and mates back in Waikerie were proud of what he had achieved in such a short space of time and optimistic about the following year.

One of Mark's most memorable moments from his first AFL season was his stellar performance at the Club Champion award night, although he concedes his mother may not agree. Eager to fit in with the group and to show that he was as worldly as any of them, he became involved in a drinking game – and later wished he hadn't.

Seated at a table with Sean Tasker, Simon Tregenza and several of the other younger players in the group, Mark found himself committed to a game that called for any player who polled a certain number of votes in a particular match to skol a glass of beer. Beer gave way to red wine as the evening progressed and, as the event was covered on live television, the skolling game found its way into lounge rooms right across the state.

Back in Waikerie, Murray and Carolyn Ricciuto began to shrink down in their armchairs while watching their son's antics as the game gained momentum. No one in the auditorium came over to Mark to tell him to slow down, so he wasn't aware that his behaviour was upsetting anyone. It seemed that every time the TV cameras were on him, he was throwing back a glass of red, to the amusement of his team-mates, who started throwing money on the table to encourage him to keep up the pace. Not only did Mark poll a few votes that season, he also received three votes from Bruce McAvaney for best on-ground that night!

Mark was definitely a bit hungover for the SANFL Grand Final motorcade the next day, and recalls being thankful he was the passenger and not the driver. He was quite amused, and very surprised, that he'd created a cult following for himself, which would stick with him throughout his career. Perhaps a lot of supporters could see that this was a very normal human being. Not only did he play hard on the field, he played hard off it as well!

4

A DREAM REALISED

A regular selection at half back by the start of the 1994 season, Mark seemed to have found his niche in the Crows lineup. His pre-season was solid and he looked forward to an exciting second year of senior football. Despite the disappointment of losing to Essendon in the 1993 finals, there was still plenty of optimism around the club and everyone was determined to push hard for another finals assault. The lineup was much as it had been the previous year and, with the experience they had gained and the lessons they had learned from an unsuccessful major round, expectations were high, both within and outside the club.

The season started well enough with a 66-point drubbing of Carlton in front of 45,000 at Football Park. After winning well in four of their first six encounters, things were running more or less to plan. The Crows lost their way from that point, however, incurring big losses against Essendon, Hawthorn and North Melbourne, and embarking on a worrying downward spiral. They finished the minor round with just ten wins, not enough to carry them through into September, and it seemed some major restructuring was in order. Graham Cornes left the club, and a few senior players hung up their boots. This was to be the first of several reshuffles that would have both positive and negative impacts on the club.

While during his tenure Cornes had rarely conceded a point on anything to do with football or his team, and would never admit to being wrong, he had always handled the media well and projected a strong image for the club. A teetotaller, he had enforced strict drinking bans if the team had six days or less between matches, which hadn't made him overly popular with those players who liked to imbibe. Nevertheless, he established a strong playing list during his time at the helm and helped set up a culture that should have stood the Crows in good stead going forward.

Contrary to the Crows' overall team performance in 1994, Mark Ricciuto had had a very strong season. He finished third in the Club Champion award behind Shaun Rehn and Tony McGuinness and collected his first senior All-Australian jumper – a considerable achievement for someone who had played fewer than 40 games of AFL football. He had become the consummate half back flanker, with the ability to negate both small and tall forwards. Playing a direct style of footy was exactly what Mark enjoyed and, despite his youth and relative inexperience, he moved quickly into the upper echelon at the Crows. It was at this time he signed a five-year contract, which was standard procedure in that era for players with obvious long-term futures. Most of the up-front money from this deal went into buying property at Waikerie as a stake for the future.

The Brownlow Medal presentation at the conclusion of the 1994 season turned out to be another memorable occasion for Mark and a few of his team-mates, but not for the usual reasons.

The Adelaide contingent arrived in Melbourne just after lunchtime on the day of the event and checked into the Carlton

Crest Hotel. Chris McDermott and Tony McGuinness, the club leaders both on and off the field, instructed the lads to get settled into their rooms and then meet down in the hotel's front bar. While their wives and girlfriends were off having their hair and makeup done for the big night, the players planned to have a few beers, perhaps a punt on the horses, and to chew the fat about the Brownlow and which Crows were expected to poll well.

Those few beers ended up being a dozen or so each. The plan had been for everyone to meet in the hotel foyer at 6.15 ready for the dinner, but it wasn't until just before six o'clock that Mark decided to draw stumps at the bar and head upstairs for a shower and shave. Before he was allowed to leave the group, however, he had to down a tequila 'shooter'. On top of a bellyful of beer, it made shaving and tying his tie rather more difficult than usual.

And the drinking didn't stop there. The Crows boys came up with a game that saw them drinking far more than most at the dinner. Each time one of them received a Medal vote, they had to down the contents of their glass immediately. The same applied if their direct opponent in a given round scored a vote. By the end of the count, few at the Crows table could scratch themselves. Mark's most vivid memory of the Brownlow aftermath was staggering into the hotel kitchen while trying to locate his room, which was several floors away. Fortunately, the hotel security guard found him and escorted him there, just as Carlton's Greg Williams was collecting his second Brownlow Medal. There would be several unscheduled bathroom visits during the night and a sore head the following morning.

The arrival of Robert Shaw at the Adelaide Footy Club in 1995 is something most personnel and supporters will want to forget. The Crows had taken a lot of backward steps in 1994 and the decision had been made to replace Graham Cornes with someone with a strong background in the Victorian Football League and

AFL. Shaw had proven himself as a tough, determined footballer in his playing days, but he was unproven as a top-level coach. Giving him the senior job was always going to be a gamble. Players such as Andrew Jarman were excited at Shaw's appointment, as he projected a 'street fighter' image and promised to inject a level of toughness into the squad which many thought was lacking.

Shaw had played 50-odd senior games for Fitzroy over seven seasons, and had coached the club from 1991 to 1994, but his win/loss record with Fitzroy didn't inspire confidence from within the Crows' supporter ranks. Although Graham Cornes hadn't achieved as much during his time as head coach as some would have liked, he had been highly respected, and there was considerable scepticism over Shaw's appointment from day one.

Mark was one of the regular players the new coach targeted to lift the Crows' physical presence. Along with renowned tough man Wayne Weideman, he was given a licence to raise the level of on-field aggression. Although this didn't phase Mark at all, it essentially changed his playing style. He was forced to play several positions – full forward, centre half forward and on the ball – in which he hadn't had much experience, and he found the whole process very unsettling. It seemed that much of what he had accomplished under Cornes had gone out the window, and he rates 1995 as one of his most forgettable years with the Crows.

Shaw's insistence that the players play more aggressively had seen a few of them bulk up, and Mark was one of them. His general fitness was below the level he had been accustomed to under Cornes, and he became increasingly frustrated as his career appeared to stall instead of moving forward. Mediocrity was never on Mark Ricciuto's agenda and he admits to losing his way a bit during the second year of Robert Shaw's tenure.

So despondent and disillusioned did he become, in fact, that he seriously considered giving the game away for a while. He recalls watching State of Origin Rugby League on television and wondering what it would be like to switch codes. That game had its own appeal, with plenty of hard running, serious tackling and a whole new set of skills to be learned. Shaw had upset the Adelaide applecart so drastically, even giving up the game Mark loved seemed preferable for a time.

Playing football at the top level might not always be the 'beer and skittles' proposition he had become accustomed to, Mark realised. Each season prior to 1994 had been a vast improvement on the last, enabling Mark to work steadily towards his ultimate ambition of becoming a great footballer. Then, it all came tumbling down and it hit home that AFL footy can be something of an emotional roller-coaster for those involved deeply and passionately in the game.

Admittedly, a few long-term injuries hit the club hard during Shaw's first year, particularly the loss of top-level ruckman, Shaun Rehn, with a serious knee injury. Rehn was, in Mark's opinion, one of the best big men ever to play the game, and losing him set the team back dramatically. But Shaw seemed to have trouble coping with the top job, having difficulty in several areas. At times he would be animated and highly excited, while at other times he would be moody and uncommunicative.

It was very much a period of treading water – or, as some observers would say, going backwards. The Crows' players list was still strong enough to be competitive and to play finals football, but they badly underachieved. Neil Kerley, Mark's former coach, sensed that things were on the slide. He was worried that Shaw was trying to change Mark's natural playing style in order to fit a game plan that simply wasn't working. Kerley understood the importance of structure and discipline in a football club, and didn't want to interfere; however, he felt compelled to say something to Mark in confidence. He advised him to model his game on that of the Sydney Swans skipper, Paul Kelly. Kelly was tough and uncompromising, yet he was supremely fit and could run all day as an on-baller. Kerley had always known that this was the way Mark had to play, not as the muscle-bound 'enforcer' that Robert Shaw had him pigeon-holed as.

The Adelaide media sharpened its collective arsenal of knives when Shaw's second year in control proved even less fruitful than his first. Mark sensed that Shaw was becoming as disenchanted with the whole scenario as the club and its supporters were with him.

Things came very close to boiling point between Mark and Robert Shaw during a match late in the 1996 season. The Crows were trailing badly and when Mark gave away a free kick in the opposition's goal square, the coach dragged him to the bench. Mark insists the free kick came from a bad umpiring decision and says he was livid when the runner told him he had to come off. He hadn't done a lot wrong in that match and recalls calling Shaw a few choice names under his breath as he ran to the dug-out. In that era there wasn't the rotation system currently employed by all clubs to give on-ballers a rest; if you were benched, you usually sat out the rest of the match, and that's exactly what Mark did. He had been made an example of, and he didn't like it one bit.

Considering the frustration that had crept into the club, and the general despondency Mark was feeling about football during that period, Shaw's decision to bench him couldn't have come at a worse time. So angry was he in the change-rooms after the game, he feared he might punch Shaw if he so much as mentioned the free kick. He felt so disillusioned with the effect Shaw's coaching was having on the football club he loved so much, he says he doubts that he could have contained himself.

Looking back now, of course, Mark is relieved that the

confrontation didn't occur. He feels that few of his team-mates at that time would have jumped in to defuse the situation. In fact, there might have been a couple that would have joined him! It would have been an emphatic review of Shaw's performance, but perhaps not an appropriate one.

Despite finishing seventh and sixth in the Club Champion awards, in 1995 and 1996 respectively, Mark was unhappy with his form, and the general morale of the club seemed at an all-time low. The Crows' underperformance for much of Shaw's time at the helm – they won just nineteen out of 44 games – drew plenty of heat from the media and supporters, who expected much more after what had been clearly evident in 1993. Most were relieved when Shaw was shown the door, and excited when the news broke that South Australian football legend Malcolm Blight had signed to take over.

It had been a dark period in the Crows' short history, with Mark struggling to find form and fitness and the club desperate to re-establish itself as a genuine force in the AFL. Despite the fact that Shaw had been a flop as senior coach, Mark concedes that his subsequent career, which spans two decades and four clubs, indicates that he must still have plenty to offer as an assistant and administrator. But there's a huge difference between the roles of head coach and assistant coach, and Mark believes Shaw simply didn't have what it takes to make the next progression.

5

UPPING THE ANTE

The news of Malcolm Blight's appointment soon after the conclusion of the 1996 home-and-away series sent a wave of excitement through West Lakes. Blight's status in South Australian football had been legendary since he emerged as a brilliant player with Woodville in the SANFL, then went on to achieve greatness with North Melbourne in the VFL. There had been few more decorated players in the game than Blight, and although he hadn't been able to pull off a Premiership while coaching Geelong, most observers felt that would change with a playing list as talented as Adelaide's.

One of Blight's first, and most controversial, decisions as coach was to axe three of the club's iconic players, Andrew Jarman, Chris McDermott and Tony McGuinness. These players had been seemingly untouchable, with a list of achievements as long as West Lakes Boulevard, but history meant little to the new coach. Like everyone else, Mark was shocked when he learned of the sackings and particularly that of Chris McDermott, who had been his captain, mentor and close friend. He concedes it must have been a tough call for Blight, as it was inevitable there would be a huge public backlash, but Mark says he has always admired this aspect of Blight's character: he carefully considers any decision before he makes it, and then he sticks by it, regardless of sentiment or external pressure.

Lifting both the fitness and skill level of the Crows would be Blight's prime objective from the moment he set foot in the Adelaide change-rooms, and he would be the major influence in getting Mark's football back on track. He pulled Mark aside before the 1997 pre-season for a long talk about his future and the role he would be expected to fill. Blight told him that if he continued to play the way Robert Shaw had insisted – bulky, and with extreme physical aggression – his career would be over at age 26 or 27. He expected Mark to drop some weight, regain his peak fitness and be able to run out a game in the mid-field. In fact, Blight questioned the overall fitness of the squad and, in conjunction with newly arrived fitness coach Neil Craig, designed a lengthy and strenuous program to address the issue.

The Crows trained on Max Basheer Reserve and on the roads around West Lakes for thirteen weeks prior to Christmas, as compared with just five or six weeks these days. There was no mandatory end-of-season time off during that era and the pre-season started before the '96 SANFL Grand Final had been played.

October had traditionally been reserved for relaxing, which essentially meant drinking and eating. It was obvious to all from the outset that Malcolm Blight saw the potential in the squad and meant business. After the frustration of not winning a flag with talented players at Geelong, he was determined to take the Adelaide Football Club all the way in his first season.

Despite the toughness of the new campaign, Blight's arrival was a welcome breath of fresh air for Mark Ricciuto. He felt the new direction, and rekindled enthusiasm, from day one. Neil

Craig pushed the squad hard, with two- and three-hour running sessions three times a week. Like most of his team-mates, Mark soon found himself in the best physical shape of his career. He was lean, trim and felt like he could run all day, which was just what the new coach had planned. His assertions that 'a fat blowfly is a slow blowfly' and 'it's better to have an empty house than a bad tenant' certainly had a marked influence on the squad. Neil Craig was determined to make the Crows a fitter unit. Mark had these words firmly in mind as he put in the road miles, sometimes stopping to vomit from exhaustion, but determined to reach peak physical condition.

While Blight did plenty of research on the opposition, he didn't thrust it down his players' throats unless it was really warranted. Instead, he relied heavily on his vast knowledge of the game and confidence in his squad and game plan. He played golf once a week, which enabled him to escape and relax. Without that release, Mark feels Blight wouldn't have been anywhere near as effective a coach.

By this stage of his career, Mark had developed a strong sense of self-belief. He knew he was good enough to beat any opponent, and he never hesitated on the football field in any contest, which always provided him with an edge. Because he also coped well with extreme pressure, his goal kicking at vital stages of a game was controlled and reliable.

Although he rarely spoke one-on-one with his squad, Malcolm Blight was a terrific communicator. Training drills, specific instructions and game plans were always crystal-clear. As long as Blight didn't take him aside from the rest of the group, Mark knew he was going well. When the coach felt he needed to address a significant problem with an individual player, he would do so privately, firmly and constructively, and always ended his chat with them on a positive note.

Also unlike some of Mark's other coaches, Blight always considered himself a chance to get a kick among his players on the training track. There was often time for some humour at training when the occasion was right, and he liked nothing more than recounting tales from his playing days, such as his famous after-the-siren goal – the kick from 70 metres, or was it 80 or perhaps 90 metres out? The distance that kick covered always grew by ten metres each time Blight retold the story. Blight had been one of Mark's boyhood heroes, and he immensely enjoyed hearing about matches he recalled watching, such as the famous drawn VFL Grand Final of 1977. The mood was always positive with Malcolm Blight as coach, and it would show in the Crows' performance in 1997 and 1998.

The home-and-away season kicked off well for the Crows, and Mark was in sparkling form in the mid-field. He had never been a regular on-baller in the past, either at Waikerie or West Adelaide, and this presented a whole new set of challenges. He was now playing on the AFL's elite and was expected to be able to match it with the likes of St Kilda's Robert Harvey, Sydney's Paul Kelly and Footscray's Scott West. Without losing much of the physicality for which he had been steadily building a reputation, Mark took on all comers and was in top form when groin soreness started to worry him. At first it was just a 'niggle' that didn't slow him down much at training or during matches, but towards the middle of the 1997 season it flared noticeably and he realised he was in trouble.

He was selected in the South Australian squad for a mid-year State of Origin match and concedes now that he shouldn't have played. Mark had always been proud to represent his state and he didn't hesitate to line up against Victoria, but he pulled up very sore from that eight-point loss and was soon looking down the barrel at time away from footy. His first halves were fine, but after cooling down at half time he had trouble with mobility in third quarters, and struggled to run out each game. Malcolm Blight decided to rest him in round 21 in the hope of freshening him up for the finals series, but he returned the following week and was able to contribute little on the field.

With the major round pending, the groin injury looked set to shatter Mark's plans and destroy everything he had worked hard for since the previous September. He underwent intensive physio treatment at the club in the hope of coming up for at least one finals game, but to no avail. He recalls lying on his back on the floor at home and not being able to get to his feet. Reduced almost to tears, he decided there and then that his 1997 season was over and groin surgery should be scheduled as soon as possible.

Mark's reparative operation was a first for a South Australian AFL footballer, with two conjoint tendons and two hernias fixed simultaneously. He was released from hospital on Preliminary Final day in a wheelchair and went straight down to Football Park to see the Crows take on Footscray. To his delight, his team-mates rallied strongly in the second half to come from six goals down and pinch the match by two points, qualifying the Adelaide Football Club for its first-ever Grand Final appearance. Mark was elated that the Crows would play off for the Premiership the following week, but felt bitterly disappointed at having to watch, rather than play.

It all seemed like a bad dream. He had played in several Grand Finals in the Riverland competition and had never been forced to watch from the sidelines when he could have been out in the middle. He had led the 1997 Brownlow Medal voting to round 16 and was in career best form; to have things fall in a heap so drastically ate at him like a mob of fire ants. He felt strangely conflicted; one minute he wanted the boys to get out there and kick St Kilda's butt, and the next he wasn't sure he wanted them to win without him. He felt guilty when his thoughts ran along these lines, but was simply devastated at not being able to play. His world had been turned upside down. During the match he cheered as hard as any Crows supporter when the team scored a goal, but he simultaneously felt dismay. He joined his elated team-mates at the Premiership dinner that evening but left early, feeling strangely left out. Mark still finds it difficult to explain the conflict he felt. Tony Modra, Peter Vardy, Simon Tregenza and Matthew Liptak also missed that day, and Mark has wondered if they felt similarly torn between elation and despair.

When his mates who had played in the Grand Final team had their Premiership ankle tattoos done, Mark spent five hours having an aggressive-looking tattoo drawn on his left shoulder. The pain helped divert his attention from the disappointment he felt at having missed out on the match he had dreamed of playing since he was a youngster.

Mark's groin injury had been the result of over-use and could be attributed to the vastly increased amount of training the squad had done under Malcolm Blight and Neil Craig. Five other players had similar operations at season's end, but Mark concedes it was the Crows' overall fitness level that enabled them to run over St Kilda and ultimately claim the club's first Premiership.

6

A SECOND CHANCE

Mark was in good shape for the 1998 pre-season campaign. His groin repair had been successful, and never before had he felt the sort of fire in his belly that propelled him into 1998. Missing out on a Grand Final appearance was the ultimate incentive. Although the players all knew that winning back-to-back flags in the competition would be tremendously difficult, there was plenty of optimism at the Crows. Improvements had been made to the squad, and again the general fitness level was there on which to build a good base. Maybe, just maybe, this outfit would be good enough to do what no one had done since the glory days of Hawthorn in the 1980s.

History will show, however, that Malcolm Blight's troops started the 1998 season poorly, winning just two of their first six games. In round two against St Kilda at Waverley Park, Blight was keen to make the point that no one in the Crows' lineup, regardless of reputation, was immune from spending time off the field if performance warranted. At one stage, he had Mark, Darren Jarman, Nigel Smart and Shaun Rehn all on the bench together. This was the much-publicised 'million dollar bench' which featured prominently in the Adelaide media. Blight hated losing more than any other coach Mark had ever played under, and he wasn't a lot of fun to be around after a poor team performance. Blight expected and would accept only the best from every player who represented the club.

Midway through the season the Crows' performance steadied, and eventually they ran out the minor round with thirteen victories. They travelled to Perth in round 22 to take on the West Coast Eagles, thinking they would have to win that match to play finals football. However, the results of other games in that round fell Adelaide's way. On the eve of the West Coast match they celebrated like kids at a birthday party when they discovered a finals berth was assured. No alcohol, of course, just fairy bread and party pies. The Crows went on to beat the Eagles by 25 points and entered the major round feeling confident.

However, they faltered badly against Melbourne on the MCG in the First Qualifying Final and were fortunate to get a second opportunity. Under the system in force today, they would have been eliminated. Training intensified from that point onward, which ran contrary to the way coaches normally approach a Finals campaign and caused the odd murmur of unrest from within the playing group. There was a lot more hard running and competitive work than there had been for several weeks, but Blight's decisions were never to be questioned. The Crows completed a tough week on the track and then travelled up to Sydney to tackle the improved Swans on their home deck.

It was a dismal night, with consistent heavy rain. The Adelaide boys ran through the tunnel and on to the Sydney Cricket Ground just as the pre-match fireworks display was winding down. As they did so, the rain was pelting down, the ground was covered with mud and the air was filled with smoke from the fireworks display. This was to be a do-or-die game and it was as if they were entering a combat zone. From the front of the pack, Mark yelled, 'This is going to be like Vietnam!' Going into battle is exactly how the Crows approached the game. Peter Vardy carved up the Swans' defence that evening and Adelaide ended up comfortable winners. This meant that the team would continue on its seemingly endless road trek, taking on the Bulldogs next in Melbourne and playing away from Football Park for the fourth consecutive week. The media had blown up the fact that Footscray were still smarting from the two-point loss inflicted on them by the Crows in the 1997 Preliminary Final and that the Bulldogs would pull out all stops to turn the tables. There was plenty of tension in the air as the two sides entered the MCG arena, but the much-awaited re-match turned out to be anticlimactic. Adelaide played sparkling football, demolishing the hapless Bulldogs by 68 points. Mark played well, but it was the rising superstar, Andrew McLeod, who stole the show with seven goals.

Malcolm Blight took Mark and Peter Vardy off the field with ten minutes to play and a Grand Final berth well and truly assured. The pair hugged each other in disbelief before the final siren had sounded. Mark's body was still in good shape and, barring a freak accident at training or some other unforeseen mishap, he would play in his first-ever AFL Grand Final. He was determined that if his team were good enough to ultimately win the flag, he would soak up every bit of the atmosphere, every moment of excitement and every ounce of the glory.

Mark slept fitfully for the first couple of nights that week. It was a nervous time, but gradually he came to terms with what lay ahead. The Crows would have to travel for the fifth week in a row, which was unusual in the competition at that time, but everyone in the club, from players to property stewards, was ready for the challenge. Mark felt as fit as he had ever been, and was both physically and mentally prepared to take on the might of North Melbourne. North had won ten games in a row leading into the Grand Final and, with Wayne Carey, Glenn Archer, Anthony Stevens and Corey McKernan all in blistering form, overcoming the Kangaroo juggernaut was always set to be a daunting assignment.

Mark was sitting on the toilet in the Crows' change-rooms on Grand Final day when an F/A-18 Hornet fighter jet swooped over the arena, making the stadium shake and helping him get the job done quicker! The scene was set for an afternoon none of the Adelaide Football Club personnel would ever forget. The Crows began sluggishly, with North Melbourne dominating the first half of the game in general play but failing to capitalise on the scoreboard. Mark had kicked a goal early, but otherwise hadn't made much of an impact. As had become the norm, he was being tagged closely by Adam Simpson and was finding trouble breaking free to play as he knew he could.

The mood in the Adelaide rooms at half time was subdued, and Blight realised he would have to find something special to arrest the Kangaroos' dominance of the match. The deficit was 24 points and, had North kicked more accurately, the game may have been beyond retrieval, but Blight hadn't lost hope. North had left the door ajar with their poor goal shooting. He urged his charges to throw caution to the wind and have a real crack in the second half. He assured them that, if they could get back to the sort of football they had played against Sydney and the Bulldogs, and if the bounce of the ball went their way for a while, they were still in with a chance. Playing on at every opportunity would be their approach in the second half, he said. Finally, Blight reminded them how fit they were. They knew they had all worked harder on the track than any other team in the competition and that this could be the trump card if they could get back within striking distance.

Mark has no doubt it was Malcolm Blight's inspiration, motivation and absolute confidence in his players' fitness that renewed their self-belief at half time. They had entered the rooms at the end of the first half with long faces, but they emerged to meet the second filled with excitement and fresh enthusiasm.

Early goals in the third quarter provided exactly the sort of impetus Blight had been looking for. In a truly remarkable transformation, Adelaide fired off 13 scoring shots to two in that term, to lead by a couple of points at the last change. North Melbourne's older legs were beginning to feel the strain, and during three-quarter-time Blight again emphasised his players' superior fitness. Mark knew at that point he was just half an hour away from his first AFL Premiership. The huddle was as animated as he had ever seen, his team-mates' faces looked fresh, and there was a hunger and determination he had never before seen in a group of footballers.

The Crows increased their lead just three minutes into the final quarter and from that point onward, never looked like being headed. They had all done what the coach requested at half time, with flow-on football and non-stop running eventually wearing the opposition down. The 35-point victory was easily the sweetest in Mark's career. With the game well beyond doubt at the twenty-minute mark and the Crows pulling further away, there was time for celebration even before the final siren. Every goal brought with it a glorious sense of exhilaration, and, for the first time that afternoon, Mark allowed himself to soak up the adulation of the Adelaide fans. His family and close friends were among the 94,431 spectators who packed the MCG, and he thought fleetingly of the thousands more back in the Riverland who were about to share his elation. He was only minutes away from becoming part of an AFL Premiership team and experiencing the feeling in football every player craves. His last Premiership was at the

Barmera Oval for Waikerie in front of a couple of thousand people. Things were a bit different this time around.

One of Mark's favourite football photos was taken when he accepted his Premiership medallion and saluted all who adored the Adelaide Crows. He realised immediately how fortunate he had been; most who play a full AFL career never get to stand on the dais on that special day in September and he was determined to savour the moment. Andrew McLeod picked up a second Norm Smith Medal as the best player on the ground, young Simon Goodwin collected his second Premiership medallion after playing fewer than 40 games, Peter Vardy got to be part of it all after missing out with Mark in 1997, and North Melbourne discard, Mark Stevens, was compensated in no uncertain terms for having missed the Kangaroos' Premiership in 1996.

Mark Ricciuto had turned 23 mid-season and had already achieved more than he had ever considered possible in football. He won his first gold jacket as Adelaide's Club Champion, finished fourth in the Brownlow Medal count and collected his third All-Australian jumper. That Premiership feeling continues to sit somewhere in the back of his consciousness, as it does with most who were part of that historic team and are still playing today. It's a feeling that has driven Mark ever since and far outweighs the money, the accolades and the other more tangible benefits that come with playing elite-level football. Whether or not Mark climbs on to the MCG dais again on Grand Final day before he retires is entirely in the lap of the gods, but being able to hoist the Premiership Cup as club captain would certainly be his crowning achievement.

7

RIDING AN EMOTIONAL ROLLER-COASTER

With most on the Adelaide Football Club's list having played in one or both of the back-to-back Premierships, Malcolm Blight knew that his biggest task in 1999 would be maintaining focus and enthusiasm. No club had won three flags in a row since Melbourne in 1955, 1956 and 1957, and doing so in football's modern era is seen as being close to impossible. With sixteen teams in the competition and a salary cap system that now prevents the powerful clubs from 'buying' Premierships, things are certainly a far cry from the days when one or two clubs could dominate a decade of football.

Blight's credibility with his squad at the start of the new season was unparalleled in the Adelaide Football Club's history. No previous coach could handle the media with such aplomb. Known around Adelaide as 'the Messiah', he had the ability to answer questions in a way that always showed the club in a good light, and he rarely got a reporter offside. Everyone seemed to love him, from members of his playing squad all the way down to the casual Crows fan, and Mark recalls 1997 and 1998 as being his happiest time at the Crows since he played his first game in 1993.

As amiable as Malcolm Blight was, however, he didn't hesitate to tear strips off someone if he thought it would benefit the cause, or to pull a controversial move if he thought it might confuse the opposition. He was definitely a thinking coach, who wasn't afraid to try something new or radical if he thought it might give his side an edge.

Although he encouraged his players to enjoy their wins, Blight expected them to be home at a reasonable hour, and to keep their partying to within sensible limits. Provided it didn't interfere with their performance, he didn't mind the squad having a beer or two, but anyone who obviously flaunted this small window of freedom was in for a thorough dressing-down. He also allowed his players some latitude on the field if the situation warranted, and didn't mind them having a crack at a torpedo punt at goal if they considered they were just outside drop punt range. This is the way he had played his own football, and he encouraged all in his squad to do likewise. Blight knew that his charges needed to enjoy everything about the game if they were to perform at their peak, and if that meant cutting them a bit of slack after hours, so be it.

But even before the first ball was bounced in 1999, the atmosphere in the Crows camp had changed. Despite the dual Premierships, the team hadn't been a dominant force in the home-and-away series in both 1997 and 1998, and had played its best football in the major round both years. Mark knew that it wouldn't take a lot to drop off the pace and fall back in the pack, and that's exactly what happened. The Crows crashed from being Premier to finishing thirteenth, which stands as an AFL record – a record no one at Adelaide is keen to acknowledge.

Mark felt that Blight didn't really want to be at the club in 1999. That's not to say he was to blame for the disastrous collapse, but he had achieved in Adelaide what he had failed to achieve in Geelong and appeared ready to bow out. Blight's influence had been the most significant in the Crows' short history, and Mark is certain that without him, those back-to-back flags would still be a pipedream.

Like most who were with the Crows between 1997 and 1999, Mark learned a lot from Malcolm Blight. He learned that a combination of extreme fitness, smooth skills and quick thinking would win far more football matches than it loses. Two Premierships in three years pretty much sums up Blight's contribution as Adelaide Football Club's greatest coach to date.

When Gary Ayres accepted the coaching job with the AFC for 2000, everyone associated with the club sat up and took notice. Playing for Hawthorn during one of Australian Rules Football's greatest eras, Ayres had been a tough defender and had a reputation for being equally as tough as a coach. He had taken Geelong to a Grand Final in his first year in charge, but had missed out on a Premiership. Like Malcolm Blight, he saw the talent still on the Crows' list and jumped at the opportunity to move to Adelaide and assume the reins. Coming from a successful club like Hawthorn and almost winning a flag with the Cats, his credentials seemed exactly what the Crows needed. Although Mark considered Malcolm Blight close to irreplaceable, Ayres' appointment was also exciting and he looked forward to leading Adelaide with renewed enthusiasm. But before his first pre-season campaign had even begun, Ayres' move to live in Adelaide was made difficult by serious family health issues, which put tremendous pressure on the new coach.

The Crows kicked off the 2000 home-and-away season disastrously, with five consecutive losses and any hopes of playing in September all but gone. Contrary to the general form of the team, however, Mark was in scintillating touch. He averaged 26 disposals per game for the season and was high in the best players most weeks, as were Andrew McLeod and Simon Goodwin, but the Crows could manage only nine wins for the year and finished in eleventh position.

Mark was handed the club captaincy for the 2001 season after being deputy vice captain for the previous four years. Leading the Crows was something he had dreamed about since his debut, but had never thought would become a reality. Coming off a very poor season in 2000, things weren't in good shape at the club and he knew there would be a lot more to being captain than simply tossing the coin before each match. Ayres was under pressure to elevate the Crows to a more acceptable position, and he was certain to share some of this pressure with the senior players. Mark felt confident enough to do the job, and to do it well, gaining a lot of inspiration from his memories of Chris McDermott and Mark Bickley at the helm. Both had been the most committed clubmen Mark had met and seemed the perfect models for any new captain.

That year's pre-season competition provided Mark with an early stumbling block that would go on to plague him for quite some time. Midway through the first match against the Western Bulldogs he cracked two ribs in a heavy clash. Despite being pretty sore for a few days afterwards, he came up well enough to play in the second game. However, he struggled for breath after sustained bursts and knew that things weren't right. This trend continued as the home-and-away season got under way, and in round two he was forced from the ground with an alarmingly high heart rate and a noticeable lack of energy. After being examined by the club doctor, he was ordered to stay off the ground. His heart was racing at 200 beats per minute after being benched, and still recorded a dangerous 110 bpm – 50 beats higher than it should have been – after sitting out the entire game.

The following week was spent taking medical tests. Tests on Mark's blood, pulmonary and cardiac function showed nothing abnormal, which was both surprising and frustrating. His aerobic capacity remained limited, which seemed absurd, given the amount of endurance training he had completed with the squad over the summer. He would get through training with an 80 per cent effort and be able to front up for a match, but when asked to put in a full 100 per cent during a game, he would tire quickly and be forced to come off the ground periodically to recover. He complained constantly that he couldn't get enough oxygen into his lungs, but despite further tests on his lungs and heart, the club doctor couldn't pinpoint anything to explain the condition.

Mark consulted the highly regarded naturopath Lyn Crossman, and embarked on a liver cleansing diet to eliminate the possibility that toxins might be interfering with his system. His team-mate and housemate at the time, Brett Burton, commented that, while there might have been a shortage of breath in Mark's lungs, there was certainly no shortage of wind from downstairs!

After all this testing and no sign of improvement, Mark began to feel that the medicos didn't believe what he was telling them. Gary Ayres thought the ailment might have been stress-related, which was certainly not the case. Although no one ever questioned his sincerity, Mark suspected (falsely, as it turned out) that they doubted him, which was probably the most frustrating thing of all. It was a desperate and anxious time, with the only obvious source of his condition being the rib fracture he had suffered several weeks previously. One hypothesis was that the ribs hadn't healed properly and the nerves in the area had become 'confused' and wouldn't allow the brain to expand the rib cage to protect the injured site.

With this in mind, Mark organised regular physiotherapy in an effort to break up the scar tissue that had formed around the rib fracture. At Mark's own expense, he also flew regularly to Mildura to visit a chiropractor named Ron Keys, who was a former head trainer at Carlton and something of a legend in treating football injuries. Keys had a background in medical autopsies as well as a reputation for knowing how to fix the human body when no one else could. Quite a few of the AFL clubs used Keys to treat injured players, and Mark knew he was in good hands as soon as he met him.

After a couple of visits, Keys' diagnosis was that the nerves surrounding each of the fractured ribs had become displaced. When this was corrected, intensive physiotherapy would be needed to facilitate the healing process. There would be no 'quick fix'. Mark remembers those treatment sessions with Adelaide-based physiotherapist Steve Saunders as being extremely painful, but gradually his lung capacity returned and he started to run out games again. By that stage, however, much of the 2001 season had passed him by. The Crows finished eighth after an inconsistent home-and-away series and failed to advance beyond the First Elimination Final. Mark's inaugural season as club captain had been less than auspicious. He had averaged 19 disposals per game and all he could do was put the season behind him and look forward to 2002 with renewed optimism.

Mark picked up another All-Australian jumper after showing exceptional form in 2002. His consistency was remarkable and, with no significant injuries impeding his progress, he contributed strongly to the Crows' steady improvement. He played his 200th game in round eight that season against the Kangaroos at Manuka Oval in Canberra. It was one of the coldest days he can ever recall on the footy field and typical of the Australian Capital Territory in late May. He doubts the temperature climbed into double figures at any stage during the match, which made playing especially difficult. Mark started the game at full forward and was picked up by Kangaroos strong man Glenn Archer, whose primary stopping tactic was punching Mark's hands away every time the ball came in overhead. Adelaide lost to the Kangaroos by 17 points, and new recruit Ryan Fitzgerald suffered a career-ending knee injury. It was a milestone match to be remembered for all the wrong reasons.

The Crows made it through to the Preliminary Final after a dramatic come-from-behind against Melbourne, but ultimately were stopped by Collingwood in what was both a spiteful and controversial match. Top performer Tyson Edwards was knocked out by Jason Cloke, which set Adelaide back dramatically. The 28-point loss to the Magpies, and yet another Grand Final opportunity missed, was hard for Mark and his team-mates to accept. The Brisbane Lions would go on to record their second successive Premiership, and Gary Ayres' frustration was destined to continue. Mark's average disposal rate of 22.5 was well up on the previous season and he had kicked a career-best 35 goals for the year.

Floating bone chips in his left ankle severely restricted Mark's preparation for the 2003 season. He missed most of the pre-season competition and took the field for the first time as Adelaide headed into the Wizard Cup Grand Final against Collingwood. Mark tossed the coin at the start of that game, then ran to the bench. With limited games under his belt, he played in short bursts, but still managed to hold the Premiers' trophy aloft at game's end. His team-mates gave him plenty of ribbing for hogging the glory of a Wizard Cup win, but after missing out on one Premiership back in 1997, he wasn't going to let this one slip by.

With a week off for all AFL clubs prior to the commencement of the 2003 home-and-away season, Mark was sent to play for the

Woodville/West Torrens Eagles in a trial game. He desperately needed game time and, although an inter-club trial was far from ideal, he was grateful for the opportunity. This was his first match in the SANFL for over a decade and he felt a little awkward. The match was against Port Adelaide at Alberton. Although Mark copped a bit from some of the 200-odd Port fans in attendance, the match provided him with a competitive hit-out.

Wayne Carey came to the Crows from North Melbourne in rather controversial circumstances that year, providing Adelaide fans with a burst of optimism. The club had finished third the year before, won a pre-season Premiership, and picked up one of the greatest forwards the AFL had ever seen; the recipe seemed in place for the Adelaide Football Club to return to the list of long-term winners. Mark's form, despite a less-than-ideal preparation, was red-hot. In fact, featuring regularly in the best players and polling strongly in the various media awards, he seemed at the pinnacle of his game.

Mark and Wayne Carey became close friends during that season. Both from the country, they had a lot in common and spent time together away from football. They shared enormous mutual respect and although Carey's contribution was restricted by injury, his influence and experience were critical to a strong home-and-away series for the club. He brought a lot out of those he played with and helped Mark develop as an effective forward. Carey says he has played with few team-mates who are as professional and held in such high esteem as Mark. As soon as he arrived at West Lakes, he knew the Crows were in good hands. Like former team-mate Glenn Archer, Carey says Mark is the ultimate on-field leader. He is super-skilled, courageous, plays the game as hard as he can, and will hand out a bump or two when the time is right, but his major attribute is his ability to lead by example.

The Crows finished the 2003 minor round with thirteen wins and nine losses, but couldn't overcome the Lions in Brisbane to make an impact in the finals. Mark Bickley, the club's inaugural Premiership captain, hung up his boots after the Gabba loss. Despite the Crows' failure to advance in September, the Monday evening of Grand Final week provided Mark Ricciuto with one of his greatest football moments.

Touted for several weeks by the media as one of the Brownlow Medal favourites, Mark considered himself an each-way bet in the game's most prestigious individual award. His year had certainly been very consistent, and kicking a few goals would have made the umpires more aware of his presence than in seasons past. However, Collingwood's Nathan Buckley and Sydney's Adam Goodes were the big tips around Melbourne.

Ultimately, sharing the stage at the Melbourne Entertainment Centre with Buckley and Goodes was a moment Mark – and most other South Australians – will never forget. There was hysteria in Waikerie when the final round of votes had been revealed and Mark was announced joint winner of the 2003 Brownlow Medal. It was a sweet moment for Crows fans after their team had failed to produce when it really counted. Mark also picked up his second Club Champion award and the Best Team Man trophy – the first time anyone at the Crows had taken out the quinella.

It wasn't until after Mark won the Brownlow Medal that Gary Ayres first complimented him on his achievements. Ayres, like Malcolm Blight before him, never got really close to any of his playing squad, despite having the occasional beer with them if the occasion warranted. In retrospect, Mark feels that some of his team-mates might have performed better under Ayres if he had been able more often to give praise where it was obviously due. Having said that, Mark and Ayres remain good friends today.

Again, things didn't go to plan for Mark during the pre-season of 2004. While playing a game of 'British Bulldog' at a training camp at Strathalbyn, he broke his right thumb in a contest with ruckman Rhett Biglands. Both lined up at opposite ends of the Bulldog course, then Biglands took off, flat out, in an attempt to get past Mark and reach his home territory without being brought down. Rhett is a big guy with a 100-kilogram-plus frame, and when Mark's thumb copped the full brunt of this bulk in an awkward tackle, it snapped like a carrot. Thumb injuries are as debilitating as they are painful and this set him back for a while with ball work. Fitness wasn't an issue, as he spent plenty of time on the exercise bike and running, but with his right lower arm in plaster, using the football should have had to wait a few weeks. However, Mark was back at Strathalbyn the day after the accident and trained with his arm in plaster, catching the ball with his left hand and disposing of it with his left foot.

All was healed, and Mark was itching to play again, by the time the 2004 season opened. But it was to be yet another frustratingly poor year for the Adelaide Crows. They lost their first four games and seemed to be on a downward spiral, but rallied mid-season and thrashed Hawthorn by 86 points on the MCG. This was Mark's 250th game – he kicked three goals and racked up an imposing 35 possessions – but, that milestone aside, he could find little to get excited about. Further injury forced Wayne Carey to call it quits after round 12, having kicked 24 goals and looking in good form; and a week later Crows' stalwart Nigel Smart decided to hang up his boots as well. Adelaide was sitting well out of the top eight with a win–loss record of four and nine at that point, and it came as no real surprise to learn that Gary Ayres had opted to join the growing list of departures.

Ayres' main flaws as a coach, Mark believes, were his inability both to inspire and to cater for a wide range of personalities from within the playing group. There are many footballers who don't need a lot of positive feedback in order to perform consistently, but there are also quite a few who do, and these were the players who didn't achieve under Ayres. Although Adelaide's general performance had lifted during Ayres' time at the helm, Mark feels that the team's improvement could and should have been faster.

Gary Ayres' departure after round 13 of the home-and-away season of 2004 saw his former assistant, Neil Craig, take over as caretaker. Craig had been at the club for eight years (excluding the time in 1999 he spent helping out with the Australian Cycling Team in preparation for the Sydney Olympics). He was highly respected in all quarters, and it didn't take long before even the Victorians stopped calling him 'Neil Who?' and began taking notice. Craig has an incredible work ethic. He was, and still is, always the first at the club before training, and is invariably the last to leave. He demands a lot from his assistant coaches and rarely thinks of much else but football. His enthusiasm and level of involvement rubbed off on all around him at the club from the moment he took control. Suddenly the mind-set of the squad changed, with everyone becoming more positive.

Craig led the Crows to a strong victory over Melbourne in his first game at the helm, but his interim appointment didn't arrest the alarming decline. He would go on to try a lot of young players in the Crows' lineup during the last rounds of 2004. An alarming injury list, and the retirement of some experienced campaigners, essentially set these youngsters up for a crack at the top level in 2005. Several of them have since gone on to become regulars and are now touted as the real future of the Adelaide Football Club.

Three weeks into Craig's stint as interim head coach, the team travelled to Brisbane to take on a full-strength Lions outfit and came away with a 141-point drubbing. Mark recalls feeling totally helpless at the Gabba that evening, leading a side that was seriously undermanned and devoid of confidence, and being able to do little to curb the brilliance of opponents Voss, Lappin, Black, Akermanis, Power and Lynch. Adelaide finished the season with just eight wins from 22 starts. Mark's contribution as leader had again been strong, averaging better than 24 disposals a game. He came second in the Brownlow Medal behind West Coast's Chris Judd and won his third Malcolm Blight Medal as Club Champion. This was Mark's seventh All-Australian selection and his first as All-Australian captain.

When Craig was appointed as head coach for the 2005 season, Mark's fifth as club captain, optimism again returned to West Lakes. Craig's incredible work ethic rubbed off immediately on all around him and things began to turn around quickly. Several of the youngsters who had been 'blooded' in the second half of 2004 started to show form, the enthusiasm of the entire outfit increased, and Crows members and supporters sensed that good things lay ahead.

Always documenting, analysing and reviewing the progress of his squad, Craig leaves nothing to chance. He introduced heart-rate monitors, tracking systems, lactate testing, in-flight humidifiers, ice vests, training communication helmets, and a host of other innovations designed to provide his players with a vital edge. Mark believes that Craig has brought a whole new science to football, setting standards that the other clubs have been forced to follow.

Craig also recognises the value of speaking with top coaches in other elite-level sports and constantly reminds his players of the need to be the best they can be. According to Mark, Craig values greatly the input of his top six or seven players – the guys who have been at the coal face for ten years or more and who know as much if not more about the game than he does. It was Craig who initiated the Club's Leadership Program, which Mark regards as one of the most significant steps forward in the Crows' history. The program utilises the expertise of senior players, involves some of the so-called second-tier players, and generally makes everyone a lot more answerable for everything they do.

One very significant initiative for the 2005 season was the establishment of the leadership program, which made everyone at the club accountable. In previous years, too much had been left to too few people, and Craig and his senior panel decided to spread the load around and involve all the players. The senior group would be known as the 'Backbone' players – guys who had been around for three seasons or longer – and they would be asked to assume a lot more responsibility in several areas. A few in this category had been flat and uninspired under Gary Ayres, and the new coach was determined to bring them out and make them aware of exactly how important they were to the wellbeing and future of the Crows. Those players who had been at the club for just one or two seasons would be known as the 'Crushers' and they, too, would be asked to make a more significant contribution under this program.

Ray McLean, an expert in the field of leadership and team-building and author of the book *Any Given Team*, was brought in to consult on how best to initiate the Leadership Program. He had worked closely with Alan Stewart at Central Districts, where his input and advice had strengthened that club, and also with the Sydney Swans. In fact, he still works closely with Paul Roos in Sydney and consulted with both the Swans and Crows simultaneously for some time. The program revolves around the basic premise that everyone has a role and responsibility, from club captain all the way down to the youngest recruits, and that the opinions and ideas of all personnel are important. Everyone is accountable for their actions, and absolute honesty is vital for the program to work. So successful has the model proven in the AFL that at least a third of the clubs have now adopted it. It has also found its way into Rugby League, Rugby Union and the National Basketball League.

When Ray McLean came to the Crows and met Mark for the first time, he was immediately impressed with his outlook and obvious commitment to making the Adelaide Football Club a stronger and better place. McLean says that without a character as highly regarded as the club captain embracing the Leadership Program, it would never work. It also needs a coach as progressive and forward thinking as Neil Craig, and when McLean saw coach and skipper together, he knew his model would be successful at Adelaide.

One of the Leadership Program's most revealing and enlightening aspects is its feedback component. This involves an individual player coming up with three words he would use to describe himself, and three words he would like his team-mates to use to describe him. As he is making this list, his team-mates are deciding on the three words they feel best portray him. Quite often, of course, the lists don't match and this provides the player concerned with an accurate view of where he stands and what he should be thinking about in terms of improvement.

The 'start, stop, keep' philosophy is part of this process and represents things the team thinks an individual player should either start doing, stop doing or keep doing. It depends totally on an honest, open forum, where everyone has the right to express an opinion. Ray McLean says that, when he first came to the Crows and sat in on meetings involving the coach and players, they were pretty much dominated by Mark and Neil Craig. However, as the Leadership Program began to flourish and gain acceptance, the

.meetings began to open up and communication improved at all levels of the playing group.

All of this takes guts in an open forum, and Mark says it forces the players to have their own house in order before they start criticising others. It's a very confrontational process, but it provides immediate feedback from which no one is exempt. At most clubs the first- and second-year players have a settling-in period, during which they find a level of acceptance they can build on as they play more games and become more experienced. However, McLean's Leadership Program doesn't allow for this at all and, regardless of the fact that new players may be a little shy and reticent, they are still expected to go through the same process as the captain and senior team members.

Like many of the other senior players around him, Mark was astounded at the difference the program made in a short space of time. Suddenly there were a lot of so-called second-tier footballers putting their hands up, making the sorts of decisions they hadn't made before and contributing in ways that surprised everyone. This spilled over into games and propelled Adelaide to its first Minor Premiership, with 17 wins and superior percentage to the West Coast Eagles. With virtually the same playing list that had floundered in 2004, Adelaide forged ahead with confidence and, at times, arrogance. The 110-point thrashing of Collingwood at Football Park in round 21 was a perfect example of a team that believed in itself, and the club entered its eleventh finals campaign confident and ready to take on anyone, anywhere.

There would be one notable omission from the Crows' team for the first final, however. In round 22, with Adelaide travelling to Perth to fight it out with the Eagles for the Minor Premiership, Mark Ricciuto was reported and eventually suspended for striking Adam Selwood. This suspension was shattering, both for Mark and the club, and he insists he was harshly done by over the entire incident. An errant kick in after a West Coast point lobbed over Mark's head forced him to turn quickly and run at top pace to recover possession for Adelaide. Unfortunately, Selwood ran in to contest, but was tripped accidentally and fell forward as he and Mark closed on the football. Instead of collecting his opponent in the chest region as contact was made, Mark's elbow found Selwood's head and he went down heavily. He insists there was no malice in the incident at all and that the whole set of circumstances was unfortunate, but the AFL Tribunal disagreed and banned Mark for the first final. The suspension could have been far worse, with a three-match ban initially imposed, but it was reduced to one match on appeal and Mark had no option but to cop it and prepare himself for the remainder of the major round.

A small consolation for Mark was being presented with the much coveted Tool of the Week award on the Channel Ten program *Before the Game*, which undoubtedly sits proudly with all the other awards he has picked up during his career. The award was his when, shortly after the Selwood incident, he took a mark inside the 50-metre zone, his jockstrap broke and he suffered a well-publicised wardrobe malfunction. This was a significant feat, given that football shorts are now considerably longer and looser fitting than in the Warwick Capper days!

With ten consecutive wins under the belt, but without the leadership of its greatest player, Adelaide struggled to capitalise on a general ascendency in play against St Kilda in its first home final. That eight-point loss sent them to a second home-town final against Port Adelaide and then to Perth, where they would have to overcome the vastly improved West Coast Eagles to secure a Grand Final berth. Although he concedes that losing one player will rarely affect the outcome of any football game, Mark is confident the Crows would have beaten St Kilda in the first final if he had been out there, and that untimely suspension still haunts him. Being able to lead and inspire his troops during that disappointing performance against the Saints just might have been enough to get them over the line. Given the Crows' impressive record against Sydney, had they fronted up against the Swans on Grand Final afternoon, Club Premiership number three may have been achievable. They wouldn't have had to travel to Perth to play in a Preliminary Final and would have been in perfect shape for a Premiership assault. All of this is academic, of course, and finishing third was a bitter pill for all at Adelaide to swallow.

Having been part of the team that threw away a Premiership chance in 1993, missing the Grand Final in 1997, going close in 2002 and now bowing out in 2005 after showing so much promise, the loss at Subiaco cut Mark to the bone. Such opportunities at this level of elite sport are rare, and Mark sat in front of his locker in tears for half an hour after the game. Although he had tried hard to avoid it, and put off fronting the media for as long as he could, his eyes were red in the post-match press conference. He had climbed back on to that emotional roller-coaster, where frustration, disappointment and a sense of guilt over his suspension combined to make this the most bitter of all pills to swallow.

These finals lowlights aside, however, 2005 had been another year of great personal achievement for Mark Ricciuto. He averaged over 24 disposals per game, collected All-Australian jumper number eight and was announced All-Australian Captain for the second year in a row. As far as individual accolades and awards were concerned, his collection was becoming truly enviable. Now easily the most decorated player at the Adelaide Football Club, Mark would again lead the Crows in 2006. The new coach was now more experienced, the playing list was strong and, with so much unfinished business to take care of, Mark looked forward to his fourteenth season as much as he had his first. Well aware that his career was winding inexorably towards its conclusion, Mark knew that he, and a couple of other senior Crows, were running out of chances for another flag.

Although his body was beginning to show a few signs of having played the game at the top level for fourteen years, Mark's resolve during the 2006 pre-season had never been stronger. He managed his best time ever in a three-kilometre run before the Christmas break, which gave him plenty of confidence at age 30. Many of the Crows' younger brigade, including Brent Reilly, Trent Hentschel, Nathan Van Berlo and Nathan Bock, had advanced to the next level and there was an air of optimism within the playing group that rubbed off on everyone. The media touted this as the most talented Crows squad ever, and it seemed that all the club needed to succeed, apart from continuing its work ethic, was more of Neil Craig's coaching magic and some luck with injuries.

Mark had a minor groin operation mid-January and resumed training with the group in good spirits, but he experienced some worrying hamstring soreness early in his first session. He had never had a hamstring issue in his entire career and immediately sought treatment. He thought that the mandatory rest period after his groin surgery would have eliminated any hamstring problems, but the problem became more severe as training escalated and was eventually diagnosed as hamstring tendonitis. More difficult to overcome than a regulation hamstring strain, this is a typical over-use injury and one that set Mark's pre-season well and truly on its backside. He took no part in the pre-season competition and, with limited preparation, looked in danger of missing the beginning of the home-and-away series.

Reaching the Grand Final of the 2006 NAB Cup pre-season competition had never been a real priority during the pre-season build-up, and Mark is certain the Crows could have defeated Geelong that evening if they had lined up with their strongest team. However, the plan from round one of the NAB series had been to expose as many promising youngsters as possible to top-level football and an eight-point loss was as pleasing as any defeat can possibly be.

Most observers, and particularly the media, were surprised when Mark was named in the Crows 22 to play in the season opener against Collingwood in Melbourne. With his hamstring tendonitis well publicised and no NAB Cup game time to fall back on, the 'armchair' critics had a field day over Neil Craig's decision to play the skipper in round one. It was a Monday night game (the first in AFL history) at the Telstra Dome before a huge crowd and an unprecedented television audience, and although the Crows' pre-season form had been strong, they went in slightly as underdogs. As expected, the Melbourne media considered Mark's selection a huge liability. He had trained just three times in the lead-up to the match and most predicted he would toss the coin and run to the bench. However, in a huge show of faith, Craig sent Mark to full forward for the opening bounce. It was a move that would pay off.

In a masterful display that showed how versatile the Adelaide captain had become, Mark kicked six goals three and won most of the media votes as best on ground. The Crows prevailed in a stirring game of Australian Rules Football that would set the trend for much of the home-and-away series. Mark missed rounds five and six with his first genuine hamstring strain, but returned and continued to play up forward and kicked enough goals to justify the coach's decision to keep him out of the centre.

Hamstring tendonitis would plague Mark for much of the season, restricting his training and fitness level and virtually precluding him from rejoining Tyson Edwards, Simon Goodwin,

Scott Thompson and Robert Shirley in the mid-field. Despite his on-ball absence, however, the Crows' dominance throughout the minor round began to worry many in Victoria. After eight consecutive victories and sitting well clear on top of the ladder after round fourteen, they were installed as short-priced favourites to win the Premiership – odds that hadn't been seen since the glory days of Hawthorn in the 1980s.

That particular round was also significant for another reason: it was Mark Ricciuto's 300th game. As anticipated, the Adelaide media build-up to this milestone match was typically frenzied. Never before had Mark felt so pressured by requests for interviews, press conferences and live appearances. There was even a commemorative coin and a life-size Ricciuto head cut-out made available by *The Advertiser* newspaper. All of this attention took a toll, and although Mark was proud to have achieved 300 games, he was also relieved when it was over and all the fuss had died away. Those 300 games had taken just thirteen years and 83 days to complete – the fastest ever in VFL/AFL history.

The first cracks in Adelaide's seemingly invincible armour appeared when the team travelled to Perth in round fifteen to take on the West Coast Eagles. Craig's training regime had been unrelenting and the Crows played that day with heavy legs and weary minds. Mark considers this the club's worst performance since 2004, when it had been humiliated by Brisbane at the Gabba by 141 points, and it marked the beginning of a poor month of football. Several big names, including McLeod, Hart and Burton, were missing through well-publicised injuries, and there was an air of tiredness within the playing group that worried everyone. Most AFL teams go through flat spots at some stage of the season and manage to climb back up again, but for Adelaide to lose form and suffer injuries to key personnel leading into the finals was a major blow.

If they had been despondent after being eliminated in 2005, they felt totally shattered in 2006. To be so far ahead of the pack for three-quarters of the season and then to bow out in this fashion was devastating.

Despite struggling badly towards the end of the minor round, however, Adelaide rallied to defeat Fremantle by five goals at AAMI Stadium in the Second Qualifying Final. This gave the club a much-needed week's rest before taking on the West Coast Eagles – again at home and before a sell-out crowd. In stark contrast to Adelaide, the Eagles had found their best form for the season exactly at the right time, and everyone concerned with the Crows knew West Coast would be a formidable opponent.

Leading by 22 points at half time and due to kick with a substantial breeze in the third quarter, the Adelaide side was in good shape to beat the Eagles and advance to the Grand Final. Despite the absence of several star players due to illness or injury and the poor lead-up form, it appeared they might just overcome the odds and have their first crack at a Premiership in eight seasons. However, history tells us this didn't happen. West Coast took control from the first bounce after the long break, ultimately running over the Crows, who simply ran out of legs and finished the season in third position for the second year in a row. Mark was close to playing against the West Coast and, if the Crows had got through, would definitely have taken his place in the Grand Final.

Most South Australians had never heard of parvovirus before it was eventually diagnosed as the cause of Mark's physical problems late in the 2006 season. He had first noticed a general tiredness and reduction in energy in the week leading up to his 300th game, but he put it down to the milestone match build-up and the added pressure of having to cope with the unrelenting media attention. However, over the ensuing month he seemed to have at least one day a week when he felt ill and woke up in bed sweating. Mark recalls driving down to training one Saturday morning before a Sunday home game and having to pull the car over to dry retch. He felt awful, but trained anyway and then sought help from the club's medical staff. Their first thought was that he might have contracted some virulent strain of stomach bug, which would run its course and leave him free to resume playing, but when Mark's health deteriorated further, the medicos became concerned and ordered a complete range of diagnostic tests.

His blood work immediately showed the presence of a virus, but its actual identity was a little more difficult to pin down. Ross River virus, glandular fever and even chronic fatigue syndrome were investigated, but none really matched the whole gamut of symptoms, which, by this stage, had worsened dramatically. Mark had little or no energy, his joints ached, he felt periodically nauseous, and there was very real concern not just for his immediate playing future, but for his long-term health. He lost weight through being unable to keep food down and was confined to bed until an answer could be found.

It was a call-in to a local radio station from someone who had suffered the same symptoms as Mark that finally unlocked the mystery. Parvovirus is very uncommon in adults and it's still unclear as to how he actually contracted the illness. One hypothesis was that the infection was transferred through contact with a youngster at a football clinic or function, and Mark suspects it probably occurred during the week leading up to his 300th game. He'd had unprecedented contact with strangers during that period, signing hundreds of autographs for young fans and, as this is when he first felt ill, chances are one of those wide-eyed kids unwittingly passed on the virus to their idol.

To compound matters further, a dose of hepatitis came with the parvovirus, turning Mark's eyes yellow and giving his skin a jaundiced appearance. With his immune system way down, and his liver compromised and struggling to fight off the virus, his general condition deteriorated to a point where a specialist all but ruled him out of the Crows' finals campaign. Feeling as low as he did at that point, tears welled in his eyes. The only reason he was still playing football was to be part of a second Premiership side and this dream was now all but gone.

The only cure for parvovirus is rest, so Mark went home, turned off his phone and shut himself away from the world. He watched the complete series of *Rocky* movies, every episode of *The Sopranos*, and tuned in to the Sky Racing Channel whenever a horse of interest was running. He delegated responsibility for his various business interests to others he knew he could trust, and relied on family, the Adelaide Football Club and his fiancée, Sarah, to keep his life running as best it could without his involvement.

The year had been yet another in a string of disappointing years for Mark Ricciuto and the Adelaide Football Club. The captain had missed seven games – the most ever in a single season to that point. Despite his health issues, however, Mark had kicked 44 goals and made a strong contribution to the team effort. Hopping on and off that dreaded emotional roller-coaster was becoming something of a habit and he wasn't sure exactly how much more he could handle.

8

SARAH

In 1994, seventeen-year-old Sarah-Jane Delahunt had arrived in Adelaide from Port Augusta, where she had been the last of three children born to Irene, who owned a clothing store, and Mick Delahunt, a train driver. Sarah had decided against going to university, but the lack of employment opportunities in her home town had convinced her to think about moving to Adelaide. As is often the case when country-born teenagers relocate, it was difficult to leave both her immediate and extended family, though they were all supportive of her decision. So, with a couple of bulging suitcases and a tear in her eye, she headed south to the Big Smoke. Sarah was the first of two Delahunt children (the second being her brother, Chris) to move to Adelaide, and these days her parents live in the city as well.

Some part-time modelling and a sales job at the Just Jeans outlet in the Westfield Arndale Shopping Centre suited her nicely at that stage and, although she missed her family and friends, she soon adjusted to the city lifestyle and looked ahead to an exciting future.

Always a Crows supporter, Sarah was excited one day to learn that Mark Ricciuto was signing autographs in the shopping centre where she worked. Wearing her Just Jeans badge, she lined up along with a crowd of other young Adelaide fans, in hopes of meeting the star player. Soon after the autograph-signing session, Mark walked into Just Jeans intending to buy some clothes. He and Sarah struck up a conversation and Sarah found him pleasant and approachable. He also bought $300 worth of clothing, which pleased Sarah's boss and earned her a handy sales bonus! There was an obvious attraction, even from that first meeting, and the two would always enjoy a wave, a smile and sometimes a chat if they ran into each other after-hours in a city nightclub or restaurant.

Keen to get into business administration, Sarah eventually left Just Jeans and applied for a traineeship at Macweld Industries, an engineering company, where she quickly settled in. She would ultimately spend twelve years with the company. Sarah thoroughly enjoyed her time with Brett Duncanson and the Macweld team, who treated her more like family than a staff member. She loved the Duncanson children and became like an older sister to Jacob and Emily. There were just twelve employees at Macweld when Sarah started with the company and more than 150 when she eventually left. In her time there she had progressed from administration trainee to manager of administration. Duncanson was on the Port Power board, and there was always a lot of good-natured rivalry from both sides.

At that stage, Mark and Sarah both had steady partners, so their friendship remained casual. One evening, Sarah bumped into Mark while she was out with some girlfriends and invited him and his mates to a party at her friend's place. It was here they first exchanged phone numbers, but the two then drifted out of each other's lives for a couple of years. It wasn't until Sarah and her long-time boyfriend eventually parted ways in 1999 that she decided to give Mark a call. She found his phone number on the drinks coaster she had put away some years before, but when she dialled the number it was no longer in service.

Keen to re-establish contact, Sarah found Mark's parents' number in Waikerie in the phone book and eventually summoned the courage to ring them. She introduced herself, and explained that she had cousins living in Waikerie, Matt and Brenton Kay, whom Mark knew. She hoped this connection would jog Mark's memory. Instead of asking for Mark's new mobile number, she decided to leave hers in the hope that his parents would pass it on and he would call her. Sarah didn't really expect to hear from Mark; it had been quite a while since the two had spoken, and she had no idea if he was still with his previous girlfriend or had even moved on to another relationship.

He phoned the very next day.

Mark was in the middle of a break-up at that time, and the idea of having someone else to talk to obviously appealed to him. Sarah went overseas for a while that year and Mark was becoming even more intensely involved with the Crows, so once again they temporarily lost contact.

Mark and Sarah's relationship finally blossomed in 2000. After years of being little more than casual acquaintances, they officially became a couple and things went along nicely for quite some time. Early in 2003, however, they decided to separate for a while. Mark needed to be clear in his own mind that she was the right girl and that it was the right time in both their lives to make the sort of commitment he had always considered very important.

Those ten months apart were very difficult for Sarah. She missed him terribly, having long since decided that Mark was the man she wanted to spend the rest of her life with. She had known that from the first time they had kissed, when she felt a very special connection. There was intermittent contact during their time apart, so when Mark phoned her just before the 2003 Brownlow Medal night and asked her to accompany him, she was surprised but accepted the invitation happily.

As this was by far their highest-profile date, and they hadn't seen a lot of each other that year, Sarah was understandably nervous. Mark being named a joint winner of the Brownlow Medal that evening added to the euphoria of the occasion. Sarah remembers the event as a high point in their life together, although she says the three days after the Brownlow evening were 'a bit of a blur'.

From that point onward, their relationship went from strength to strength. It was as if Mark's period of soul-searching and introspection had finally come to an end and, for the first time, he knew exactly where he wanted to be. Sarah was naturally delighted, as her feelings towards Mark had only grown stronger. Soon the couple became inseparable.

On New Year's Eve in 2005, Mark and Sarah were on their annual end-of-year houseboat holiday with a 50-strong crowd of friends on the Murray River. The boats were pulled into the shore near Overland Corner and all on board, including several of Mark's Crows team-mates, were preparing to see in the New Year in style at the Overland Corner Hotel. At about 10.30 pm, Mark suggested that he and Sarah take a walk down by the river and phone their families to wish them a happy new year. Sarah thought she was about to get lucky, and she did, but for a different reason – they got engaged!

When they had put some distance between the rest of the party and themselves, Sarah could sense that Mark was nervous and quite obviously had something on his mind. But it wasn't until he began fumbling around in his pocket and eventually produced a small black heart-shaped box that she realised exactly what was going on.

Sarah

When Mark asked her to marry him, Sarah was speechless. It was done with typical country style. 'What do you reckon? Do you think we should get married?' he asked. It took Sarah a few seconds to compose herself enough to respond. Instead of accepting his proposal immediately, she asked him if he was really certain that this was what he wanted. This was her dream – what she had been longing for, but had never really expected – and she had to be sure that Mark's feelings were as strong as hers. When he replied that he was absolutely sure, Sarah joyously accepted his proposal. There were tears as he slipped the engagement ring on her finger.

There could be few better ways to bring in a new year than by announcing an engagement, particularly an engagement that friends and family on both sides had long been hoping would take place.

Sarah and Mark set a wedding date for the late spring, after the football season had ended. Both being very family-oriented people, they talked about having children immediately. Four, five or even six kids would be on the agenda, and they agreed to start sooner rather than later. In March 2006, Sarah discovered she was pregnant. She and Mark were ecstatic at the news, as were their families and close friends. However, as Sarah would be eight months pregnant at their planned wedding date and it would be just a little hard to be fitted for her dress, the wedding was deferred. On 16 November 2006, Sophie Jane Ricciuto came into the world.

9

THREE SPECIAL PEOPLE

Having special mates – mates you can rely on through thick and thin – is vital to most of us, and when we find them, we generally hit it off straight away. Having been in the limelight since he was a teenager, Mark had countless acquaintances and casual friends, but there were two people he considered to be his best mates – Joe DeVito from Waikerie and Matt Dawson from Adelaide.

Both of these mates would pass away within a couple of months of their 30th birthdays – Matt shortly before and Joe shortly after. Their deaths had a profound effect on Mark and on the way he viewed the world. Being a pallbearer at both funerals and experiencing true grief for the first time affected him greatly.

Matt Dawson was born in Whyalla and, like many country lads, moved to Adelaide to further his education. Brought up in a caring Catholic family with high moral standards, Matt had a great outlook on life. He knew what was right and let that guide him, but he also enjoyed a good time more than most. Although he wasn't a football nut, he enjoyed the game. He also loved most of the other outdoor activities Mark had pursued since childhood. And like Mark, Matt was keen on business and had a firm idea of where he was headed in life.

The Ricciuto–Dawson friendship blossomed and provided Mark with a much-needed escape from the high-pressure world of AFL football. He was always a lot more comfortable away from the limelight and the rigours of professional sport, and loved the fact that he could be anonymous with Matt. The two went fishing together at Port Pirie and Whyalla, as well as at the Dawsons' shack at Lucky Bay, near Cowell on the Eyre Peninsula. In turn, Matt's visits with the Ricciutos in the Riverland also provided plenty of enjoyable moments. The two would regularly have dinner together and maybe go into the city once or twice a week to eat at Amalfi, their favourite restaurant.

Maintaining a balance between the expectations and pressures of elite sport and some measure of normality is something a lot of young athletes struggle with. Matt Dawson provided that normality for Mark, and it's a fair bet the reverse situation applied.

Mark grew up with Joe DeVito at Waikerie. Their grandmothers were sisters, but despite a two-year age difference, the boys were much closer than most second cousins. Because Mark played football out of his age group, Joe was in the same junior teams at Waikerie. When they weren't running around the oval, the pair and several other mates were fishing, yabbying or annoying their parents.

Joe DeVito lived life at a hundred miles an hour and put 110 per cent effort into everything he attempted. When the two boys reached their late teenage years and Mark moved down to Adelaide, the relationship remained strong. Whenever Mark had a day off,

A young mum and dad in the late 1980s.

The Ricciuto children: Lisa aged six; Mark, eleven months, and Craig, three years old.

Early days – Mark and Craig having
a kick in the backyard.

Mark backing his first winner.

Yes, it does get hot in Waikerie.

Ten cod caught in one net? You better believe it! *From left:* Kym Lehmann, Mark, Mark's dad, Phil Neilson and Kevin Mackereth, 1981.

Mark sharing a coffee with
Nonno Nicola.

Nicola, the proud
grandfather in 2001.

Showing cousins Julian, centre, and Pip, right, how to grade apricots, 1984.

Mark representing the state primary school team, 1987.

Wax on, wax off – taekwondo exam, 1987.

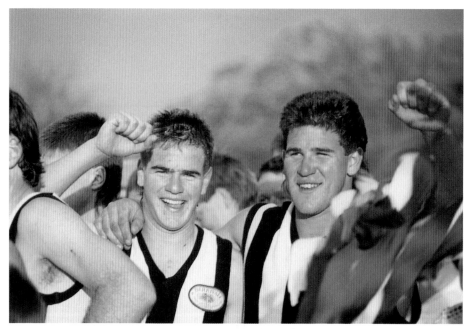

Brothers in arms moments after Waikerie's first Grand Final win in seventeen years, 1991.

Mark running onto the field watched by young supporters, 1993.

Leaping high – playing for the Adelaide Crows at Football Park, 1993.

Mark's drinking mentors, Simon Tregenza, left, and Sean Tasker, right, on a New Year's holiday in Darwin, 1993.

Mark and some of the Waikerie boys show Adelaide Crow Simon Tregenza, left, a few shooting tricks, 1994.

Mark sidestepping Mark
Bickley, 1994.

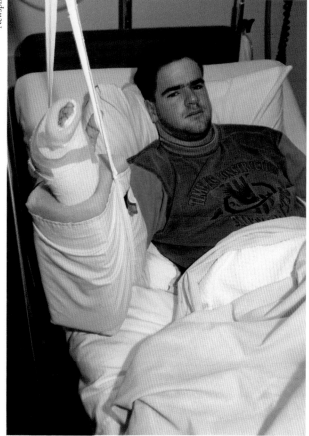

November 1994 – recovering
in hospital after severing a
tendon.

Cooling down before a game against Melbourne, February 1995.

Mark celebrates the Crows' thrilling ten point win over the West Coast with team-mate Greg Anderson.

West Coast Eagles player Peter
Matera is taken out by Mark during
a game at AAMI Stadium, 1995.

Mark in action – he didn't always
have a mullet or a mohawk! 1995.

Relaxing with Chopper. Mark had recently won the Merv Agars *Advertiser* Medal, 1996.

Mark, Bill Kelly, centre, and Andrew McLeod, right, with a bumper catch at Marion Bay, 1997.

Harvesting a 40 kilogram tuna on one of the Lukin vessels, 1997.

The author and his fishing apprentice with a catch at Marion Bay.

Celebrating after another goal in what was one of Mark's most memorable games of football, beating Sydney at the SCG in 1998.

the Waikerie boys would go fishing together or maybe rake a few crabs at Ardrossan. Joe ran a 100-acre (40-hectare) grape block for his father near Waikerie, which was demanding work, and he, too, appreciated the release when he could take the day off to meet his best mate on or by the water.

Always a mad fisherman, Joe became a dedicated theorist in an attempt to lift his fishing game. Mark preferred not to record the statistics, as it made embellishing the facts easier. Joe recorded his catches in a diary, mounted a barometer on the wall to check the effect of air pressure on his catches, and generally delved deeply into the science of fish behaviour. Mark found amusing the fact that one minute Joe would be running amok, having a drink and a bet, and partying with his mates, and the next he would assume his 'professor' mode and get back to investigating the vagaries of angling. He was always over-the-top and considered himself an expert on many things, which the pair often laughed about.

Joe never needed much arm-twisting to get away and spend time with Mark. Usually all it took was a phone call if the crabs were running, or if there were some fish to be caught in the river or along the coast. Joe was always willing to let the grapes look after themselves for a couple of days if he could see there was a good time in the offing. The pair were big on spontaneity.

About the only thing Mark found hard to deal with where Joe DeVito was concerned was his allegiance to Port Adelaide (the Crows' local adversaries in the AFL). The two were always at each other about footy and decided on a standing bet of $1000 and the occasional bottle of Penfolds Grange Hermitage. At one stage the Showdown bet (for games between the Crows and Port Power) was for an expensive aquarium set-up, which Joe collected gleefully. Showdown wagers were fine for Mark in the early days when the Crows had the wood on the Power, but not quite so enjoyable when the tables were turned. At one stage Port had won six Showdowns in a row and the standing bet was starting to become a financial drain.

Joe DeVito and Matt Dawson had met through Mark and had also become good friends, completing a triangle that looked set to remain in place forever.

The phone call from Matt Dawson's family came just before dawn on a Friday morning in December 2000. Matt had been out late the night before and must have drunk too much. He had passed out on the front porch of the family home at Kensington, and had choked on his own vomit. When Mark arrived at the house a few hours later, Matt had been dead for some time.

In shock at the sight of one of his closest mates lying dead on the ground, Mark wandered around, dazed and unsure of quite what to do. There was an air of total disbelief among the family and friends who had gathered in the Dawsons' front yard. Mark had to be at Crows training in a short while, so he left and drove to Football Park. The squad was scheduled to complete a triathlon that morning, and although Mark's still not quite sure how he did it, he finished the gruelling session without mentioning to anyone at the club what had happened just a few hours earlier.

It wasn't until the post-training stretch-down session that the full impact of Matt Dawson's death hit home. Midway through the recovery period, Mark was forced to escape to the toilets, where he broke down. Being captain of the club, he didn't want his team-mates to see his grief – at least, not until he was ready to deal with it – and he stayed out of view until he was composed enough to change his clothes and leave.

Things weren't the same in many areas after Matt had passed away. Family functions were different, nights on the town were different and, with his mate gone, Mark experienced an indescribable void in his life for the first time. He can only imagine what it would have been like for Matt's family, as Matt was the eldest of four children and had always been the dominant one. To have him snatched away under such tragic circumstances must have been excruciating for those left behind.

Matt's mother gave Mark a bracelet to remember her son by, and it's something he holds dear. It's about the only piece of jewellery Mark hasn't managed to lose, which says a lot about the bond that still exists between the two mates. In February 2007, Mark was throwing a crab net over the side of his boat when, to his horror, the bracelet came off his wrist and went over the side, too. When he retrieved the net, the bracelet was entangled in the mesh. He was able to wash it off and put it back on, after which he looked skyward and broke into a wide grin. Despite his paranoia about sharks, Mark believes he probably would have stripped off and gone over the side to retrieve the bracelet if fate hadn't intervened and rescued it for him – or, more likely, he would have paid someone else in the boat to do the retrieval job!

A few months before Matt's passing, Mark had noticed a gradual change in his friend's behaviour. He began doing a few things that Mark didn't approve of, which caused their relationship to sour slightly. Mark now feels that Matt somehow knew he was going to die and had made the decision to try to fit as much as possible into his life before it was taken away. There was tension between the two, which escalated to the point where they didn't talk much for several months. This upset Mark, who likes to resolve personal issues as soon as they arise and to restore harmony before any long-term damage is done.

This rift compounded Mark's grief. To have lost his mate while the pair still weren't on speaking terms upset him terribly. Just before Matt's funeral, Mark sat down and wrote him a lengthy letter, which spelled out exactly how he felt about the distance that had opened between them and how sorry he was that their differences couldn't have been settled. He slipped the letter into an envelope and put it into Matt's hand during the open coffin viewing. Somehow, Mark felt the message would get through to Matt and that it wasn't too late to repair their relationship. It all felt a bit weird, but it was the only way he could think of to maintain the much-needed bond with his old mate. It also provided Mark with at least some small measure of closure, and he now thinks back on only the good times that he and Matt Dawson shared.

Joe DeVito had always been a bit of lad and, although the term is often used loosely, Mark and his circle of friends considered him to be something of a local legend. He enjoyed nothing more than a bet and a drink with the boys, and got himself into a bit of strife from time to time; nothing major, but enough to cause the odd argument with his father. Deep down, however, Joe was a great guy who was in the process of settling down and looking ahead to an exciting future, when his life, too, was cut short.

Joe had always wanted to travel, and he was particularly keen to see Italy and to look up relatives he had never met. In 2003 he booked a comprehensive European holiday and took off on the trip of a lifetime. He also bought a brand-new black Ford XR8, indulging himself as he'd never done before. Mark feels that this was all a bit out of character for Joe, as he had always been conservative with money, but he didn't think much more about it until after Joe's passing.

Joe had been in high spirits after his long-awaited overseas adventure. One day, soon after his return, he was outside gathering firewood, when he fainted and knocked his head quite severely. After regaining consciousness, he managed to drag himself into the house and got a lift to hospital, where he was admitted immediately.

The first Mark knew of all this was when he received a phone call from his brother, Craig. Joe had been diagnosed with a blood clot, which had caused the blackout, but it didn't sound all that worrying. His family had been in to visit him, and Mark had phoned from Adelaide. Joe seemed to have suffered little from the mishap, and was laughing and joking in his typical fashion. For some reason he still can't explain, though, Mark had a bad feeling. He kept thinking about Joe that night and hoped that the Waikerie doctors had been correct in both their diagnosis and prognosis.

When the phone call came early on the morning of 3 September 2003 and Mark learned that his mate and second cousin had died, he went into shock. It was later determined that Joe had died from deep vein thrombosis, most likely acquired from prolonged air travel. Apparently, he had displayed a few symptoms of the condition during the weeks prior to his death, but no one had picked up on them. The clot had formed in his leg, then moved slowly to his lung, which ultimately caused respiratory failure.

Like most who knew him, Mark was shattered by Joe DeVito's death. Within a painfully short space of time, Mark had lost two of the people who meant more to him than just about anyone outside his immediate family – and both in freakish circumstances. Joe had died on the Tuesday night before the Crows' first final in 2003 against the West Coast Eagles at Football Park. Mark was simply too distraught to train the following night and again recalls breaking down in the toilets after the match. He sought grief counselling from within the club for the first time, which helped him cope to some degree, but it wasn't until he got back to Waikerie and could meet with Joe's parents and close mates that he could really come to terms with his emotions.

The fact that no one had seen Joe's death coming made the whole situation even more difficult to come to grips with. As had been the case when Matt Dawson had passed away, Mark recalls that the most difficult part was talking with Joe's parents and seeing their grief. Everyone knows that children are supposed to bury their parents, not the other way around, and for Joe to die at 30 from something as obscure as DVT seemed almost impossible to contemplate. Mark and all the Waikerie boys were at Joe DeVito's wake, which was held around a campfire on the DeVito property the evening before the funeral. The wake turned out to be a celebration of Joe's life, rather than an occasion for mourning his death. Mark had to leave Waikerie shortly after the funeral to get back to training.

Most of his close mates went fishing on Joe's property after the funeral and, as if Joe was sending them a message, they caught a big Murray cod on his rod and reel. Mark felt he had received several other 'messages' from both Joe and Matt Dawson after their deaths – a feeling he has always been at a loss to explain. So profound were these messages, in fact, he decided to visit a clairvoyant in 2006 in an attempt to find some answers.

The clairvoyant told Mark that he had two men standing behind him, one of whom had been ready to die; not so the other. She told Mark that Matt Dawson had received the letter Mark had placed in his coffin (something only Mark and Sarah knew he had done) and that he understood its contents and that everything was okay with their relationship. The clairvoyant also told Mark that the second person standing behind him was 'pissed off' about dying with so much still left to do in life. She passed on the message that Mark should keep up his good work on the football field and should think of him each time he enjoyed a cold beer. Apparently, Joe was annoyed that Mark hadn't remembered the second anniversary of his death.

Mark is 100 per cent certain the clairvoyant knew nothing about the letter he had placed in Matt's coffin, nor could she have had prior knowledge of certain other events, most of which were known only to Mark.

Mark took a lot of comfort from the clairvoyant's 'messages' from Matt and Joe that they would look after him whenever he was in trouble – sort of like guardian angels. Mark still talks to both of his departed mates, which he feels is one way of dealing with the grief that still haunts him.

Mark won the Brownlow Medal just a couple of weeks after Joe DeVito's death. The Crows had been eliminated from the finals race after showing plenty of promise, and it was a very emotional time. Mark's not sure exactly how he held it together that night when he stood before his peers to accept the medal he shared with Nathan Buckley and Adam Goodes. Rarely before had he experienced such an overwhelming mix of emotions. He felt that he wanted to publicly dedicate the Brownlow win to his mates Matt Dawson and Joe DeVito, but knew he would be unable to maintain his composure if he attempted to do so.

His acceptance speech ended up being pretty much off the cuff and centred around the most important things in his life: family, friends and football. Many who watched that historic Brownlow presentation would have picked up on Mark's emotional state, though few knew the real reasons behind it.

Learning to cope with death had become part of Mark's development as a person. There's an old adage that says when someone close to you dies, a part of you dies with them, and Mark feels this is right on the money. There's no doubt that a small part of Mark Ricciuto died along with his two best mates. Although he occasionally feels robbed that they are no longer around to share life with him, he is consoled by the thought that Joe and Matt are still looking down on him and that someday they might all be together again.

* * *

A third very special person in Mark's life, but for completely different reasons, was his grandfather, Nicola. Always family-oriented, and tied strongly to the Italian way of doing things while growing up in the Riverland, Mark had a close affinity with his '*Nonno*'. Nicola had done some hard things in his early years, such as packing up as an eighteen-year-old and moving to a new country, in part to escape the political tyranny of his homeland. He had worked under difficult conditions for years before ultimately establishing himself in the Riverland and starting a family. Mark admired his grandfather's courage, as well as his pride and his determination to make a good life for his family and future Ricciuto generations.

Mark often wonders what it must have been like to do what his grandfather did, which was truly daunting for someone so young; he had no English, no car, just one friend, and no certainty about where the next meal was coming from. Whenever things get a little tough for him now, Mark often recalls stories his grandfather told him of the 'early days' and his own situation doesn't seem quite so bad.

According to Carolyn Ricciuto, Mark was and still is very much like his grandfather. Nicola was a tough man, driven constantly by the will to succeed. He was a strict disciplinarian who wasn't afraid to give his children or grandchildren a crack if he considered it was warranted. But he was always fair and thought the world of everyone close to him. Like most immigrant fruit growers of that era, and particularly those who had started from scratch, Nicola Ricciuto was an extremely generous man. Whenever he would leave his block and go into town to church, he would take as much fresh produce as he could spare and distribute it to people in need. Looking after both family and community was of paramount importance to him, and this is something that has flowed down through the Ricciuto generations and is readily evident in both Mark and his father, Murray. There was always a big bag of fruit left at the West Adelaide Football Club for all to share, and when Mark started playing for the Crows, Murray would load the boot of the Commodore with peaches, grapes, apricots and oranges, and deposit them at the front desk.

As well as passing these traits on to his family, Nicola taught Mark and his brother and sister to have fun. He taught them to play cards, to drink in moderation (this one did slip Mark's mind on occasion), to keep fit, and to enjoy and encourage the company of others. He could still arm wrestle and do chin-ups until late in life. Always a staunch Catholic, he went to church every Sunday and encouraged his family to do the same.

It wasn't until he was in his late eighties that Nicola began to show obvious signs of growing old. Mark had always seen a lot of his grandfather in himself and took pride in the fact that he had done, or at least tried to do, most of what 'Nonno' had advised. It saddened the whole family when the onset of dementia forced Nicola into a nursing home, which he hated with a passion. Murray had to take his father's car keys away when he began driving at high speed in order to avoid being overtaken on the highway. A phone call from one of his Waikerie mates informing Mark that his grandfather had just been seen doing 160 kilometres an hour in an 80-kilometre zone was the final straw and essentially forced the family's hand in curtailing Nicola's driving. He had always been an extremely competitive person, and his phobia about being overtaken while driving, combined with old age and impaired reflexes, was obviously a recipe for disaster. Mark watched on sadly as advancing years gradually caught up with the man he loved and admired so much. He could see the frustration and helplessness in his grandfather's eyes and it cut him to the quick.

Nicola Ricciuto died on Mother's Day 2001, aged 91 in a frail state. The days of chin-ups and arm wrestling were over, and Mark had no doubt he was ready to pass on when the time ultimately came. Mark and his cousin Julian delivered the eulogy at their grandfather's funeral, which was easy to write, but infinitely more difficult to read. There was no doubt that Nicola had been a rock in the Ricciuto family and was very highly respected in his local community. A better role model, Mark says, would be near impossible to find and he still draws inspiration from his '*Nonno*' in both football and business.

Losing three of the most important people in his life in the space of just a few years was certainly tough for Mark to cope with. Tears still well in his eyes when he thinks or talks about Matt, or Joe, or Nicola. He is in no doubt that they will continue to be a strong influence on him until the day he joins them.

10

THE SHOWDOWNS

When, back in late 1996, Port Adelaide had entered the Australian Football League, the South Australian football dynamic had changed forever. One day South Australia was a single-team state and the next it was a duopoly; it was something a lot of died-in-the-wool Crows fans would find difficult to come to grips with. Depending on where your football allegiances lie, Port's move into the Big League was a controversial issue. They had made an unsuccessful – some say underhanded – bid before the Crows had even been born, but they'd had to wait for the end of 1996 until both the timing and the entry criteria were right.

Despite what most Crows fans believed, Adelaide needed a second AFL club at that time. A single entity is under constant scrutiny, so when Port Power arrived on the scene, it immediately took some of the pressure off the Crows. It obviously suited them well, as they subsequently won back-to-back Premierships in 1997 and 1998.

According to Mark Ricciuto, the Showdowns – when the two South Australian teams face off – have always been very special footy matches. Like most others, Mark didn't really know what to expect from Port when they entered the competition. Their coach, John Cahill, had previous VFL experience, as well as nine SANFL Premierships and a playing résumé anyone would be proud of. The inaugural Power squad seemed to boast plenty of talent, too, but no one knew whether all this would be enough to make them a competitive unit in their first season at the top level.

The Adelaide Crows, along with their legion of supporters, found out in no uncertain terms on 20 April 1997. As anticipated, the build-up to that round-four match drew a huge amount of media attention in South Australia. The term 'media frenzy' doesn't really do that lead-up week justice. Mark recalls that each time he turned on the television or picked up a newspaper, the weight on his shoulders increased. The Crows were expected to win, and to win well. No one, not even the most one-eyed of Port supporters, really expected the result to go any other way. A team that had been involved in just three AFL matches up against another that was in its seventh season? It was billed as the ultimate David meets Goliath event, but with Goliath expected to be triumphant!

There had been little time and opportunity for rivalry to build up between the Crows and the Power, but that didn't prevent tension mounting between the opposition camps. At that stage you were either a Crows fanatic or a Port fan led on by blind faith; there could be no middle ground. Despite the best efforts of Malcolm Blight and the Crows' hierarchy to play things down and treat the two teams' inaugural Showdown as just another four-point match, Mark recalls that the pressure and tension affected everyone involved. Everywhere he turned, someone would implore him not to let 'the dark side' have a sniff of the leather that fateful Saturday afternoon. There was always someone who wouldn't be able to go home and live in a street full of Port supporters if the Crows lost, or another who had wagered a considerable amount on Adelaide, or someone else still who had picked the Crows in the office football pool. These people, each of whom represented a hundred thousand others, had agendas of their own that depended heavily on an Adelaide victory in the match. Although Mark would probably dismiss these pressures today, he was fully aware of them in 1997.

Showdown I turned out to be a gruelling affair, punctuated by plenty of tough clashes and melees, with the pre-siren punch-up in the goal square between Scott Cummings and Rod Jameson being undoubtedly the best-remembered off-ball incident. Losing that game by 11 points really hurt the Crows, not just because they felt they had let down their supporters, but because it saw them on the Premiership table with one win and three losses – hardly the sort of start to the season new coach Malcolm Blight had been looking for.

Mark gave his team-mates a bit of a 'spray' back in the dressing room after the game, telling them in no uncertain terms that a performance of that standard was totally unacceptable. If Adelaide wanted to go places in 1997, they would have to raise the bar in a hurry. One win from four matches placed the Crows in danger territory and in a hole from which even someone like Blight would have trouble extricating them.

Mark recalls the coach walking into the rooms a few minutes after the match and writing a large number '18' on the whiteboard. Blight was obviously upset over his team's inept performance in such a significant game, but he didn't say too much at first. None of the playing group knew what the mysterious number '18' signified, until Blight explained there were eighteen more rounds of football to be played before the finals. This meant there was still time for his group to get it together and play the sort of footy they had previously and which he knew they were capable of. Contrary to what most of the squad had anticipated, Blight put a very positive spin on things – probably the most positive reinforcement any of them had seen from a coach after a loss – and his words turned out to be right. There was still a lot of football ahead in 1997 and his attitude that day certainly demonstrated the faith he had in the Adelaide squad.

The Crows evened the ledger four months later with a slogging seven-point victory on a wet and windy day. They trailed by four goals at three-quarter time, which, given the conditions, seemed an insurmountable deficit, but through sheer guts and determination, they held the Power scoreless in the final term and kicked four goals six to steal the four Premiership points.

The Crows' seven consecutive Showdown losses, between round 22 of 2000 and the corresponding round in 2003, were hard to swallow and made Adelaide a difficult place to live for their die-hard fans. This run also made life tough for the Crows boys. As the pressure from outside mounted, so did the tensions within.

Adelaide's seaside suburbs have come alive in recent years, particularly the strip from Grange through to Glenelg. Henley Beach, about midway between the two, has become something of a hub for alfresco dining, with several top-class restaurants, bistros and cafes attracting thousands when the weather is right. Henley Square, within a stone's throw of the beach and jetty, is now *the* place to be if you enjoy a glass of red and a gourmet meal.

Right in the middle of Henley Square is the Ramsgate Hotel – an old pub that has been renovated and modernised to fit the new beachside atmosphere. Like most hotels along the coastal strip, it is very well patronised when the skies are blue and the air is warm. Such were the conditions when some of the Crows and Port Power boys came together in April 2002 in what has become easily the most well-documented off-field incident involving the rival Adelaide-based clubs.

The two teams had played off in Showdown XI on the evening of Saturday, 27 April and, as usual, the match had been close, hard and very physical. The Power prevailed by eight points. The Adelaide boys weren't in the best frame of mind over the loss, and decided to drown their sorrows the following afternoon down at Henley Square. The Showdown had also been Simon Goodwin's 100th game, so there was at least some cause for celebration. Each Crows player who turned up at Henley brought along a good-quality bottle of red to toast their team-mate's milestone.

What with the weather being so nice and Henley Square providing the perfect atmosphere for a temporary escape from the world of football, the Crows boys let their hair down at an outdoor cafe. After a number of full-glass toasts to 'Goody', the red wine supply had dwindled alarmingly and Ben Nelson decided to wander across Seaview Road to the Ramsgate Hotel bottle shop to replenish supplies.

When he eventually returned, it was with the news that a few of the Port Power players were also enjoying a drink in the balmy autumn sunshine. It didn't take long for Mark, Simon Goodwin and the other Crows to decide to go across the road for a chat. Mark denies that he and his mates had any intention of starting anything. They were all feeling relaxed, and it seemed like the ideal opportunity to congratulate the Port lads on their win and maybe even buy them a beer (just joking!). But everyone who became involved had drunk more than they probably should have and this was always going to play a key role in what happened next.

Josh Carr, who had played a couple of seasons for Port Power to that point and had become one of the AFL's most effective taggers, was among the Port contingent at the Ramsgate. He and Mark had developed a bit of on-field history in Showdown matches, as Carr was invariably given the job of shutting the Adelaide star out of the game, which often meant employing a few tactics no running mid-fielder would appreciate. Mark concedes that Carr was not only very good at the tagging job, but also had enough talent to win his fair share of the ball in his own right. The two had been involved in some heated clashes since Carr's first match against the Crows in 2000 and there is no doubt that the Ricciuto–Carr contest alone drew a lot of people to Showdown matches.

Heavy tagging of prominent players has become part and parcel of modern football, and Mark copped plenty virtually each time he took to the ground. He says Carr was one of the best taggers in the business and that he was forced by Carr to change his game in an attempt to get around all the close attention without giving away free kicks. The primary role of any tagger is to get inside an opponent's head and distract him from playing in his normal style, and Josh Carr did exactly that to Mark on a couple of occasions. Mark recalls being 'dragged' by Gary Ayres early in one Showdown match after giving away a couple of costly frees – which, of course, was the ultimate victory for Carr. He knew he was going to have to put his ego in his back pocket and try to cope with Carr's unwanted attention as best he could. If he didn't, the other clubs would pick up on it in no time and Mark would be under more tagging pressure than he could handle.

Of course, with Carr wearing Mark like a glove on the playing arena and constantly dishing out as much 'niggle' as he could physically get away with, their relationship was always a little strained. During a match there were seven umpires and a dozen television cameras maintaining a close eye on proceedings, so physical aggression had to be kept within the rules of the game, but away from Football Park things were naturally far different.

With alcohol fuelling a lot of what would be said when Mark and Josh Carr met up in the Ramsgate that Sunday evening, the scene was set for an explosive confrontation.

The major thrust of Mark's initial conversation with Carr inside the hotel was that things off the football field might not always be as ordered and scrutinised as they are during a match. In other words, Carr might find he wouldn't get away so easily with harassing him, now that they weren't at Football Park. Mark had obviously been frustrated by the constant digs in the ribs, toe stomping, sharp elbow jabs and a dozen other tactics used on him by Carr.

Josh Carr had been having a casual chat with Kane Johnson in the Ramsgate's front bar when Mark joined in and the tone of the conversation changed somewhat. Mark obviously had a few things he wanted to get off his chest, and what started off as a spirited verbal exchange inside the hotel soon escalated to a push and shove, which ultimately made its way outside into the car park and attracted a crowd of a couple of hundred intrigued spectators. Mark recalls practising his tackling technique, as he spread-eagled Carr over the bonnet of a Ramsgate customer's new Mercedes! The same couldn't be said of the others involved, and a number of blows were exchanged. However, the scuffle was over in ten minutes or so, and both the Port and Adelaide players were in the process of leaving the Ramsgate when the police arrived. Mark assured the attending officers that no one had been injured and that the whole affair was done and dusted, which seemed to satisfy them. Had the media not grabbed hold of the incident and milked it mercilessly over the course of the following week, the whole Ramsgate rumble probably would have faded away as quickly as it had begun and ended.

Relieved that the altercation hadn't gone any further, and that police action had been avoided, Mark decided he had better let the club know what had happened. As captain, the last thing he wanted was to be involved in a media-driven controversy, but he could see it coming and telephoned the club's football operations manager, John Reid, to fill him in. Reid did his best to divert the media scrum when it inevitably descended, but to no avail. Where the Adelaide Crows – and especially their captain – were concerned, an incident like this was grist to the mill and the Ramsgate brawl soon dislodged everything else from newspaper and television news headlines.

Respected football journalist with *The Advertiser* Michaelangelo Rucci, and practically any other journalist who was given the opportunity, had a field day with the story. The interstate press jumped on the incident with similar gusto, but by far the most spectacular reaction came from Channel Nine's *The Footy Show*, with Sam Newman and the crew playing it up as only they can do. It's not often that the Victorians are even remotely interested in what happens in football on the South Australian side of the border, but it seemed there was enough 'biffo' and scandal in this one to get them excited.

Fines were handed out to Mark and Josh Carr by their respective clubs and, of course, the AFL weighed into the affair by insisting that those involved were appropriately disciplined. Although they hadn't done themselves any favours with the AFL or their own clubs, neither Ricciuto nor Carr seemed to cop much criticism from the football public. 'Boys will be boys,' appeared to be the general reaction, and it's a fair bet that most Crows and Power fans revelled in the knowledge that their respective 'hard nuts' had gone at it, head to head, away from Football Park.

However, while Mark and his team-mates had apparently escaped serious consequences from the club, their girlfriends were after their scalps. When the melee erupted in the hotel car park, and the police arrived soon after, the lads' first priority was to put some distance between themselves and the Ramsgate as quickly as possible – and they completely forgot about the girls. The women had seen that something had attracted a crowd of onlookers, but were unaware that their menfolk had been at the centre of it. The lads had quite a bit of explaining to do to sort that one.

Prior to the 'rumble' at the Ramsgate, many people in South Australia hadn't known the hotel existed. After the resulting media onslaught, they would have to have been blindfolded, bound, gagged and locked away in a cellar not to have heard the pub's name a hundred times. The Ramsgate couldn't have bought the sort of publicity they received on national television, including *The Footy Show* that week. Mark and his business partner, Simon Goodwin, who had interests in the Alma and Kensington hotels in Adelaide, would often joke later that any future inter-club altercations should take place at one of their own establishments, rather than provide free publicity to the opposition!

Josh Carr and Mark didn't talk for a while after the Ramsgate affair, but once the dust had settled and their mutual respect had returned, the pair were soon on speaking terms again and now look back on the whole affair with some bemusement. (It's ironic that their next off-field meeting would also be at the Ramsgate, on 'Mad Monday' at season's end. This time, however, there would be no bad blood; just handshakes, a few laughs and more than a few beers. Had it been held at the Alma, though, who knows what might have happened!)

The Ramsgate brawl certainly heightened the rivalry between the Crows and Power. It left the supporters in both camps in no doubt that there was still plenty of feeling between the two Adelaide AFL teams. Josh Carr's determination to stop Mark in Showdown matches has been well documented and although their relationship has been 'testy' at times, Mark admires Carr's courage and resolve. He also has great admiration for Carr as a footballer and the fact he would always stand up and be counted in big games, and regards him as one of the prime movers in securing Port Adelaide's 2004 Premiership. Like Mark, Carr likes to play the game as hard and as tough as possible, and it's little wonder he fitted into Fremantle's side so readily after returning to Perth. Mark also considers Port players such as Josh Francou, who won three Showdown Medals, Warren Tredrea, Nick Stevens and Matthew Primus, who always presented Adelaide with a major headache, as being real stars who were firing during the early part of the new millennium. Mark has a lot of respect for these and several other of Port's front-line players, and he expects that the same would apply from their side of the fence.

Although Carr, Francou, Primus and Stevens are now missing from the regular Showdown lineups, Mark says Port is still very strong, right around the ground. It used to be just Peter Burgoyne they had to watch in the mid-field, but now it's his brother Shaun as well. Brendan Lade has developed into one of the game's best ruckmen; Warren Tredrea, despite injuries, is still as potentially damaging as ever; and newcomer Danyle Pearce looks like being another top-class mid-fielder.

Like Essendon and Collingwood, or Fremantle and the West Coast Eagles, there will always be rivalry between Adelaide and Port, and it will continue to bring people to the football each week.

Although Mark says Malcolm Blight, Gary Ayres and Neil Craig, his three coaches since Showdown games began, have invariably played down the home-town rivalry aspect of these matches, he knows there was always something special about those matches for them as well. As much as the coaches, including Port's Mark Williams, might like their squads to treat an upcoming Showdown as just another match for Premiership points, they are aware it's virtually impossible to do so.

Adelaide didn't resume control of the Showdown matches until 2005 and went on to record four successive victories. Three of these were by big margins; and, as was the case when Port had its run of wins, the trend was definitely in line with the strength of the respective playing lists. Adelaide was flying through 2005 and 2006, while Port struck a bit of a rough patch, but still managed to beat the Crows by 14 points in round 21 of 2006. Mark was down with the parvovirus and didn't play in that game; he also missed Showdown XXI, early in 2007, as a result of his chronic back problems.

The mood in the change-rooms after a Showdown victory was always just that little bit sweeter than after a win against an interstate side. Apart from the rivalry between home-town teams, this is probably because a victory releases some of the pressure that accompanies others' expectations. The same applies in reverse after a Showdown defeat. After losing to the Power, it's always just that little bit harder for the players and the coach to front up to Crows supporters over at The Shed or to complete media commitments. In fact, going to ground for a few days after a loss would be the preferred option but, of course, the Adelaide media would never allow the losers a luxury like that.

Mark's personal form in Power–Crows matches has generally been very good. He won the inaugural Showdown Medal in 2000 (the medals weren't presented until Showdown VII), then again in 2004 and 2005, equalling Josh Francou's record. He also finished high in the Crows' best players on nine other occasions, indicating that he coped well with the added pressure of these games. He was club captain for fourteen of the 22 Showdowns played until the time of writing.

Mark has no doubt that the Showdown rivalry between Adelaide and Port Adelaide will continue to intrigue and divide South Australians for as long as football is played there. Fremantle/West Coast 'Derbies' have already reached a similar level in Western Australia, and it's inevitable that Sydney and Brisbane will each have a second club one day, to create more interest in our 'non-football' states. Mark isn't sure how many more Crows/Power games remain on his football radar, but he would certainly like to hold that Showdown trophy aloft at least once more before he hangs up his boots.

11

THE PHYSICAL TOLL

It is every football club's dream, regardless of league or level, to have its best 22 players on the deck each week. In reality, of course, this rarely happens and it seems the further up the football tree you look, the greater the role injuries play in success or failure. When you get to the top of that tree, the AFL, injuries can determine the outcome of vital games and, at times, whole seasons.

Australian Rules Football has always been among the toughest, most physically demanding team sports in the world. It's tough on both body and mind, and only those totally prepared in both areas can hope to succeed. Even after the best preparation and with the most advanced medical services available, however, most AFL clubs go through any given season with significant injuries to key players. It's how they manage and cover these injuries that often determines the outcome.

There can be no doubt that injuries have played a big role in Mark Ricciuto's football career. Like most who play the game hard, many of Mark's injuries have resulted from heavy ground-level collisions. According to those who have coached him, there are few players who train with more dedication. All of Mark's coaches say his work ethic is equal to the best they have seen on the training track, and that his ability to push through pain is truly outstanding. But it's a fact of life that some players over-train, and Mark is in no doubt that at least some of the injuries that have kept him off the field over the years have resulted from exactly that.

When he looked back over a detailed list of his injuries sustained while with the Crows, Mark was surprised. He knew he had been in and out of hospital a few times for various repairs and had missed a few games over a career spanning fifteen seasons. However, it wasn't until Adelaide Football Club's Dr Brian Sando went back through his records that the true extent of the list was revealed. Dr Sando has been with the Crows since they entered the AFL competition. While Mark has suffered his share of injuries, he says, there are plenty who have fared worse.

Brian Sando has provided for this account of Mark's career a complete rundown of his injuries, starting from his first ankle sprain in 1993. This wasn't a bad sprain and healed quickly enough to enable him to play the following week. He also suffered his first facial injury that year, which required several stitches to repair. Since that time he has had more than a dozen facial, oral or scalp lacerations that needed Dr Sando's handiwork, a couple of which were quite nasty. Some of Mark's friends say that the facial injuries have made him more attractive! He has also collected half a dozen concussions, the most serious of which put him in hospital overnight. Blurred vision after heavy knocks was a regular part of the deal throughout his career.

The first hint of hamstring soreness came late in 1993, but it wasn't significant and was treated effectively with ice and massage. Hamstring injuries are common among footballers, and are foremost in the minds of most AFL fitness coaches and medical staff. It doesn't seem to matter how modern footballers are trained and how carefully they are managed, hamstring strains and tears will always be a part of the game. In extreme cases, such as with Adelaide's Matthew Liptak and Simon Tregenza in the late 1990s, hamstring injuries have proven career ending.

The only injury recorded in Mark's medical notes by Dr Sando during the 1995 season was a left ankle sprain, but he also had an extraordinary series of corked thighs that year. Players at all levels of football cop 'corkies' from time to time; in fact, this is one of the most common injuries in just about any contact sport. However, throughout the course of the 1995 season Mark seemed to suffer more heavy knocks to the thighs than ever before. This may have been the result of the new role Robert Shaw had asked him to play – a more physical type of game that caused him to 'bulk up' and be involved in a lot more heavy ground-level contests.

Mark recalls his thighs being so sore after some matches, it often took him four or five days to recover. This seriously restricted his training and forced him to undertake lengthy 'icing' periods after both games and training. He also had to wear 'Rhino' pads to protect the injured areas. Despite all the recovery sessions and protective equipment, the corked-thigh issue became quite significant. Once an area is deeply bruised on several consecutive occasions, it becomes very tender and prone to further injury with minimal contact. Mark recalls not even being able to touch his thighs on some days, but, determined not to miss any game time, he continued to play in pain. He says corked thighs may sound innocuous, but if they are bad enough and consistent enough, they can certainly make a footballer's life difficult.

The 1996 season was relatively injury free, but midway through 1997, a historical year for the Adelaide Football Club, Mark suffered his first serious injury – one that would go on to have a profound and long-term effect on his career. In July he began to experience groin soreness, which he reported immediately to Sando, and was given a series of cortisone injections. The cortisone provided only limited relief, however, and by the end of the home-and-away series his groins were so bad, he was ruled out of the Crows' finals campaign. This was a terrible blow after playing so well for much of the minor round, but there was simply no way he could expect to continue without reparative surgery. (As soon as he decides to retire, Mark will be heading to hospital for further groin surgery in the hope of clearing up the problems that have plagued him since 1997. On a couple of occasions he has had golf-ball-sized lumps appear in his groin, the result of internal infection, and has even had a couple of intact stitches pop out through open skin wounds. Naturally, this sort of eruption has been extremely painful and unpleasant.)

Having conjoint groin repairs and two hernias fixed at the same time certainly knocked him around, but the surgery enabled him to get back on track in time for 1998. Apart from a labrum tear of the hip joint that cost him a couple of games, 1998 turned out to be an injury-free year and, of course, provided Mark with his one and only Premiership medallion to date. He says the Premiership was the only thing that could have compensated for the frustration he still felt from the year before, and that he will always remember the joy that came with holding aloft the Premiership Cup.

The following year, 1999, saw a broken nose, courtesy of an errant 'spoil' from North Melbourne's Glenn Archer, and a minor ankle sprain. During summer training leading into the 2000 season, however, he began to experience some problems caused by the double hernia operation he had undergone over two years before. Stitch abscesses had formed around the site of the internal hernia repairs, which are essentially infections emanating from the deep stitches inserted to hold the hernias together. These abscesses concerned Sando, and he organised for Mark to have the sinuses surrounding the hernia repairs cleaned out. There was a lot of pus oozing from the repair sites, which was potentially dangerous. Soon after an apparently effective clean-out procedure, however, Mark developed a bacterial infection in the same area and was admitted to hospital. It seemed those hernia repairs would haunt him for some time.

As newly appointed club captain, a heavy blow to the chest in a pre-season game in 2001 set Mark back considerably. He was keen to lead his team from the front, but cracked ribs and associated respiratory difficulty made this one of the most trying injuries of his career. He could play in short bursts, but he simply couldn't run out a whole game and struggled to overcome the injury for much of the year. A slight hamstring strain and the first real sign of lumbar soreness followed that season, making his fitness less than ideal for a new captain.

By far Mark's most significant ankle injury occurred against the Bulldogs in the opening round of 2002. This one needed quite a bit of treatment, including cortisone injections, and cost him two matches. He came back against Essendon at Colonial Stadium in round four with so much ankle strapping, he says he felt like he was running on a wooden leg! A serious tongue laceration that evening was the first of several he would suffer over the course of his career. Against the advice of all medical staff, Mark has never worn a mouthguard and so is always prone to oral injury.

Although he had suffered slight hamstring tightness over several years, these began to trouble him more frequently in the middle of the 2002 season. He was diagnosed with hamstring tendonitis for the first time, which required successive cortisone injections in August and considerably hampered his on-field performances. Tendonitis is far more difficult to treat and harder to get over than a straightforward hamstring strain. Post-season surgery was ordered in November to clean out floating bone chips in Mark's right ankle. By this time, he was getting used to short stints in hospital and mandatory periods of recovery.

Soreness in his left ankle forced him back into hospital in February 2003 to have yet more bone fragments removed. The ankle had locked up badly during the club's annual pre-season trial game against SANFL club Norwood, and it was obvious something had to be done – and in a hurry. It couldn't have come at a worse time, of course, with the AFL pre-season competition about to kick off, but there was simply no way around it. Despite the setback, Mark was back in action by round one and opened strongly with a 28-disposal game against Fremantle. A back sprain mid-season, followed by a corneal abrasion from an accidental finger in the eye, caused some temporary discomfort but no loss of game time, and he finished the season very strongly to be joint winner of the 2003 Brownlow Medal.

There was further surgery on both ankles after the 2003 season had ended, this time to clean out more floating bone fragments and generally to tidy up what were becoming very troublesome joints. Mark remembers running on grass late in the season and feeling like he was running on concrete. There was obviously a lot of bone-on-bone contact within his ankle joints, which, had it been left unrepaired, may have led to permanent, long-term damage. Most would be unaware that Mark climbed on to the stage to collect his club Best and Fairest award at season's end with both ankles so heavily strapped, he could hardly feel his feet. Most would also be unaware he was wearing his club suit and sandals!

Tackling Rhett Biglands at a 2004 pre-season training camp at Strathalbyn proved something to avoid in the future, as the resultant thumb fracture seriously interrupted summer training. Thumbs are by far the most difficult of the digits to get right after a breakage, and this one was both painful and frustrating. After reparative surgery, Mark was back at Strath' two days later and on the bike with Charlie Walsh.

A fractured nose late in the 2005 season was Mark's most serious facial injury, but it didn't prevent him from leading the Crows to a finals campaign that, had they had a bit of luck, could have resulted in the club's third Premiership.

Hamstring tendonitis returned in his right leg in the 2006 pre-season, seriously restricting his training for three months. This injury required multiple cortisone injections, while the others were assisted to some degree by physiotherapy and massage. Mark missed rounds five and six with his first ever hamstring strain and the tendonitis seriously curtailed training, which certainly affected his overall form and fitness. A second nasty tongue laceration late in the year reinforced the need to wear a mouthguard. Mark could actually stick his finger through his tongue, but still there would be no mouthguard.

Up to the time when the much-publicised onset of parvovirus put paid to Mark's finals aspirations in 2006, he had missed seventeen matches due to injury or illness and two through suspension.

After recovering from parvovirus and watching Sarah give birth, Mark channelled his thoughts to pre-season 2007. He was in such good condition that he achieved a personal best time for the three-kilometre time trial, proving to himself and the rest of the club he was ready to get back into it.

In pre-season training, Mark began to experience chronic lower-back problems. The injury was diagnosed as a minor tear to the disc between the L3 and L4 vertebrae, but its effect was anything but minor. If persistent tendonitis and contracting parvovirus the year before had been frustrating, this back complaint was proving a disaster. No player, and especially a club captain, wants to miss big slabs of football as his career draws to a close. Everyone associated with the Adelaide Crows shared Mark's anguish as the back injury dragged on.

Leading the team from the medical room is, quite obviously, far from ideal. Had his preparation for 2007 not been so strong and so positive after recovering from the debilitating virus and had the players not voted him their preferred skipper during the pre-season training camp, Mark probably would have handed the club captaincy over to the next in line. In his view, it doesn't matter how mentally strong you are, how highly respected you are, or how well you can communicate with your team; it's essentially impossible to lead them effectively unless you're out there with them in the heat of the battle.

Fortunately, Adelaide's leadership group of Nathan Bassett, Tyson Edwards, Simon Goodwin and Brett Burton were capable of picking up the slack created by Mark's on-field absence. Aware of this, he opted to retain the captaincy and embarked on a consistent treatment program for his troublesome back.

Early in the season, on a couple of occasions, it seemed to be on the mend and Mark was hopeful of returning to the team. However, persistent relapses forced him back on to the 'indefinite' injury list, and there were plenty of doomsday prophets who predicted he had played his last game. Mark's frustration as the 2007 season appeared to be slipping by was quickly turning to despair. He says it's one thing to have an injury with a probable recovery time frame, as you then have a fair idea of when you will be playing again; it's quite another to suffer from something that is classed as 'indefinite'. Mark describes these types of injuries as ones that 'get you in the head'. You become disillusioned, and even pessimistic, he says. You begin to doubt yourself, particularly your ability to play again at the same level and to be a strong team contributor, and it's almost as draining emotionally as it is physically.

Mark has always been mindful, when off the field injured, not to let his frustration and dejection become obvious to his team-mates, and especially not to the younger ones. Remaining upbeat is part of his role as club captain, and this has definitely been a lot more difficult whenever he has been confined to the medical room. When ill with parvovirus, Mark was overwhelmed by the volume of support he received from fans, AFC members and hundreds of people he didn't know. He says it's this sort of support that keeps many top-level sportspeople going in the face of adversity.

On 1 June 2007 Mark made his long-awaited comeback to AFL football against Melbourne on the MCG. He hadn't played since round 20 of the previous season and his return to the Adelaide lineup was the cause of much celebration among Crows fans across SA. Unfortunately, his inclusion couldn't prevent Adelaide from going down to previously winless Melbourne, but Mark contributed strongly with two goals and pulled up well after the match. It seemed he had silenced the media doomsday prophets who had all but written him off as a football has-been.

The ability to rehabilitate and recover has become a huge part of AFL football, and Mark considers himself lucky to have been in such good hands at the Crows. Without the expertise of the AFC medical staff, he would certainly have missed more games than he has. He says the volume of physiotherapy, chiropractic care and therapeutic massage now available is crucial to all AFL clubs. The ability to keep all players on the field is vitally important, and in this area Adelaide is second to none.

One of Mark's least favourite, but undoubtedly most effective, therapy tools for muscle and soft tissue recovery is the ice bath. Crows players regularly undergo ice bath sessions, where they stand waist-deep in water of between zero and six degrees Celsius for eight minutes at a time. It's painful and generally unpleasant, but it's very effective in minimising intra-muscular bleeding and promoting rapid dispersion of bruising.

The Crows' Maintenance and Core Stability Program, which helps strengthen muscles in the pelvic area, has also proven very effective. This is a preventative program that all team members are involved in three times a week, regardless of where or how they play. Mark says it's probably the most boring component of training and provides few, if any, tangible benefits in the short term, but that it definitely helps over the course of a long and demanding season. According to doctors and physiotherapists, it's an absolute must in modern football.

Never a fan of swimming, Mark was forced to do a lot more than he would have liked during his periods of injury in 2006 and 2007. Crows swimming coach Glen Beringen has always had to drag Mark out of a hiding place to get him in the pool for rehabilitation sessions, which he hates with a passion. He may be a champion footballer, but he is no Ian Thorpe. Charlie Walsh, former Olympic cycling coach and on the training staff at Adelaide, also saw a lot of Mark while he was out injured, pushing him hard on the bike to maintain aerobic fitness and build up the appropriate muscle areas.

Mark admits to being 'a little grumpy' at times during 2006 and 2007 as the injuries started to pile up, and says he is extremely grateful for the understanding, care and support from those around him – particularly Sarah. He's aware that most of his latest injuries are the result of a body that's been worked very hard over fifteen gruelling seasons of top-level football. Mark knows that, despite his recent return to form, his body is crying out for a break. Much as he dreads the thought, that break may have to come sooner rather than later.

12

FOR STATE AND COUNTRY

Mark had just turned nineteen when he represented South Australia for the first time at the Senior level. He had played in the Under 12 State Schoolboys team, then for the State Under 15s, and for two years played in the Teal Cup, so he was no stranger to wearing the tri-colours of South Australia. Still, when he made the Senior squad in his second year of AFL football, he was over the moon. Being part of the best football team his state could muster was a thrill in itself, and particularly as that side comprised his boyhood idols. (He says he managed to restrain himself from asking for autographs in the change-rooms.) Stephen Kernahan, Craig Bradley, Mark Naley, the Jarman brothers, Tony Hall and John Platten would all be his team-mates that evening. The opposition was equally talented, and again the 'Big V' representative side was full of players Mark regarded as the cream of the competition.

Things were a little different then in the AFL, of course. The competition was fiercely intense and professional, but probably not quite to the same extent it is now. Most AFL home-and-away matches were played on Saturdays and Sundays, and State of Origin matches were often played mid-week, putting an enormous amount of strain on those involved. Having star players front up for three games in seven days is something no AFL club would even consider doing now, which is the main reason State of Origin slipped off the program after 1999.

Mark represented South Australia with distinction in 1994, 1995, 1996, 1997 and 1999, but concedes he shouldn't have played in 1997. That match exacerbated a developing injury – which ultimately cost him a place in the Crows' historic first Premiership team. He was selected again the following year, but this time declined on injury grounds. He had a few mid-season 'niggles' that he simply needed to get right, and the decision to miss the interstate clash turned out to be the right one. The second half of 1998 was a stellar one for Mark, with a Premiership medallion and club Best and Fairest trophy capping off a season to remember.

By this stage, State of Origin was losing popularity, especially with the sixteen clubs involved in the competition. With the game becoming more intense and physically demanding all the time, wedging an interstate match into an already demanding schedule became increasingly difficult. No one was surprised when the AFL put the State of Origin concept on hold. The matches had been a great spectacle over many years, but the game had now evolved to a degree where they simply no longer fitted.

With rest and recovery now more significant than ever before, Mark feels that the State of Origin series will struggle to make a comeback. It has been proposed that these matches could be played at the end of the season, but there are now compulsory players' breaks to consider and a host of other non-negotiables that consume much of the time between the conclusion of one season and the beginning of the next. Mark believes the only possible structure that would allow State of Origin matches back on to the calendar is to have two byes – one after seven rounds and a second after round fourteen – that would be a week off for all players. The State of Origin match could be played on the Thursday night prior to the first bye, enabling all involved to have at least nine days off before the next home-and-away fixtures.

Although Mark was always keen to be involved at the interstate level, he knew that the Crows' hierarchy weren't overly happy with him, or any of the other top-line players, committing to represent their state. This is indeed a pity, as Mark believes that elite sporting personnel should always aspire, and be trained, to represent their home state and, ultimately, their country. He feels for today's crop of top-line players, such as Matthew Pavlich, Chris Judd, Ben Rutten, Daniel Kerr and Jonathan Brown, who have never had the opportunity to represent their home states. For Mark, there are few more significant moments in football than playing in a winning State of Origin side. State of Origin Rugby League is still as strong as it ever was, and Australia has always fielded competitive Rugby Union and soccer teams at the international level, so it seems somehow incongruous that the same no longer applies in our most popular football code.

The State of Origin match Mark recalls most vividly took place on the MCG in 1995. E.J. ('Ted') Whitten, a former Footscray Football Club player generally regarded as one of the greatest-ever AFL footballers and a passionate advocate of State of Origin, who was dying of prostate cancer, did a lap of the 'G' to farewell his fans. There was scarcely a dry eye in the house. Lockett, Ablett and Dunstall had then proceeded to tear the Croweaters apart on that rainy afternoon. Whitten died just a few weeks later. Mark considers playing in that game a highlight of his career, and he regrets that a depleted South Australian side couldn't put up a better showing against Victoria on the day. However, with Ted

Whitten virtually dying in their arms, he concedes that no one would have beaten the Victorians that day; they were so highly motivated, it would have taken an army to stop them.

In a nutshell, Mark feels that State of Origin football began its demise as soon as the Victorian Football League became the Australian Football League. It's virtually state playing against state every weekend now, and although the 44 players competing in each match will never be as talented as those chosen in a representative game, the standard is still extremely high.

International Rules Football matches between Australia and Ireland fall into much the same basket. Mark was chosen to play for Australia for the first time in 1998 on a tour of Ireland. He was proud to have been selected, but as the squad was due to fly out just a week after the Grand Final, his emotions were mixed. He had just played in his first ever AFL Premiership side and was looking forward to at least a month of basking in glory, not training, and catching up on a few quiet beers, but there would be hardly any time to celebrate before packing his bags and jetting off to Europe. The last thing he – and Shaun Rehn, Ben Hart and Nigel Smart, who had also been part of the Crows' Premiership side – wanted just then was more training, more curfews and, ultimately, more football. But they had made the commitment, so off they went.

There was never the same intensity with preparation for International Rules matches as there was in the domestic competition, which was at least some consolation. There was total commitment on the field, of course, but the Aussie lads were allowed to go out and party, except on the night before a game, and party they most certainly did.

Robert 'Dipper' DiPierdomenico was a very prominent member of the touring party. Because he had been part of the first Australian squad to play International Rules in 1984, and had developed something of a cult following in Dublin, he took charge of most of the 'social' arrangements. The other lads were bemused to find their Italian-Australian colleague revered as a local legend in Ireland. Drinking for long periods, and then training hard for a match, wasn't the ideal physical preparation, and it ran contrary to the way things worked back home, but the Aussie boys did it in grand style. The more relaxed atmosphere reminded Mark a little of playing football back in Waikerie. He has joked that, in the AFL, trainers bring out oranges at three-quarter time; whereas in the country, trainers bring out ashtrays.

The result of that two-match series was one game each, but Ireland won on points aggregate. Mark scored a couple of 'unders' in the second Test, collected a bottle of very expensive French wine as best player, and thoroughly enjoyed the fast and physical nature of the hybrid football code. According to Collingwood captain Nathan Buckley, who was also on tour in Ireland in 1998, Mark was one of the few Aussie players who could kick the round ball 'inside out', achieving optimum distance and accuracy. This was the kicking technique used by the Irish themselves. Buckley also feels that the Irish – who are not easily scared – were quite intimidated by Mark, regularly opting out of contests in which he was involved.

However, it was still the social side of the Irish tour that stood out as the highlight for most of the visiting contingent. Downing pints of Guinness became an art form and although there were drinking curfews in place, they weren't rigidly enforced. Most of the Australian players drank as much in Ireland as they would have if they had been on a traditional end-of-season footy trip with their own clubs. It may take a fair bit to scare an Irishman, but it takes very little encouragement to get them out for a beer – an attribute the Aussie boys loved!

One of the things from that tour Mark still smiles about was Shaun Rehn's huge contribution. Shaun is an intense sort of guy, and there was no doubt he looked forward to tangling with the Irish on their home soil. He had just completed a sensational year with the Crows, winning a Premiership medallion and stamping himself as the best ruckman in the competition; he wasn't amused at being left out of the Aussie side in the first Test at Croke Park. Unlike with Australian Rules, guys the size of Rehn don't really fit in the round-ball game, and it was only because the coach, Leigh Matthews, understood Rehn's eagerness to be involved that he included him in the second scheduled match.

Leigh's instructions to Rehn were simple; his job was to line up against the Irish ruckman, win the tap from the first throw up, then run off to the bench. He would get a chance to do this again at the beginning of the second half and that would be the extent of his contribution. Naturally, Rehn wasn't all that happy about being out there for less than a minute in each half, but he understood his coach's instructions and ran out on to Croke Park to get things rolling for the Australians. Unlike the centre circle arrangement in our game, there are only two players from each side involved in starting the game and on this occasion the Aussie pair were Shaun and Mark. Understandably, his Australian team-mates had ribbed Rehn about his significance in the overall scheme of things and warned him not to lose the all-important first throw up.

With teeth clenched, back hunched over and an expression that could intimidate the toughest in the AFL, Shaun Rehn prepared to get things off to a flying start for his country. However, in the round-ball game the referee doesn't blow his whistle and hold the ball aloft while the siren blows. He simply blows the whistle and throws the ball up simultaneously – pretty much the same as in basketball. Rehn hadn't been aware of this and was still barking last-minute instructions at Mark when the referee threw the ball in the air. He mistimed his run-in completely, the Irish ruckman tapped the ball clear, and the opposition were deep in attack before Rehn knew what had happened. Mark says he could hear Rehn cursing and swearing all the way to the bench, where he had ample time to think about things before his second contribution after half time. To ease his own frustration over the incident, Mark dropped a shoulder into the Irish captain and sent him to the ground, which incensed the 80,000-strong crowd and set the tone for a spirited match. One afternoon, while en route to training between the two matches, Mark recalls hearing a disgruntled Shaun Rehn say, 'I wish this bus was heading for the airport.'

Nigel Smart, Mark's Crows team-mate and his room-mate for the tour, was one casualty of the hectic drink/train/play cycle of the 1998 Irish tour and was unable to play in the second Test due to self-inflicted illness. Burning the candle at both ends certainly took its toll on Smart. Mark says that, although all involved were very serious about the game when they were out on the park, the players were also very serious about their partying. Unlike more recent International Rules exchanges, where a lot of younger players have been given the chance to represent their country, the earlier series involved the cream of Australia's football talent. If you made the All-Australian side, you played against the Irish, which Mark enjoyed doing immensely.

Other than during these annual trips to Ireland, the country's elite footballers rarely got the chance to rub shoulders, exchange football stories and enjoy a beer together. Most of the guys liked to have a bet occasionally, and playing cards became a very popular pastime, particularly during the lengthy plane trips to and from Ireland. 'Dipper' recalls that the card game kicked off in the airport lounge prior to departure, then resumed once they were in the air. A few of the Australians were lying on the floor of the plane, playing cards, so that the cabin attendants had to step over them to serve food and drinks to the other passengers. The game was 500, which is played in pairs. 'Dipper' and Simon Goodwin teamed up against Mark and Andrew McLeod. After more than twenty hours in the air, Mark and McLeod came out well in front – a gambling debt Mark insists has never been paid. In 'Dipper's' version of the same event, it was Mark and McLeod who lost the marathon game of 500 and still owe him ten dollars!

Another of Mark's fond memories of the 1998 Irish trip was playing cards with Australia's elite footballers and administrators at a huge round table in an authentic medieval castle. Wayne Jackson, Wayne Carey, Robert Harvey and Peter Everitt were at the table – players Mark respected and admired greatly, but whom he'd never before had the opportunity to spend time with in a social situation. For a lad from Waikerie, it was all a bit surreal and he made the most of every second of the tour.

Mark went back to Ireland in 2000, and this time the social rules and regulations were a bit tougher. There was a strict midnight curfew, and no alcohol was to be consumed two days prior to any match – restrictions that made sense, but which weren't well received by most of the touring squad. One afternoon Simon Goodwin, Andy McLeod and Mark took off for a bit of sightseeing. On spotting a betting shop, they poked their heads inside and decided to have one drink and a wager on one race. That one drink became a couple, and then a couple became a few more. Although the Adelaide trio made it back to the team hotel before the midnight curfew, they did so with stomachs full of beer. It was very easy to get caught up in the atmosphere of the place, the visitors found. The Irish are very friendly, welcoming people, who worship Aussie sportsmen, so having just a couple of drinks and retiring for an early night was always going to be a problem.

The Aussies won both matches of the two-Test series before a combined crowd of 96,000 people. This was Mark's last taste of playing football overseas.

With State of Origin shelved after 1999 and further touring of Ireland off the agenda, Mark could concentrate on his major objective – captaining the Adelaide Football Club to its third AFL Premiership. He feels privileged to have represented both his state and his country, and hopes that some day, in some way, both State of Origin and International Rules can again find a place in the Australian football calendar so the younger generation can experience what he has.

13

THE BROWNLOW MEDAL

Ask any elite footballer – or, in fact, any elite team sport player – about the significance of individual awards over team achievements and they'll give you the same answer: there is simply nothing like standing on the dais at the MCG on the last Saturday in September and having an AFL Premiership medallion placed around your neck. Mark Ricciuto was there in 1998 after the Adelaide Crows had won the second of their back-to-back flags, and he still regards it as the sweetest moment in his long career at top level. Although all who play in the AFL aspire to being part of a Premiership team, only a select few will ever reach those heights.

Even more select is the group of footballers who have played in a Premiership *and* won a Brownlow Medal. Mark's individual form had been very consistent since breaking into the Crows' lineup in 1993. Regular All-Australian selections and, ultimately, the All-Australian captaincy, indicated the esteem in which he was held by his peers, and so it came as no shock – certainly to South Australians – that Mark figured in a three-way tie for the Brownlow in 2003 with Collingwood's Nathan Buckley and Sydney's Adam Goodes.

Mark first began to attract the attention of the umpires back in 1997. There are some who play great football, week in and week out, without scoring many Brownlow votes, and others who seem to collect votes after mediocre performances. Mark cites Wayne Carey and Simon Goodwin as examples of brilliant footballers who never received the recognition from the umpires he and others believed they deserved. Carey, in particular, is still rated by most as the best footballer ever to play the game, yet he never figured prominently in the Brownlow count. The highest vote tally Carey ever managed during his fifteen-season/271-game career was twenty in 1998, finishing some twelve behind the eventual winner, St Kilda's Robert Harvey.

When Malcolm Blight came to the Adelaide Football Club after the 1996 season, he encouraged Mark to drop a bit of body weight and, without losing all of the aggression that had become his trademark, to approach football in a slightly different way. Dropping a few kilos and improving his aerobic fitness would enable him to play a greater on-ball role, and it was this change of direction that ultimately made him a more complete and effective footballer. Blight's influence, and that of the Crows' new fitness coach, Neil Craig, simply can't be overstated. Mark polled eighteen votes in the Brownlow in 1997 finishing fifth, and most knowledgeable observers agree he would have given the award a real shake that season if a chronic groin complaint hadn't intervened. He played the last eight minor-round games under extreme duress and ended up watching from the grandstand as his team-mates won the club's first Premiership against St Kilda.

Mark's good form continued in 1998, when he played consistently for the entire season and finished fourth in the Brownlow count with an impressive 21 votes. The umpires were finding it difficult to ignore his influence on the game; although always hard at the ball and body, he was fair in the contest and rarely, if ever, questioned an umpire's decision.

The Crows had poor years between 1999 and 2002 but Mark's form went the other way, reaching a new level in 2000, when he polled highly in both the Brownlow Medal and the AFC Club Champion award. Adelaide won thirteen home-and-away matches in the 2003 season – the best result with Gary Ayres as coach – and although they couldn't go on with it in the finals, Mark was well pleased to be playing the best footy of his life.

As was to be expected, only the Adelaide media gave Mark a good chance of becoming the Crows' first Brownlow Medallist. Nathan Buckley and Adam Goodes were the favourites with both interstate media and bookies. Both had enjoyed terrific seasons; especially Goodes, who had gone from being a good player to a great player in a short space of time and was one of the hottest properties in football. Buckley had been right up there with the game's best for quite a while, and most considered it was only a matter of time before he grabbed a Medal.

Mark was in the top five with most sports bookmakers and went to the 2003 presentation expecting to do well in the count, but not figuring on polling with the likes of Buckley and Goodes. The Adelaide contingent and their partners flew to Melbourne in time for lunch and a few beers, and all looked forward to an enjoyable evening. With the Crows out of the finals race, they could all let their hair down a little and enjoy the AFL's hospitality. Mark had learned a lot since the 1994 Brownlow Medal dinner and wouldn't be repeating his form of that night.

Mark polled a few votes early in the count, plateaued a little mid-season, then came home with a wet sail to be part of the Medal's first-ever three-way tie. About halfway through the count, audio technicians came to the Crows' table and fitted Mark with a radio microphone, indicating that something was afoot. Mark decided to back off the beers a little, just in case. As the count neared its exciting conclusion, more and more TV cameras began to appear on the auditorium floor, with cameramen rushing between tables to catch the facial expressions of those polling well. There were up to half a dozen players in the race, with just a couple of rounds to be counted. Only at this stage did Mark allow himself to think he had a chance. Buckley had been just one vote ahead with one round remaining, and Goodes had been a further vote behind. The Crows had played Port Power in round 22 and lost by 16 points, but Mark had been judged Adelaide's best that night by local media commentators and, despite the loss, figured there might be one umpires' vote in it for him.

That prediction turned out to be spot on, and when Goodes picked up two votes in the same round, it brought the house down. Mark wasn't at all prepared when AFL's CEO, Wayne Jackson, announced that Adam Goodes, Nathan Buckley and Mark Ricciuto were the joint 2003 Brownlow Medallists. After all the hugs, handshakes, kisses (surprisingly, one from Ben Hart!) and general mayhem at the Crows' table had subsided, Mark rose rather unsteadily to his feet and walked to the stage for the official presentation. He was still shaking his head in disbelief as he climbed the steps to join Buckley and Goodes.

It all seemed quite surreal. What he had thought would be just a fun, relaxing and entertaining evening had suddenly been turned completely upside down. Ever since he had discovered Australian Rules Football, he had dreamed of winning its highest honour, but never for a moment had he considered that dream would ever come true. He had no prepared speech, but managed to get by without forgetting to thank anyone. Nathan Buckley, always the consummate professional, delivered an eloquent acceptance speech, but the shy and retiring Adam Goodes struggled through and was obviously relieved when the official presentation was over.

Mark's brother, Craig, had been watching the Medal count on television at home. He was in the process of giving his one-year-old daughter, Charlotte, her evening bottle before putting her to bed, but the count was so tense and exciting, he let her fall asleep in his arms. As the last round of votes were counted and the three-way tie was announced, Craig flew up out of his chair, forgetting about his sleeping daughter, and had to make a difficult juggling catch to stop her falling to the floor. Tears filled Craig's eyes as his little brother accepted the Brownlow. Charlotte, who had been so rudely awakened, also started to cry. Craig sensed Mark's highly emotional state immediately and spent the next two hours answering phone calls from just about everyone he knew.

Mark says the true impact of his Brownlow win didn't sink in until the next day, when his head had cleared and he had regained his composure. He received hundreds of congratulatory text messages from friends, family and others associated with the Crows; so many, his mobile phone battery went flat before he could read them all. It was at that point he considered his Brownlow win a just reward, not only for the hard work he had put into his football over a decade at the top, but also for those who had helped him along the way. This was something he could share with everyone at the Crows, everyone back in Waikerie and, ultimately, everyone in South Australia.

Mark says he felt honoured to share the victory with two opponents; in fact, he says, it made things a lot easier to handle. Always one to appreciate the company and friendship of others, he really enjoyed having his name mentioned alongside two greats of football's modern era – two guys he has enormous respect for and with whom he will always have a special bond. Mark and Adam Goodes had several beers together after the count, but aside from the obligatory champagne toast, Nathan Buckley, who would be playing in the Grand Final just five days later, celebrated with water.

One aspect of the Brownlow Medal evening Mark really enjoyed was the opportunity to meet and talk with many of the AFL/VFL's past greats. Guys like Bob Skilton, Peter Moore, Barry Round and Keith Grieg had all been his boyhood heroes, and to be considered as an equal in their company was indeed an honour. It felt good just being in the same building as these men, he says, but to have joined their elite group was close to incomprehensible. Like all past winners, Mark is now guaranteed an invitation to every future Brownlow Medal dinner.

The Brownlow Medal meant many things to Mark. Although he doesn't feel it really changed his life, it certainly validated the decision he made at an early age to put football first and to pursue his dream of becoming a top-level player.

Mark isn't sure what he should do with the 2003 Brownlow Medal itself. He had his 1998 Premiership medallion, his Premiership guernsey and his Club Champion award from that year all mounted together and framed to go on the wall, but he simply keeps the Brownlow in a drawer at home, bringing it out only when he is required to wear it at special functions or when friends ask to see it. It's precious, but personal. He swears there is no truth in the rumours that he wore it around the house for the next six months.

Mark finished second in the 2004 Brownlow count behind West Coast's mercurial Chris Judd, actually polling one vote more than he'd scored to win in 2003. Craig Ricciuto says he took the precaution of putting toddler Charlotte to bed early that night.

Mark had enjoyed a really good season in 2005, but injuries would intervene and seriously affect his performance in '06.

Like all the Brownlow winners before him, there is no doubt that Mark Ricciuto would trade 'Old Charlie' for another Premiership medallion. That's simply the way of things with those who put their club and team above personal achievement.

14

THE CHANGING FACE OF FOOTBALL

They say a week is a long time in football, so fifteen years must seem like an eternity for Mark Ricciuto. As one of Adelaide Football Club's longest-serving players, he has seen both his club and the game change dramatically. The same is true of the way the game is now administered, according to Crows chairman and long-serving former CEO Bill Sanders. It is obvious to most football observers that what the AFL now dishes up at winter weekends is a far cry from the way it used to be. Football has seen an overall lift in professionalism in all areas, enabling it to maintain its status as one of the world's premier team sports. Changes have occurred both on and off the field

In the last decade and a half, there have been many changes in the way the game is played. Some of those changes have improved it and others, arguably, have held it back; but there is one constant – the attitude and dedication of all who compete at the highest level. Like all of his team-mates, Mark is always 110 per cent committed once he crosses the white line. The passion and determination to win at all costs has always been – and will

135

always be – the underlying premise in AFL football. Those players who don't display that level of commitment simply don't make the cut.

As the demands and pressures of modern football have increased, so has the amount of time that everyone involved is required to spend in preparation. When Mark first started with the Adelaide Crows there were five pre-season training sessions during the week, kicking off at around 5.30 pm and continuing through until 7.30 or 8. Another session on Sunday morning would last for a couple of hours, totalling six training periods for the week. These days it's two sessions a day, Monday to Friday, and another on Saturday, essentially doubling the track time and club contact time. This doesn't mean double the workload, however. Training for the modern game now involves a lot more variation, including recovery, stretching, pilates, weights, swimming, cycling and yoga – on top of the usual skills and endurance work. There are few players who now hold down jobs away from football, as the time commitment is simply too demanding.

During the season, a typical week for Crows players after a Saturday evening game would look something like this. (There are slight variations if the team plays on a Friday night or Sunday.)

Immediately after the match, each player spends ten minutes on the exercise bike, ten minutes stretching and a further ten minutes in an ice bath. There are often two or three injured players who spend the entire night at the club for consistent treatment under the supervision of medical staff. These players will sleep with an automatic icing machine strapped to the injured site. This timer-activated machine pumps ice-cold water for twenty minutes every two hours and is closely monitored by head trainer, Vince DeBono, who doesn't sleep at all until the following day.

Sunday morning is all about recovery. Most uninjured players begin with sets of six 60-metre stride-outs and then hit the pool, where they swim 25-metre laps, either walking, jogging or lunging through the water for each 25-metre return leg. Those with sore spots spend more time in the ice bath, while those who have escaped the match unscathed will spend a minute in the ice and then two minutes in warmth to stimulate blood flow and help eliminate waste products. There is more general icing for up to twenty minutes and compression bandaging for players with obvious sore spots.

On Monday morning, those with injuries report to the medical staff at eight o'clock. It's then another recovery session for the whole team, which includes 30 minutes of low-intensity running and swimming. This is followed by 30 minutes each of supervised stretching and massage. Players write on the medical room whiteboard how many physiotherapy sessions they think they will need during the course of the week for optimum recovery.

At 2.30 on Monday afternoon the whole squad sits in on a game review meeting, during which most of the positives and negatives from Saturday's match are discussed. By this stage Neil Craig and the other specialist coaches have spent hours reviewing videotapes of the game. This meeting usually takes an hour, and quite often club CEO Steven Trigg and operations manager John Reid will pop in to share their thoughts with the coaches and players.

A light, low- to medium-intensity skills session for uninjured players follows at 3.30. Those with injuries spend this time on the exercise bike or in the lap pool.

Tuesday morning training kicks off at nine o'clock with a half-hour core stability session, which has become a big part of the overall training regime. This is designed to minimise soft tissue injuries and the risk of an unstable pelvis, and associated complaints such as osteitis pubis.

A maintenance session begins at 9.30; it's designed to strengthen the sites of previous injuries and is very specific. Those with a history of rolled ankles, for example, might use a 'wobble board' at different levels of intensity to shore up and reinforce ankle ligaments.

A one-hour weights session, designed by Chris Hinck, is next on the Tuesday agenda. Each player has his own weights program and is expected to complete at least two sessions a week. Mark, Ben Rutten, and other players who like to maintain strength without bulking up too much, will complete only one or two sessions. A meeting of the club's Leadership Group follows at noon.

Wednesday morning at eleven o'clock the squad breaks into groups for an areas meeting with their specialist coaches. At these meetings the forward line players, mid-fielders, rucks and backline players can each discuss their own sets of issues from the previous week's game.

At midday the entire squad comes together for the week's main meeting. This is a 'general housekeeping' forum and is head coach Neil Craig's opportunity to tackle important issues from the previous weekend's game and to make suggestions about things that he feels need to change. Injuries to various players are explained to the entire squad, and the coach then outlines the format and specific drills planned for the main training session to follow. Craig often uses video to explain drills; once everyone is out on the track, it's expected that all drills will be fully understood.

Neil Craig prefers the term 'rehearsal' to 'training', as he believes the old adage, 'you play the way you train', and regularly incorporates a lot of competitive work and game-oriented drills into practice sessions. Craig uses 'rehearsal' time to get his players to learn to make the right decisions – something that is crucial to success in modern football. The main session concludes at around 2.30 pm and then it's back inside for some stretching, bike riding and an ice bath before heading home or staying on for weights or extra medical treatment if required.

Officially, Thursday is the players' day off, but there are quite a few who come in for weights work, further medical attention or massage. Several players, including Mark, opt for extra massage outside the club and do so at their own expense. Some like to stay away from the club altogether on Thursdays, perhaps having a round of golf, doing some fishing or simply relaxing at home.

Mark has a standing appointment (again at his own expense) with a private physiotherapist, Steve Saunders, on Thursday afternoons and says the 40-minute session is of great benefit. He also sees chiropractor Margie Barry each fortnight for a check-up, as he feels that chiropractors and physiotherapists concentrate on different anatomical aspects and complement each other nicely.

Fridays kick off with a second areas meeting. This time each group concentrates on the strengths and weaknesses of the opposition for the upcoming match; the teams will normally have been announced by this stage, and each of the specialist coaches has a good idea of who will be playing where in the opposition camp. It's at this meeting that tags are worked out, stoppage set-ups are finalised and forward structure is planned.

The final 'rehearsal' session begins at around ten o'clock and it's usually 40–60 minutes of medium- to high-intensity drills. Some players like to go flat-out during this final practice, while others prefer to scale things back a bit and complete drills at 70 per cent pace to conserve energy. The coaches are aware of this and won't push any player harder than he feels he should be working just 24 hours before a match.

A noon team meeting takes a last in-depth look at forwards, mid-fielders and defenders, as well as the predicted opposition lineup. Structures are explained in detail, and many other signif-icant issues, such as kick-out strategies, probable opposition tags and first-quarter player rotations, are decided. 'What if' strategies are also put in place to cover contingencies such as surprise opposition positional changes or the unexpected withdrawal of a key player. Nothing is left to chance by any of the coaches, who have spent most of the week analysing the opposition and formulating plans to counter players who are in brilliant form or who have hurt the Crows in previous meetings.

Each player has his own routine leading up to a match. If it's a Saturday afternoon game coming up, Mark will watch a movie or perhaps some football on television on Friday night, but likes to be in bed by eleven o'clock. He will get up at around 8 am, read the paper and have a breakfast of organic oats or maybe baked beans on toast. He doesn't like to talk much at this time and begins focusing on the game ahead. A casual walk, stretch and maybe a bit of time with a football precede a 12.15 departure for AAMI Stadium. All players must report by 1 pm, and Mark allows 45 minutes for what is normally a half-hour drive.

If all the previous week's hard work, strategic planning and medical treatment have come together and the Crows play well enough, chances are they will have recorded another home win. It has been yet another demanding week for all concerned, but the pain, frustration, sweat and emotional drain have all been worthwhile if the Adelaide Football Club has been able to bank four more very important Premiership points.

Naturally, the pace of the game itself has increased dramatically since Mark took the field against Hawthorn in his first match in 1993. Most on-ball players these days would cover perhaps 15–20 per cent more distance than used to be the case, but the most significant change in this regard would be with half backs, backs, forwards and half forwards. Most players in these positions now use up to two-thirds of the oval during the course of a match, as opposed to maybe a quarter in the mid to late 1990s.

Aerobic fitness across the board has had to increase accordingly.

Also significant is the use of the four interchange players, who essentially hold positions like those on the ground. The bench quartet know precisely when they will rotate on and off the field, as well as the roles they are expected to play, whereas the two reserves in the older-style game were there to cover injuries or severely out-of-form team-mates. In essence, it's 22 guys now playing 90–95 per cent of the game each, as opposed to eighteen playing the entire game unless something went amiss.

Most AFL clubs now have four or five coaches (a head coach and assistant coaches), as opposed to just two when Mark started. All are full-time, which means there is now very little left to chance in knowing the opposing teams' personnel. Mark says the difference between the teams at the top and bottom of the Premiership ladder these days has never been so small; winning and losing often comes down to game plans, coaching strategies and contingency issues. It is now a thinking man's game, rather than simply a test of skill, fitness and endurance.

Since Adelaide Football Club's inception in 1991, it has had five head coaches – all from vastly different backgrounds. There can be no doubting the significance of the head coach in modern AFL football; aside from possessing an amazing knowledge of the game, he has to be a psychologist, a mediator, an arbitrator, a master tactician and an accomplished media personality. Gone are the days of simply organising Tuesday and Thursday night training sessions with a light run on Sunday mornings; in their place is a full-time, '24/7' commitment that pays nicely and expects plenty in return.

Having been involved in elite sport for many years, and always interested in the scientific side of fitness, Neil Craig's squads at the Crows have invariably been superbly prepared. Most agree that it was the team's overall fitness that enabled them to wear down the opposition in the 1997 and 1998 Grand Finals. The same applied when he took over as head coach, with all members of the playing squad in peak condition and ready to run out four quarters against any opposition.

As far as the AFC's members and general supporters are concerned, Craig has been a welcome breath of fresh air. He is acutely aware of the importance of a strong supporter base and encourages the players to acknowledge that support at the conclusion of each match. Kicking footballs out into the crowd and 'high-fiving' it with those around the fence after a win is important to the club in maintaining a high level of membership (over 50,000) and keeping crowd levels high at home games.

While he was a little rough around the edges when it came to addressing the media in his first year as coach, Mark feels Craig is now much more at ease and projects a strong, but amiable image during press conferences and interviews. Adelaide's appeal to the community as a whole has never been better and, apart from Malcolm Blight, the club coach has never been more popular.

Mark says his coaches spend more hours in analysis and planning than most outsiders would believe possible. The Crows' list of set plays is now three times as long as it was during the 1990s, particularly for organising stoppages, boundary throw-ins, kick-outs and for slowing down the tempo if the opposition gets a run on. There are also specific strategies for certain opposing teams, such as Sydney and the Western Bulldogs, both of whom play a totally different style of football. Coaches have always tried hard to be one step ahead of their opposition counterparts, but never before have game plans been so intensely scrutinised and so well organised.

It's certainly no secret that financial rewards for coaches and players have elevated dramatically since the early 1990s and that top players from most clubs are now paid in accordance with the time and effort they put into the game. AFL footballers who spend ten years or more at the top level are generally wealthy – at least, those who look after their earnings and invest them wisely. Naturally, there are also opportunities to increase one's income through endorsements and sponsorships, but Mark says those opportunities are far easier to come by for Melbourne-based players than for those from the less populous and less football-crazed capital cities.

Post-career media involvement is now much more lucrative for a select few than it has ever been. There is big money on offer for those recently out of the game who have the necessary attributes for television and, to a lesser extent, radio. Mark stresses, however, that TV is definitely the province of only those retired players who have exceptional presentation skills, and that there have been some spectacular failures in recent times. Again, most of the 'specialist comments' telecast people seem to be Victorian, and Mark doesn't see this situation changing too much in the future.

Players at most AFL clubs are now coached to handle media interviews and press conferences, whereas a decade ago each club had just a couple of elected spokesmen. It's not uncommon these days to see a first- or second-year player handling himself capably in a television interview situation or being quoted in a newspaper sports column. Media savvy is expected these days at all levels, both by the football public and the AFL.

It goes without saying that AFL clubs need enormous cash flow to operate successfully in today's financial climate, and this means heavy reliance on sponsorship dollars. As a result, players need to be more accessible to sponsors than ever, which places even more demands on their time. Considering media, sponsor-ship and charity commitments, a minimum of eleven training sessions a week, and rehabilitation time, it's not difficult to appreciate that the life of an AFL footballer in this current era is indeed a hectic one.

There are few people in the game better qualified, at least on the administrative side, to comment on the way our national game has changed than Adelaide Football Club stalwart Bill Sanders. Sanders was chairman of the Woodville Football Club for many years and was one of the pivotal figures in the amalgamation of Woodville and West Torrens in 1990. He then moved on to become Adelaide's inaugural CEO, a position he held for eleven years between 1991 and 2001. After vacating the top job at the Crows, he was elected to the board and has been chairman since 2004. No one has a more intimate knowledge of the way the club is run, how its players are looked after, and its relationship with both the SANFL and AFL. Sanders is undoubtedly the guru of football administrators in South Australia, and is still regarded by some as the best in the country.

In Mark's first year the Adelaide Football Club's salary cap for players' payments was $1.75 million to cover a squad of 52; the 2007 figure is $6.94 million for a squad of 38. Inflation aside, this is a dramatic rise, but when considered in context, it's not hard to appreciate. The Adelaide Football Club's income in the 1993 season was $6 million, and $21 million in 2007, so, in relative terms at least, the figures remain on par.

As head of the club, Bill Sanders has seen a whole host of changes in AFL structure in fifteen years, including the gradual rationalisation of the ovals on which matches are played. Gone are Melbourne's suburban grounds such as Windy Hill, the Whitten Oval, Victoria Park, Optus Oval and Moorabbin, with Victorian games now played only at the MCG, Skilled Stadium at Geelong and the Telstra Dome, which was originally the Colonial Stadium. Geelong's home ground was known throughout VFL history as Kardinia Park, but was picked by the Skilled Group as corporate naming of AFL venues gathered momentum. Adelaide's beloved Football Park is now known as AAMI Stadium, indicating the way big business is getting involved in football and, in return, generating vast amounts of income for the AFL and state leagues.

Bill Sanders recalls his early days at the Crows, when there was still a fair bit of rivalry within the squad that carried over from the SANFL competition. Players would congregate and socialise in groups, rather than as a complete squad, which was something the administration tried hard to overcome. It wasn't until a few new players, including Mark Ricciuto, came along and the team began enjoying consistent on-field success, that it started to assume its own true identity and team spirit. Finishing third in 1993 went a long way towards establishing the Crows as a respected, close-knit unit. They had no readily identified 'home base' during that era, which is a far cry from where the club sits today.

There were few years between 1993 and 2000 when something significant failed to occur in AFL football, Sanders says. The Blood Rule appeared in 1994, which dictates that any player with external bleeding must leave the playing arena immediately. Fremantle joined the competition in 1995, dividing loyalties in Western Australia, and the Fitzroy Football Club merged with the Brisbane Bears in 1996 to form the Brisbane Lions. Port Adelaide was the next to enter in late 1996 for the 1997 season. In 1998 the interchange bench increased to four players following requests from the clubs and the AFL Players' Association. Things slowed a little into the new millennium, with the sixteen-team competition stabilising and only a few rule changes grabbing the headlines from time to time.

For an administrator of the game and a close link between his club and the AFL, it has been heartening for Bill Sanders to see football grow in most areas. Home-and-away and finals matches are now attended by nearly half a million more people each season than when Mark first played in 1993. The national television audience has become astronomical, providing the AFL and its clubs with enormous financial benefits. Just about every sponsorship opportunity has been taken up, such as corporate names on footballs, players' guernseys, shorts, boots and even socks. Memorabilia is now big business, particularly through the AFL retail outlets and individual club stores. In a nutshell, Sanders has seen AFL football go from a semi-professional enterprise to a full-blown, corporate-driven business in his seventeen years as a key administrator.

Adelaide Football Club has flickered into life, struggled under adversity, stabilised, won back-to-back Premierships and, ultimately, become one of the most powerful and respected entities in the League. Sanders was there when a young Mark Ricciuto had his first kick on 30 April 1993 and he will be there, without fail, when Mark runs out in Crows colours for the last time. It's a safe bet that both will have a tear in their eye when that day comes around.

15

SIXTEEN TO REMEMBER

Most of Mark Ricciuto's 300-plus games of AFL football have been of a high quality; no player can be so highly decorated over a career of that length without incredible consistency, but there will always be a handful of matches that stand out in his mind for various reasons. Some of those are prominent solely because of abnormally high statistics, others because they were milestones, and a couple because they were simply fantastic contests.

Adelaide v. Hawthorn, 30 April 1993, Round 6,
Football Park, Adelaide
There are few footballers who don't remember their first game in the Big League. Mark's first was in round six of the 1993 season against Hawthorn at Football Park before a capacity crowd. This was very much a dream come true, particularly as it was less than two years since he had played his last game in the Riverland competition. The Crows lost that game to the Hawks, who were at close to full strength with the likes of Brereton, Dunstall, Ayres, Eade and Langford, but Mark picked up a creditable 15 disposals

and kicked a goal. It was, as he describes it, 'an addictive feeling' to play before 45,000 screaming fans, rather than the six or seven hundred who turned up to watch Riverland matches. Although he was naturally nervous on his debut, he soon felt comfortable and confident in AFL company.

Adelaide	3.1	5.4	9.11	12.16 (88)
Hawthorn	3.3	7.5	12.6	16.9 (105)

Best players: McDermott, Smart, McGuinness, Jarman, Tregenza, Anderson

Goals: Modra 5, Smart 3, McGuinness 2, Anderson 1, Ricciuto 1

Crowd: 46,689

Preliminary final, 18 September 1993, MCG

If ever a chance at glory went begging, it was the '93 Preliminary Final against Essendon at a packed Melbourne Cricket Ground. This was a match that Mark and his team-mates, as well as AFC administrators, members and fans, will remember as 'the one that got away'. The Crows blitzed the Bombers in the first half and led by an imposing 42 points at the long break, but for reasons no one has been able to put a finger on, the wheels fell off completely in the third quarter.

Despite having four more scoring shots, they ended up losing the match by 11 points, providing Essendon with a free pass to challenge Carlton the following week. The Bombers went on to win the 1993 Premiership by 44 points and Mark is confident the Crows would have beaten Carlton for the flag had they maintained their first half dominance over Essendon and progressed to the Grand Final.

Adelaide	7.4	12.12	13.14	14.16 (100)
Essendon	4.5	6.6	12.8	17.9 (111)

Best players: Modra, McGuinness, Jarman, McDermott, Rehn, Tregenza, Liptack, Riccuito
Goals: Modra 6, Brown 2, Smart 2, Wigney 1, Liptack 1, Hodges 1, Anderson 1
Crowd: 76,380

21 May 1994, Football Park

Selection in the 1994 State of Origin team came as something of a shock to Mark, but not to most observers. His form had been very consistent since his debut, and to be chosen in the same team as many of his boyhood idols was right up there among his wildest dreams. The Victorian opposition was about as strong as it had ever been, and once again Football Park was bursting at the seams with a capacity crowd.

Mark recalls that match as being one of the toughest he has ever played in. The skill level on both sides was also about as good as it gets, and those who had come to watch were spellbound by the spectacle unfolding before them. The lead changed several times late in the game, with the Croweaters ultimately prevailing by just two points. Legendary Victorian forward Gary Ablett almost won it for the Victorians with a great mark, but the siren was sounded and the game was over. Mark had played at half back that evening on a much taller opponent in Chris Grant, but picked up 20-odd possessions and figured in South Australia's best. He went out for a few drinks with players from both teams after the match, which was, in his words, 'a surreal experience at just eighteen years of age and something I will never forget'.

| **South Australia** | 2.4 | 7.6 | 9.6 | 11.9 (75) |
| **Victoria** | 3.2 | 5.8 | 8.13 | 10.13 (73) |

Best players: Bradley, Kernahan, Wanganeen, Platten, Ricciuto, McGuinness

Goals: Modra 3, Kernahan 3, Hall 2, McGuinness 1, Bradley 1, Platten 1
Crowd: 47,554

25 May 1996, Whitten Oval, Melbourne
Every now and then, most footballers have a day when they simply can't get away from the ball. Mark had one of these in round nine of the 1996 season against Footscray at the Whitten Oval in suburban Melbourne. Every bounce went his way, he seemed to be at the scene of every opposition turnover, and each time he entered a one-on-one contest, the result was in his favour. It was the sort of match all footballers dream of, but which few get to experience very often.

There were only 11,000 spectators in attendance. The Crows fought hard, but lost to the Bulldogs by 40 points. In terms of possessions, this was one of Mark's best ever performances. He racked up 20 kicks and 20 handballs from a half back flank and was clearly best for Adelaide. Tony Modra kicked seven of the Crows' 11 goals that afternoon, but it takes more than a couple of brilliant individual performances to win a football match and Adelaide simply had too few winners on the day.

Adelaide	2.3	4.7	6.10	11.13 (79)
Footscray	5.3	9.5	12.9	18.11 (119)

Best players: Ricciuto, Caven, Robran, Bickley, Modra, Brown
Goals: Modra 7, Caven 1, Pesch 1, Brown 1, Ricciuto 1
Crowd: 11,140

26 July 1997, Football Park
Mark played his 100th game against Richmond in round 17 of 1997. He had enjoyed a terrific first half of football, racking up 17 possessions and kicking two goals before the main break.

However, this was the game in which his much-publicised groin problems really came to the fore, and he knew as he ran out for the third quarter that he was in serious trouble.

Scarcely able to run at better than half pace for the remainder of the game, his impact was limited in its final stages, but the Crows still came out on top. He knew that evening there was little, if any, football left in him for the rest of the season. His first real milestone match certainly turned out to be one remembered for the wrong reasons.

Adelaide   8.3   16.4   23.7   29.11 (185)
Richmond   0.2   2.4   5.6   7.6 (48)
Best players: Pittman, Jarman, McLeod, Bickley, Caven
Goals: Jarman 7, Modra 4, Robran 4, Vardy 3, Ricciuto 2, Bond 1, Rehn 1, Koster 1, Sampson 1, Connell 1, Goodwin 1, Hart 1, James 1, McLeod 1
Crowd: 36,297

28 June 1998, SCG

Round 14 of the 1998 season was undoubtedly a defining game for the Adelaide Football Club and essentially set the Crows up for a second Premiership assault. Their record against the Swans in Sydney had been pretty good, as had their form leading up to the Harbour City encounter, and they were confident of doing well against a side headed by Tony Lockett and Paul Kelly.

Mark was selected in the mid-field that day, with the odd forward rotation planned if the game went as expected. He finished with 30 valuable possessions and three goals, and recalls the 37-point victory as one of the best overall team performances he had ever been involved in. There was a real air of confidence about the Crows after that game and, of course, this trend would continue for the remainder of the minor round.

Adelaide   5.5   12.9   14.11   18.16 (124)
Sydney   2.4   5.8   10.12   12.15 (87)
Best players: Rehn, Ricciuto, James, Koster, Goodwin
Goals: Ricciuto 3, Marsh 3, Jarman 2, Bickley 2, James 2, Bond 1,
   Hart 1, Cook 1, Thiessen 1, Edwards 1, Ormond-Allen 1
Crowd: 30,735

9 August 1998, Football Park

Showdown IV against Port Adelaide in round 19 of 1998 was one of the club's most emphatic victories against its home-town opponent. The first half was relatively even, with Adelaide leading by 22 points at the long break, but they cut loose in the second half to eventually blow the Power away by more than 12 goals. Mark picked up 34 possessions that afternoon, while close mate Peter Vardy kicked seven goals and grabbed the three Brownlow votes.

As this match was turning into a bit of a procession in the second half and Port were simply unable to arrest the Adelaide avalanche, Mark began giving Vardy heaps about cutting off other players' leads and becoming a goal hog. It's not often there is room for on-field frivolity between team-mates in any AFL match, but there are few things sweeter for any Crows player than thumping Port Power, and the Adelaide boys certainly lapped it up.

Adelaide   5.0   7.5   15.8   22.12 (144)
Port Adelaide 1.3   3.7   7.8   10.10 (70)
Best players: Vardy, McLeod, Ricciuto, Stevens, Goodwin
Goals: Vardy 7, Jarman 4, McLeod 3, Modra 2, Robran 2, Caven
   2, Edwards 1, Goodwin 1
Crowd: 46,405

26 September 1998, MCG

After missing the 1997 Grand Final through injury, Saturday

26 September 1998 couldn't come quickly enough for Mark. Adelaide had beaten Sydney and the Western Bulldogs convincingly in the lead-up to the Grand Final and was in good shape to make it back-to-back Premierships. Mark didn't play a huge personal role in the victory against North Melbourne on that historic afternoon, but he contributed well enough and was ecstatic when it came time to collect his Premiership medallion. Any come-from-behind victory is a good one, but to have climbed back from the jaws of defeat to overcome North Melbourne on Grand Final day was about as impressive a feat as most South Aussies can ever remember.

Being part of a Premiership team in the country's elite football league is regarded by most who are fortunate enough to be there as the pinnacle of their career, and Mark is no exception. Playing at the country's most famous sporting arena in front of 94,000 spectators, many of whom had travelled from Adelaide, was an occasion to cherish. Consequently, the 1998 Grand Final win is easily the most memorable of Mark's 300-plus games and will remain so unless the Adelaide Crows can snatch another one before he bows out.

| **Adelaide** | 3.2 | 4.3 | 9.11 | 15.15 (105) |
| **North Melbourne** | 4.4 | 6.15 | 8.15 | 8.22 (70) |

Best players: McLeod, Hart, Caven, Johnson, Rehn, Bickley, Jarman
Goals: Jarman 5, Smart 3, Vardy 2, James 1, Johnson 1, Ricciuto 1, Pittman 1, Thiessen 1
Crowd: 94,431

23 April 2000, Football Park

From a personal contribution point of view, Mark considers his performance against Port Power in round seven of 2000 to be his all-time best. Like many Crows players, coming up against Port often brings out the best in him and in this encounter things were no different. Adelaide had lost its first five games of the season and were looking down the barrel at a very long year before rallying against Hawthorn in round six, but Showdown VII was the match that really turned things around.

Port had outplayed Adelaide easily in the first half and was leading by a seemingly insurmountable 42 points early in the third term. The Crows piled on six goals five in the last quarter to Port's one goal three, however, and ultimately prevailed by seven points. Mark had shaken off four separate taggers during the course of the match, finished with an all-time high of 41 disposals, kicked four goals and achieved maximum Brownlow Medal votes. Rarely, if ever, had one player had so much impact on a game at Football Park.

Adelaide   4.1   6.3   8.9   14.14 (98)
Port Adelaide   6.3   10.8   12.10   13.13 (91)
Best players: Ricciuto, Robran, McLeod, Edwards, Smart
Goals: Ricciuto 4, Vardy 3, Beinke 2, Welsh 1, McLeod 1, Edwards 1, Bassett 1, Johnson 1
Crowd: 41,173

21 April 2001, Optus Oval, Melbourne
Carlton was a team that gave Adelaide consistent trouble in the late 1990s and into the new millennium, particularly on their home turf at Optus Oval in Melbourne. Round four of the 2001 season was played in atrocious conditions. It had rained in Melbourne for much of the preceding week, and there was plenty of wind as the Crows slogged it out with the Blues in a low-scoring affair.

Adelaide was winless after three rounds and really needed to make a stand or its season was destined for the scrap heap before it had even really begun. The Crows squad had been decimated by injury and there were several big name players out of form, so they decided to go for broke against a full-strength Carlton lineup. Adelaide's Leadership Group called an impromptu meeting in a room at the Carlton Crest Hotel before leaving for the oval to work out a strategy to turn things around.

Mark made a personal decision to impose a strong physical presence on his Carlton opponents from the opening bounce – and he certainly delivered. He dished out three crunching hip and shoulder bumps in the first quarter, one of which rendered big man Lance Whitnall ineffective for the remainder of the match. Mark ended up with 12 disposals for the game, kicked four vital goals, and was rated second best for Adelaide behind Simon Goodwin. This match made his most memorable list not because of Mark's personal achievement, but because the nine-point win was such a great team effort under adversity.

| **Adelaide** | 4.3 | 6.4 | 7.6 | 9.8 (62) |
| **Carlton** | 1.1 | 4.1 | 5.3 | 8.5 (53) |

Best players: Goodwin, Ricciuto, Smart, Jarman, Hart
Goals: Ricciuto 4, Vardy 3, Goodwin 1, Welsh 1
Crowd: 21,110

17 August 2001, Colonial Stadium, Melbourne

The Colonial Stadium in Melbourne's Docklands precinct is one of Mark's favourite venues. Most players enjoy playing under the roof, immune from the influence of rain or wind, and Mark had a cracker there against the Kangaroos in round 20 of the 2001 season. After suffering a rib fracture earlier in the year and struggling for quite some time as it slowly healed, he was in scintillating touch. He collected 35 possessions and kicked five goals for a best-on-ground performance in the 62-point win.

This form was a welcome relief, both personally and for the

club, as Mark had assumed the captaincy that season and needed to get his body back into shape to lead from the front.

Adelaide	6.3	14.7	18.10	25.12 (162)
Kangaroos	3.5	7.7	14.7	15.10 (100)

Best players: McLeod, Ricciuto, Stevens, Perrie, Shirley, Johnson
Goals: Ricciuto 5, Perrie 5, Stevens 5, Burton 2, Jarman 2, Smart 1, Stenglein 1, Welsh 1, Biglands 1, McLeod 1, Johnson 1
Crowd: 25,340

28 July 2002, Skilled Stadium, Geelong

Winning at Skilled Stadium in Geelong had never been easy for the Crows, and a victory in round 17 of the 2002 season was imperative. They were vying with the Cats for a position in the top four, and every player knew only their very best performance would put them in with a chance. The ground was heavy, and although Geelong had more of the ball for much of the game, they kicked badly for goal. This allowed the super-accurate Adelaide to sneak home by three points.

Mark played top football all day, kicking two goals in the first half and three more in the final quarter to finish with five and essentially sink the Cats. He recalls being physically exhausted in the change-rooms after that memorable win, but was still able to celebrate with his team-mates well into the evening.

Adelaide	6.1	7.1	11.3	15.3 (93)
Geelong	2.3	7.7	8.13	12.18 (90)

Best players: Edwards, Ricciuto, Smart, Stenglein, Bode, Biglands
Goals: Ricciuto 5, Bode 2, Beinke 2, Stevens 1, Clarke 1, Johncock 1, Doughty 1, Edwards 1, McLeod 1
Crowd: 24,325

8 May 2004, AAMI Stadium, Adelaide

Reinforcing the fact that he loves nothing better than playing against the Power, Mark did a real number on his taggers in round seven of 2004. This was Showdown XV, and the Crows were in desperate need of a win with just one victory against Richmond in six starts. It was a perfect Saturday evening, with 44,733 spectators crammed into AAMI Stadium to see Adelaide break Port's Showdown stranglehold and win by 32 points.

Mark contributed strongly, gaining 35 possessions and being rated second best for the Crows. Ruckman Matthew Clarke took top honours that night in what most consider was his best-ever performance in Adelaide colours.

Adelaide   4.2   11.6   14.14   17.17 (119)
Port Adelaide 5.2   7.3   9.7   13.9 (87)
Best players: Clarke, Ricciuto, McGregor, McLeod, Stenglein, Johncock
Goals: Johncock 4, Carey 3, McGregor 3, Jericho 2, Bock 1, Massie 1, Edwards 1, Welsh 1, Stenglein 1
Crowd: 44,733

29 May 2004, MCG

Mark played his 250th game against Hawthorn on the MCG three weeks later and celebrated with an 86-point win. Unlike several other noted footballers, most of his milestone games have been victories and this one was the biggest of them all. He won 35 possessions, kicked three goals and was easily best on the field that afternoon.

Adelaide   5.2   9.8   14.11   20.13 (133)
Hawthorn   2.6   3.8   5.8   6.11 (47)
Best players: Ricciuto, Edwards, McLeod, Hentschel, Hart, Stevens, Torney

Goals: Carey 4, Stevens 4, Ricciuto 3, McLeod 2, Schubak 2, Bock
1, Mattner 1, Hentschel 1, Clarke 1, Shirley 1
Crowd: 22,942

17 July 2004, GABBA, Brisbane

Round 17 of the 2004 season was one that Mark – and just about
everyone else connected with the Adelaide Football Club – will
remember for all the wrong reasons. They travelled to Brisbane
severely undermanned to take on the Lions, who were injury-free
and right at the peak of their performance curve. Adelaide began as
underdogs, but no one expected the game to unfold quite the way
it did. Mark says he had never felt as helpless and overwhelmed in
a game of football as he did that evening at the Gabba. Brisbane
ran riot all night, kicking an unbelievable 21 goals to two after
half time and eventually winning by a massive 141 points.

Neil Craig had assumed control as interim coach after Gary
Ayres had departed; both Wayne Carey and Nigel Smart had
retired; and things looked set to get a whole lot worse before they
got better. Mark concedes this was probably the lowest ebb in his
time at the club, but all concerned drew inspiration from it and
they bounced back to beat the Kangaroos at home the following
week.

| **Brisbane** | 3.6 | 8.11 | 18.12 | 29.15 (189) |
| **Adelaide** | 2.2 | 4.6 | 6.10 | 6.12 (48) |

Best players: Goodwin, Mattner, McLeod, Bassett, Hart
Goals: Welsh 2, Perrie 2, Burton 1, Ricciuto 1
Crowd: 33,657

3 April 2006, Telstra Dome

Mark hadn't trained at all for virtually three months when the
season kicked off and Neil Craig showed tremendous faith in

his skipper to include him in the opening match. It was the first ever Monday evening game and had an enormous television audience. Mark started at full forward against Collingwood and All-Australian defender James Clement.

Collingwood came out of the blocks well, but Adelaide slowly pegged the Magpies back and ultimately ran out comfortable winners. This match was a triumph for Mark, both personally and on a team level. He kicked six goals three in a dominant performance at full forward.

Adelaide   2.1   9.5   12.6   17.9 (111)
Collingwood 5.1   7.4   12.5   12.5 (77)
Best players: Edwards, Ricciuto, Burton, Perrie, Johncock, Goodwin, Mattner
Goals: Ricciuto 6, Perrie 3, Burton 2, Biglands 2, Bode 1, Thompson 1, Shirley 1, Reilly 1
Crowd: 35,434

21 July 2006, AAMI Stadium

Mark's most significant personal milestone, at least as far as longevity in football is concerned, occurred in round 16 of season 2006. The media hype leading up to his 300th game was unprecedented in Adelaide, with both newspapers and television building it up to incredible proportions. Mark was totally overwhelmed by all the attention, and although it was naturally flattering, the build-up made him a little nervous.

Adelaide thumped the Kangaroos by 72 points that afternoon in front of a huge home crowd, and Mark contributed with five goals to finish high in the Crows' best players.

Adelaide   4.3   7.6   14.7   19.10 (124)
Kangaroos 1.3   4.4   6.8   7.10 (52)

Best players: Bassett, McLeod, Goodwin, Johncock, Ricciuto, Biglands, McGregor

Goals: Ricciuto 5, McGregor 4, Biglands 2, Thompson 2, Bode 2, Burton 1, Bock 1, Stevens 1, Torney 1

Crowd: 47,487

16

TALES FROM THE CLOSET

It's true that most of us have a few stories – snippets from the past, if you like – that come back to haunt us from time to time. These generally range from being mildly funny to downright embarrassing, and there is no doubt that Mark Ricciuto has more than his share of such tales to call his own. And while he was a bit reluctant to pass on some of the more interesting stories, he has several good 'mates' who simply couldn't wait to expose a side of Mark that most won't know about. It should be noted quite early in the piece that Mark's friends have never been known to let the truth get in the way of a good story!

The names Jason Lehmann, Danny McMahon, Clinton 'Scratcher' Eustice and Matt Western were legendary around the Waikerie area in the late 1980s and 1990s. All except Clinton have moved away from the Riverland now. Danny is a successful financial planner in an Adelaide business owned by Mark and Simon Goodwin, Jason is working at West Lakes for the Crows, and Matt is making big money in Western Australia on the oil rigs. Like Mark, they were all sports-crazy as teenagers and when they weren't playing football, tennis or cricket, they were coming up with other ideas to make life interesting. A few of these ideas may have been frowned upon by the locals, but the lads rarely did anything illegal or inconvenient to others and it was all in good fun.

Clinton Eustice played football with Mark through the junior grades and also loved to fish, shoot, catch yabbies and ride trail bikes. He remembers a day when Murray Ricciuto took Mark, Matt Western and him to Morgan to watch a football match on the local oval, which, like quite a few country grounds, had no perimeter fence. Spectators would sit in their cars to watch the game, then usually wander into the clubrooms after the match for a yarn and a beer.

Murray Ricciuto must have had a long yarn and several beers after this particular match as, keen to continue his conversation, he threw the car keys at fifteen-year-old Mark and asked him to bring the Commodore around to the clubroom door. Encouraged by 'Scratcher' and Matt, Mark started the car and decided to give it a bit of a workout on the grassed area behind the goals before collecting his father. As often happens when three pumped-up teenagers get together, the more 'Scratcher' and Matt egged Mark on, the harder he pushed the car. He eventually lost control, skidded sideways towards the oval and ended up neatly between the goal posts.

Jason Lehmann is part of the well-known footballing Lehmann clan from Waikerie. Although he undoubtedly provided more 'dirt' on his good mate than any of the others, there were only a few snippets that made it past the censor's red pen. Now that he is working at the Adelaide Football Club, Jason spends quite a bit of time with Mark again and it would seem the pair still get up to mischief from time to time.

Jason recalls a Waikerie street parade in 1990, organised by their football club, after the annual post-season presentation night. The parade was to honour medallists in the various age divisions and, as Jason had won the senior Best and Fairest while Mark had won the Colts award, they rode together down Waikerie's main street in Jason's open-top Ford Capri. Jason remembers Mark leaning over to him as the local residents applauded and the ticker tape rained down, and whispering: 'This must be what it's like to win the Brownlow.' At that point, Jason had a sneaking suspicion that one of the two footballers in that car would go on to win a Brownlow Medal – and chances were it wouldn't be him.

Port Broughton was always a favourite holiday area with Mark, Jason and several other of their Riverland mates. One afternoon they decided to do a deal with the driver of a kiddies' train in the local Apex Park. It was one of those miniature trains with several carriages that carries one or two youngsters and runs around the perimeter of the park without the need for rails. Always on the lookout for fun, and prepared to pay for it, Mark somehow managed to con the driver into taking him and his mates out of the park and down into town. They handed her $20 and the deal was done.

So much fun was had by all on board, including the driver, that Mark came up with a further $100 for the driver to take them all the way to Port Pirie for the evening greyhound races. Remarkably, she agreed, but when a semi-trailer passed them and all but sucked the whole outfit from the road, they decided that chugging up to Pirie at twenty kilometres an hour on the open road in a kiddies' train might not be such a good idea after all.

The third of Jason's printable tales involved an evening at Byron Bay in 2005. Jason was about to marry Megan Kluska, his childhood sweetheart, and Mark was among the contingent of mates who travelled to Byron for his bucks party. Quite late one evening at a local hotel, a huge platter of local seafood was being raffled. Hungry as always after a decent drink, Mark decided the boys were going to win it. It was chock-full of prawns, scallops, mud crab, lobster and calamari – exactly what was needed for the ultimate late-night snack.

To tip the odds in their favour, Mark bought most of the remaining tickets. At that stage, the others weren't aware of exactly how much Mark had invested in the raffle, but they cheered excitedly when they found they had the winning ticket. The platter was superbly presented and the seafood looked so fresh, it must have been caught that day. The lads downed their last drinks and headed back to their apartment to devour the seafood.

Just as the cling wrap was being removed, and as the magnificent aroma of fresh prawns and lobster began to pervade the room, Mark received a mobile phone call from Adelaide. Jason isn't sure who made the call, but it was obviously quite important and Mark stepped outside for some privacy. True to form, the boys decided to try the prawns to make sure they were as good as they looked. They also needed to try the lobster and the crab and the calamari. By the time Mark had ended the call and re-entered the room, all that remained of his seafood platter was a couple of lettuce leaves and a mountain of crab, prawn and lobster shells. As he had bought $200 worth of raffle tickets to ensure the platter wouldn't go elsewhere, he was just a little upset and sulked until he eventually went to bed. Jason and the boys were understandably impressed by his generosity!

Matt Western first met Mark in the Under Tens football team coached by Murray Ricciuto. Mark went to Ramco Primary School, while Matt went to Waikerie, but they both ended up at Waikerie High and quickly became best mates. Matt recalls an amusing evening at the Waikerie Under 10s presentation night when Mark was gathering his usual trailer-load of trophies. After Mark had made his obligatory acceptance speech and had thanked his mum, dad and the rest of the world, someone in the crowd yelled out, 'Hey, Mark, where did you get your football ability from?' Without even thinking about it, or giving his son a chance to respond, Murray yelled back, 'Well, his *mother* doesn't play football!' This was typical of Murray the comedian – a trait he has always been known for throughout the Riverland.

Mark and Matt were picked to play together in the Waikerie Under 13s Grand Final at Loxton the following season. They were both involved in Saturday morning martial arts at the time as well, and on this day their taekwondo instructor had been late in arriving to present them with their green belts. This meant they would have to rush to make the football match. Matt recalls the Ricciutos passing him and his family on the highway at a speed in excess of 160 kilometres an hour. They reached the game a few seconds before the first bounce.

It was fortunate for the Waikerie Under 13s that Mark *did* make it to the Grand Final that afternoon, as he kicked six of his team's seven goals and was clearly the best player on the ground. Matt reckons he touched the football twice himself that day – once in the pre-game warm-up, and once more when he picked it up and threw it to the boundary umpire – and is under no illusions about his own football ability. Mark played in eight matches that season and scored 24 votes as best on ground in every game! Matt realised on Grand Final day just how good his mate was, and it has come as no surprise to him that Mark has gone on to be one of the best footballers South Australia has ever produced.

Matt Western's driving story from a few years later is considerably more unnerving than Mark's harmless spin-out at the Morgan Oval in his dad's Commodore. Both he and Mark had enrolled in a water-ski elective as part of the Year 12 physical education program at Waikerie High. One day, Mark was driving down to the river to go skiing at the same time as Matt was being driven back by another school mate. When they noticed each other, things became quite interesting. Matt's older brother and a few of his friends had a rather silly habit of passing each other, head on, on the wrong side of the road – a teenage driving prank with potentially disastrous consequences. Mark, Matt and several of the younger brigade had seen this on several occasions and were obviously impressed by a manoeuvre that, looking back now, wasn't all that clever.

When Mark and Matt's driver were about a hundred metres apart, Mark decided to greet them by putting two wheels over the white line; the other driver reciprocated by doing likewise. At that moment, however, neither was certain whether the other was planning on a wrong-side pass and by the time a decision had been made, it was too late. The two cars collided, head on, and both still travelling at 60 kilometres an hour. With a combined impact of 120 kilometres per hour, both drivers were fortunate they were in heavy, solid and not very valuable cars. Matt wasn't wearing a seat belt and, to this day, doesn't know how he didn't go flying from the car or hit his head on the windscreen. He remembers passing out a split second before impact and thinking, 'This is going to hurt.'

He came to just as the ambulance arrived, but as his legs were wedged between the glove box and the front seat, it took ten minutes or so to free him. Both Mark and Matt agree it was a miracle that none of the three boys involved was seriously injured. For about six months afterwards, however, every time Matt saw a car out of the corner of his eye, he would involuntarily jump back and his body would begin to shake. This became known as a 'chicken fit' and was a bit of a joke among the lads' circle of close friends.

Matt Western's family was well known in the Waikerie fruit-growing business and, like the Ricciutos, they went through a lot of tough times as produce prices fluctuated wildly due to foreign imports. Anger and frustration were common emotions throughout that period, as most were third- or fourth-generation growers and had nothing else to fall back on when their fruit couldn't be sold. Matt and Mark can both recall seeing Matt's parents in tears. The financial difficulties that many of the fruit-block owners experienced were totally beyond their control and occurred through no fault of their own.

Matt is certain that seeing his parents go through those hard times has made him a better person. It taught him the value of money, and the need to prepare and save for tough times – something that practically all of his Riverland friends now have in common. Matt also feels this is at least part of the reason that he still shares such a strong bond with Mark and other close friends of that era.

Having lunch with Mark, Murray and Carolyn Ricciuto at Football Park in 1991 was something Matt will never forget. It was just before Mark decided to sign up with the Crows, and the Ricciutos were guests of the club. Graham Cornes, the club's inaugural coach, was at their table and with him was his very attractive wife, Nicole. Typical of testosterone-charged teenage boys, both Matt and Mark were quite taken with Nicole and began kicking each other under the table.

'D'ya reckon this is Cornesy's missus or his niece?' was the first of several irreverent comments from Matt.

'How did a bloke with a head like that get a chick as cool as her?' asked Mark – under his breath, of course, which almost caused them both to choke on their mouthfuls of lemon squash.

The conversation then turned to schooling. Mark was in Year 11 at Waikerie High at the time. When Cornes asked

Murray about his son's grades and was told the lad was a straight-A student, again both Matt and Mark nearly choked on their drinks. Considering the time he spent commuting between Waikerie and Adelaide, Matt concedes that his mate did pretty well at high school, but certainly didn't achieve anything like perfect grades.

Matt was living in Karratha, in northern Western Australia, and working on the Woodside gas plant when Mark won the 2003 Brownlow Medal. Karratha is a remote settlement where, in Matt's own words, 'you live hard and play harder'. He had followed Mark's football closely during the 2003 season and knew he would poll well on Brownlow night, so he wagered $100 on him with Centrebet and, as insurance, put a further $50 on Nathan Buckley.

Matt's wife was pregnant with their first child at the time and, of course, she also had her fingers crossed that Mark would do well in the Medal count. Matt was in the backyard with a TV set, a few mates and a lot of beer as the votes were being counted. When Mark won, he could scarcely contain himself. Like a lot of South Australians that night, Matt shed more than a few tears as his life-long mate accepted the Brownlow. Crying obviously didn't fit the expected demeanour of a tough West Australian miner, as Matt copped plenty from his workmates in the backyard, but he didn't care at all. He felt frustrated at being thousands of kilometres away and not being able to hug Mark and shake his hand over the Brownlow win, so he came up with a novel way to express how he felt.

As quietly as possible, Matt pushed his Rocket KTM 620 off-road bike around the side of the house, kicked the engine into life, and took off up the street on the back wheel. 'Roo dog, you're a fucking legend!' he yelled at the top of his voice. 'And now everyone in the country knows it!'

Matt can't remember much else about that night, except perhaps his mates trying to catch him and get him off the bike before he killed himself or some innocent Karratha resident. He does recall being in the doghouse at home for a couple of days after the event, but concedes it was all worth it and he will probably do it again if Mark wins a second Brownlow or holds up the Premiership Cup as captain of the Adelaide Crows.

Sean Tasker, who played 48 games for the Crows in their first three years in the competition, provided several 'colourful' anecdotes for this chapter, but once again just a couple made it past the censor. Sean and Mark have been close friends for many years and still spend a lot of time together. Try as he might to reverse the situation, on most occasions it has been Sean on the wrong end of a Ricciuto prank and he took delight in passing some of them on.

The Taskers have a shack at Walker Flat on the Murray, where they enjoy skiing, fishing, and 'associated social activities' that generally involve drinking alcohol. Towing a 'ski biscuit' (an upmarket truck-tyre tube with handles) at speed behind the boat has always been a favourite pastime, and whenever Mark was invited to spend some time with the Taskers, his competitive nature would invariably come to the fore. Those who have ridden on a 'ski biscuit' will know they can either be towed sedately behind the boat at a sensible speed, or they can be pulled at top revs, which makes it as difficult to stay aboard as riding a bucking bronco at a country rodeo.

Mark would always assume the job of setting up the 'biscuit' course. This meant he would travel downriver in the boat and come up with a series of markers around which the boat driver would have to make tight turns. The ensuing ride would become a battle between boat driver and 'biscuit' passenger. The driver would do his utmost to dislodge the passenger from the tube, while the passenger would be hanging on for dear life until he eventually came off or completed the course.

Sean insists that Mark always designed the 'biscuit' course to suit himself. He knew his strengths and weaknesses when it was his turn to be towed, and invariably set up the course accordingly. This must have been effective, as Sean and others rarely, if ever, managed to hold on for the entire journey, while Mark was near impossible to throw out. It may also have had something to do with Mark's superior upper body strength and steely determination, of course, but Sean would never concede that point.

Sean's engagement party in 1998 was an event some in attendance may not remember, and Mark was certainly right among that group. It was held in the backyard of Sean's house and the spirits flowed well into the early hours. Despite being one of the stronger members of the Crows squad, Sean insists Mark was never good at wrestling. Although Mark may dispute the fact, Sean says he would often defeat him in training exercises that involved wrestling and he is sure Mark developed a bit of a complex about it. Well into the evening of the Tasker engagement party, and with plenty of beer on board, Mark decided to start wrestling anyone who was willing, along with a few who weren't.

It was immediately obvious that Mark was a much better wrestler under the influence of alcohol than without it, and Sean vividly recalls being lifted on to Mark's shoulder and thrown around like a rag doll. He took on all comers that night and remained undefeated.

Mark's javelin-throwing prowess was also clearly demonstrated that evening. He had been bragging during the party about how good he had been at high school athletics, and particularly about how far he could throw a javelin. No one seemed all that impressed with this, so Mark decided to put on a little demonstration to back up his words. With nothing closely resembling a javelin in the Tasker backyard, he eventually decided on a bamboo garden flare as the most likely substitute.

'Check this out, Task,' cried an inebriated Ricciuto. 'I'll show you bastards what a real javelin thrower can do.'

Naturally, the host was a little concerned at this request, but as he had enjoyed almost as many drinks as Mark, Sean settled back to see if Mark was, indeed, as good as he had boasted.

No one was quite sure in which suburb the garden flare landed, nor the five others that followed, but they were never seen again. There is no doubt that Mark's javelin-throwing abilities were confirmed at Sean Tasker's engagement party.

Brett 'Birdman' Burton, Mark's team-mate and former house-mate, couldn't wait to pass on the tale of the Ricciuto post-Brownlow nightclub bash. Understandably, Mark was the toast of Adelaide after returning with the game's most prestigious award in his possession. So significant was the Brownlow Medal win, in fact, that Adelaide's Lord Mayor, Michael Harbison, presented Mark with the keys to the city – an honour usually reserved for the likes of Olympic Gold Medallists or those who have accomplished feats of national or international significance. Mark was naturally honoured and accepted the Lord Mayor's accolades with grace.

He and quite a few friends had been drinking at a popular city nightclub. Behind the bar were a couple of guys who owned another nightclub, and they invited Mark and company to their establishment after midnight. More than a little drunk by that stage, Mark began acting like a bouncer and rallied the troops outside the second club while waiting for it to be opened. This caused great merriment among his friends, all of whom looked forward to having a private drink at an exclusive venue.

After an hour standing in line and being marshalled by Ricciuto the bouncer, however, the troops began to grow restless. When word arrived that the club owners had changed their minds about a special opening, Mark could do little except feel embarrassed and bid his friends goodnight.

Brett Burton still chuckles when he remembers that Mark could get the keys to the city of Adelaide but not to one of its nightclubs!

17

GONE FISHING . . .

Apart from his family, friends and football, Mark Ricciuto's two biggest passions since childhood have been fishing and punting.

Growing up on the banks of the Murray, Mark learned to catch fish and yabbies at a very young age. With the river as their backyard, it was natural for all three Ricciuto children to explore its backwaters, climb its willow trees and enjoy all the aquatic delights it had to offer.

Murray Ricciuto had always been a keen fisherman and it was a natural progression for his sons to follow. The river was a far different place back in the 1970s and early 1980s; the water was cleaner, there was a lot more flow, and upstream irrigation wasn't as prolific and debilitating as it is now. Although the European carp invasion was well under way at that time, there were a lot more native fish such as callop, catfish, silver perch and, of course, the mighty Murray cod.

Because the Ricciutos had a firm background as primary producers and loved nothing better than eating what they could grow or catch, manna from the Murray was often prominent on the menu. Both cod and callop were always welcome to offset the weekly grocery bill, and 'having' to go out and catch them was the perfect excuse for Murray and the boys to head off with rods or nets.

Mark soon learned to adore fishing, either with his dad, Uncle Ralph, his brother or some of his closer mates. There was no fancy tackle back in those times, as finances simply didn't allow it; they made do with a couple of sturdy rods and a handful of hooks and sinkers. As they learned more about the river and the creatures that lived in it, the Ricciuto boys became quite proficient at catching a feed; they knew the best baits to use, the prime times to go and the most reliable places to try. As they have always been, Murray cod were elusive, but Mark and Craig managed to catch plenty of redfin perch, callop and the tasty catfish.

Before Fisheries regulations tightened up along the Murray, it was legal to use two 'drum' nets per person as an alternative to traditional rods and reels. The nets were suspended between two upright posts and essentially acted like oversized funnels. If the fish were active and feeding in along the banks, they would often swim into the wide end of the net, become disoriented and ultimately become trapped.

Drum nets are designed specifically to catch freshwater fish in deep, slow-flowing rivers and, if you knew where to set them, they were very efficient. Murray Ricciuto and his friend Kym Lehmann bought a couple of nets each. They watched, listened and learned from what the commercial fishermen around Waikerie did with their nets and were soon catching fish in big numbers.

Mark loved tagging along with his father when it was time to check their carefully set nets. It was the anticipation of catching something really big that remained as the major drawcard, and

Mark always dreamed of catching a cod bigger than he was. This was quite possible, as cod have been known to reach 70 kilograms or more, and Mark often marvelled at the pictures of old Waikerie locals struggling to lift giant green fish for the camera.

The Lehmann and Ricciuto drum nets usually provided a good feed of fish for family and friends most times they were set, though the river conditions had to be right for the callop and cod to move around in big numbers. One Friday afternoon, after Craig and Mark had arrived home from school, Murray loaded them into the car and headed for Apex Park, a favourite location near Ramco. Kym Lehmann and his sons, Troy and Jason, hopped into the boat with the Ricciuto clan and they motored across the river to check their first net.

When Murray removed the two poles suspending the net and hauled back on the net rope, he could feel a lot of weight and plenty of movement from below. So heavy was the net, in fact, that Kym had to go forward and give him a hand. With six excited people in a four-metre aluminium dinghy, moving around demanded quite a bit of care. There were a few anxious moments as the two men hauled on the rope and eventually brought the net to the surface. Balancing the boat became a high priority with over 100 kilograms of kicking fish being dragged aboard.

To their delight, it contained ten magnificent Murray cod of up to thirteen kilograms, all of which were very much alive and kicking. It was quite a struggle to get the net over the side of the dinghy, but when the job was completed, the Ricciutos and Lehmanns could scarcely believe their luck. There was 'high-fiving', backslapping and cheering from all quarters, which must have been quite a sight for others on the river that afternoon. After throwing back any of the fish that were possibly females carrying eggs, the happy group motored back to where they had launched the boat and loaded it for the trip home.

Understandably proud of the catch, and happy to tell the world about it, Murray immediately phoned several mates, but none would believe him. Catching that many cod in one net was almost unheard of and, to make sure he could brag about it with credibility, Murray made sure plenty of photographs were taken.

Still in awe of what they had achieved, the intrepid six were back on the river the following Sunday morning and, as if to prove Friday evening's catch hadn't been a fluke, the same net yielded another ten cod of similar size! This time the 'disbelievers' had also shown up and they, too, were astonished at the number of big fish that had congregated in one stretch of the river.

The Ricciutos and Lehmanns would go on to catch over 50 big cod in that net over the course of the year and, to their credit, they only kept enough to cover their immediate needs and maybe one or two for the freezer. One of Murray's post-fishing traditions was to measure and weigh the fish caught, then write down all the weights on the sun visor of his old Datsun ute. Mark says that, by the end of the year, there was scarcely room left on the visor for one more notation. On the upside, every time Murray drove into the sun, he was reminded of his conquests.

The River Murray callop was another popular drum net target during that era, and one also prized for its table qualities. Like the cod, callop were always at their most active and easiest to catch as the river was rising. Mark recalls one rainy afternoon when he pestered his father for hours before Murray eventually gave in and the pair drove out to check the nets. Murray had been quite comfortable at home after a tough, wet day out on the fruit block and only relented because the young fellow had completed his homework and pleaded to spend an hour on the river before dinner.

Most of the callop caught around Waikerie at that time were

small to medium-sized fish of between 35 and 45 centimetres. Mark and Murray were astonished, therefore, when they pulled three absolute monsters from the first net. Each was as long (65 centimetres) as an open sheet of *The Advertiser* is wide and Mark guesses that the largest of the three would have weighed over three to four kilograms.

Both he and his brother, Craig, caught plenty of callop on their rods over the years as well, but it wasn't until the eve of Mark's annual New Year houseboat trip in 2006 that he cracked a really big one. Mark has always enjoyed showing visiting friends his 'backyard' and how productive it can still be and, keen to make the most of every minute on the houseboat, he baited up a couple of rods with live shrimps and cast them out overnight.

Next morning he awoke to find one of the rods severely bent over and excitedly reeled in a callop that weighed 2.9 kilograms. This was easily the biggest callop he had ever caught on a rod and, thanks to modern-day camera phones, everyone he knew had seen the photograph within ten minutes of the fish hitting the deck.

One of Mark's all-time favourite 'rod and reel' fishing adventures took place at a location aptly named Ricciuto Creek, a little tributary off the main stream that runs through the family's home property. Although it often produced the odd fish or two, it had never been regarded as a real 'hot spot'.

One Sunday afternoon, Mark, Craig, Murray and his Uncle Ralph decided to try their luck around the mouth of the creek, more because of its proximity to the house than anything else. They had felt like wetting a line, but weren't in the mood to launch the boat or to travel too far from home, so it was down to the creek with a bucket of worms for bait. They all caught a nice redfin perch with their first cast and, for the next two hours, there was scarcely a moment at least one of them wasn't hooked up.

Mark recalls the redfin being so numerous and willing to bite, he would get one on the top hook and then wait until a second fish grabbed the bottom hook. None of the family had ever consistently pulled in double headers of 30-centimetre redfin before. By the time they ran out of worms, they had 122 fish in the bag. Unlike Murray cod and callop, redfin perch aren't native fish and therefore aren't subject to Fisheries bag limits. Redfin perch are delightful fish to eat, so the anglers had little trouble giving away what they couldn't use themselves.

This unexpected haul of redfin had occurred right in the middle of the Ricciuto tomato harvest and had been a welcome diversion after many hours of stooping over vines. The only problem was that with this many fish on the bite, all Mark and Craig wanted to do was go fishing after school the next day. Their father insisted, however, that the tomatoes had to come in, so the fish would have to wait.

Compounding matters, while out with the tomato crop, the boys could see their mates riding bikes or driving cars down to the river with fishing tackle on board and knew full well that they would all be getting stuck into the redfin. The run lasted for just over a week, and Mark is unsure if it was a seasonal phenomenon or a freakish one-off event that they were lucky to stumble into.

European carp became a fact of life in southern Australia well before Mark was born. Since their arrival in the 1960s they have had quite an impact on native fish stocks, and on the wellbeing of the Murray as a whole, but for a couple of youngsters growing up at Waikerie, they were little more than an endless source of fun. Mark, Craig and their mates would regularly rig up for carp and head to Lock Number Two, where they could often be caught to over a metre in length and ten kilograms in weight. Carp may be next to useless as table fish, but they fight pretty well when hooked, which provided some sport.

Most carp sorties began by riding a trail bike down to the river, carrying just a basic handline and a can of worms for bait. Carp aren't fussy fish when it comes to bait or tackle, and there was no need for a cumbersome rod and reel. Big ones pulled hard on the line, and quite a few were simply too big for a youngster to handle. It didn't seem to matter where they fished, the boys would nearly always catch carp. Because it was close to home, the mouth of Ricciuto Creek was a handy location to try, and at times it simply teemed with the big golden fish.

Although Mark shakes his head about it now, he, Craig and a neighbour, Barry Cabot, loved to spear carp and did so regularly when the conditions were right. After a high river, tonnes of big fish would become stranded in lagoons near the family home as the water level subsided. Often swimming around with their backs half out of the water, they were easy pickings for the boys. A lot of these fish were a metre long and very difficult to subdue if the spear hadn't killed them outright.

Back in the 1970s, before the character of the Murray began to change and water levels could still rise and fall dramatically, yabbies were everywhere. Prime time to catch these succulent little crustaceans in good numbers was immediately after a flood. They would invade the backwaters to breed, then spread out into the creeks and lagoons in their hundreds of thousands. Mark liked to consider himself something of a yabbie specialist, knowing exactly where and when to find them in good supply. He had a friend who reckoned Mark was half human, half yabbie!

Yabbying wasn't just for home waters, either. It became something of an obsession for a while, and Mark and Craig were prepared to travel long distances if it meant a big haul. Mark recalls a phone call from his Uncle Ralph, who lived upstream at Moorook. Apparently, there were more big yabbies around Banrock Station (now famous for its wines) than he had ever seen before, and he advised his nephews to get up there as soon as possible.

As the river level was dropping rapidly, all the yabbies that had moved into the backwaters to breed decided to return to the main waterway via creeks, channels and swamps. This, of course, pinpointed their avenues of exit and enabled them to be caught in vast numbers. Mark remembers his dad and uncle scraping the bottom of a small creek with a length of chicken wire and literally dredging the yabbies out by the hundred. Although by no means legal by today's standards, it was a very effective method, and in one afternoon they caught well over a thousand yabbies from that creek. This was well before bag limits applied to yabbying, and none were wasted. Cleaning and cooking that many yabbies was a tedious job for all concerned, but as they tasted so delicious, no one complained too much and the job was done by nightfall. Mark still recalls metre-high piles of yabbies, the likes of which he has never seen since.

Mark's love of yabbies even lured him and several mates over the border into Victoria, where there was promise of some of the biggest in Australia. They towed aluminium dinghies to a little place called Yanac and tried their luck in nearby Lake Hindmarsh, where quality rather than quantity was the local catchcry. Mark recalls some of the yabbies they caught that weekend as being 'almost frightening'; the largest was a few centimetres longer than a two-litre Coke bottle and carried almost as much tail meat as a small crayfish. Mark doesn't have any photos, but he swears it's true.

Mark kicks the first goal in the Grand Final match between Adelaide and North Melbourne Kangaroos at the MCG, 26 September 1998.

Mark with his team-mates celebrating on the Premiership dais at the 1998 Grand Final.

Welcome to Waikerie! 1998.

Mark was a Premiership, All-Australian and Club Champion in 1998!

Mark and best mates Clinton Eustice, centre, and Matt Western, right, at a New Year's dress-up show, 31 December 1999.

Matt Dawson with Mark's dad, Murray, at the party. Matt tragically passed away in December 2000.

Mark with his late cousin, Joe DeVito, who passed away suddenly in 2003.

This was the biggest of seven white pointer sharks that Mark encountered in a shark cage expedition at Point Lincoln in 2001 – it measured sixteen foot!

Mark coming out of the shark cage needing a change of wet suit.

Newspix/Martin Neon

Finishing off another hard run during pre-season training in November 2001.

Showing off his tattoos during pre-season in December 2002.

Oops. Sorry, Simon. Mark gets rid of tagger Simon Godfrey in a match against Melbourne, March 2002.

Dishing out a 'don't argue' against the Western Bulldogs player Robert Murphy in May 2003.

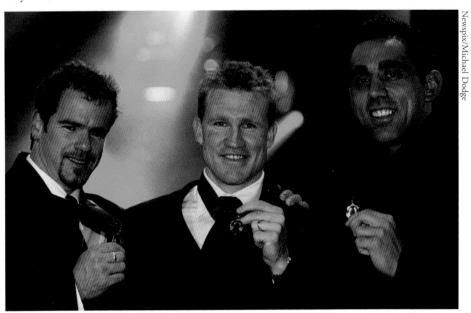

Brownlow Medal night with Nathan Buckley and Adam Goodes.

Mark and his family and friends celebrate the Brownlow win at the Alma, September 2003.

Mark Williams, left, has a joke with Warren Tredrea, Gary Ayres and Mark at the Adelaide Crows vs Port Adelaide match press conference, August 2003.

Newspix/Matt Turner

Mark and Lleyton Hewitt wave to the crowd during the lap of honour before the SANFL football Grand Final match between West Adelaide and Central districts at AAMI Stadium, 2003.

Mark with mates Andy Lehmann, middle, and Shaun Matschoss on their way to Tumby Bay, 2004.

Ninety-six yabbies in one net. Mark with the yabbie master (uncle Ralph Pope) at his Broken Hill property, 2004.

Presenting the winners trophy for the 2005 Adelaide Cup to his idol, Tony Lockett.

Owner of the Alma Tavern hotel in Norwood, July 2005.

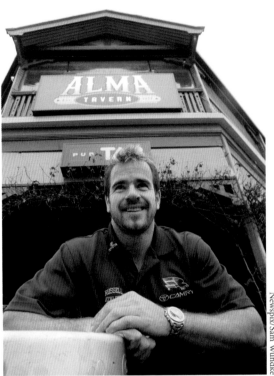

The first sale at the car yard, April 2005.

Beating Port and winning the medal as well – makes for a good day out! April 2005.

Mark and Sarah celebrating his 30th birthday with a 'day at the races in 1975' theme at the Arkaba Hotel in June 2005.

Above: The Port Adelaide Power vs Adelaide Crows showdown XV match, 2004.

Above right: Settle down, Byron. Crows vs Port Semi-final, September 2005.

Mark being chaired off the ground by Simon Goodwin and Brett Burton after his 300th game in July 2006.

On the red carpet at the Brownlow in 2006 – Sarah is looking radiant at seven months pregnant.

Mark overlooking the construction of his biggest investment to date – the Port Lincoln Hotel, 2006.

The picture says it all – a very happy family.

Mark and the boys camped out by the lakeshore overnight, cooked a barbecue for dinner, and generally revelled in the rough-and-tumble splendour of the place. Although there weren't as many yabbies in Lake Hindmarsh as back home in the Riverland, they still managed to fill ten wheat bags. When the crew rolled back into Waikerie late on the Sunday evening, they were exhausted, but exhilarated.

Mark's first real introduction to fishing in the sea came at the invitation of fellow Crows player Andrew Jarman in 1995. 'Jars' had sensed how homesick Mark was for Waikerie and his beloved River Murray, and decided that a day's fishing on the 'briny' would be the ideal remedy. It certainly worked.

As well as some huge silver trevally, the lads caught metre-long snook and mackerel, all of which fought harder than anything Mark had ever hooked before. Mark had to agree that sea fishing could be every bit as enjoyable as wetting a line in the Murray.

Catching big snapper soon became an obsession with Mark and he began accepting invitations from friends in the country to tackle them in Port Pirie and Whyalla. He vividly recalls an all-night snapper fishing session off Whyalla with his mate Matt Dawson and fellow Crows, Nigel Smart and David Pittman. He was the only one in the boat without a decent fish by daybreak. With a wager in place for the best snapper, it appeared his bad luck would also cost him financially, but it was the humiliation of going home fishless that caused him most concern. Naturally, Mark was copping plenty from the others about not pulling his weight and leaving it to them to catch a feed, when something huge suddenly grabbed his bait.

Mark knew immediately that he had hooked the biggest snapper of the trip and began giving back some of the 'lip' the others had dished out. When he finally landed his fish, he peed his pants, he was so excited, as it was an eleven-kilogram monster – easily larger than any the others had caught. Understandably, it earned him 'fish of the day' and he took great delight in collecting money from Smart, Pittman and Dawson.

Mark's most memorable fishing experience ever occurred at Marion Bay, on lower Yorke Peninsula, just a couple of days before the first Port/Crows Showdown match in 1997. He and team-mate Andrew McLeod made the three-hour drive straight after training on the Wednesday evening in order to fish with well-known local charter operator Bill Kelly. This would be McLeod's first experience on the ocean in South Australia and it certainly turned out to be a cracker. He had been bragging for quite some time about his angling prowess, and about the great barramundi and black jewfish he had caught in the Northern Territory. Mark was certain that Andy's stories were exaggerated, and Andy believed the same of Mark's stories. Of course, there was money on the biggest fish and the best bag.

Fishing in waters as deep as 80 metres, Mark and Andrew caught all manner of fish, including snapper, nannygai, blue groper, blue morwong, and even a heavyweight samson fish that tipped the scales at around eighteen kilograms. A quick stopover at Althorpe Island also provided enough squid for a tasty entrée. They brought home enough fish to feed the entire Crows squad, and Mark recalls Andrew conceding that the fishing in South Australia was *almost* as good as it was around his home town of Darwin.

Once he eventually hangs up his footy boots, Mark says there will be plenty more fishing on the agenda. Like most keen anglers, he has certain goals; and prominent among these is catching a big Murray cod on rod and reel. He has several close mates back in Waikerie who spend countless hours on the river and occasionally pull out a 60 or even 80 pounder (anywhere from 25 to 35 kilograms). For Mark a cod of this size is akin to the Holy Grail, and chances are there's a monster lurking beneath a cliff or dead tree somewhere near Waikerie with his name on it. You can bet the camera function on his mobile phone will get another good workout if his big cod dream ever becomes a reality! (One mate of Mark's reckons Mark would put it in the passenger seat of his car, put a seat belt on it, and drive it around so that everyone could see it first hand!)

18

HAVING A PUNT

It's a fact that most toddlers begin speaking with simple three-letter words, such as 'Mum' or 'Dad', and steadily increase their vocabulary from there. According to Danny McMahon, one of Mark's best friends from Waikerie, Mark started speaking in much the same way, but his first three-letter word was 'TAB'!

Like a lot of keen sportsmen, Mark has always loved a punt. Whether on the gallopers, trotters or dogs, punting has been a major recreation since he was legally old enough to place a bet (or maybe even before!). On several occasions, he has taken this to the next level with the ownership of greyhounds, trotters and racehorses.

Before delving deeper into his punting life, it should be made clear that gambling never has been, and never will be, an obsession for Mark Ricciuto. He has never bet more than he can afford to lose, and he regards betting as a social activity to be enjoyed with close friends. Like most punters, he enjoys the wins and feels sorry for himself when he loses, but it's all in good fun and will never dominate his existence. Mark's gambling stories are many and varied but, almost without exception, they involve a group of mates, a few drinks and a good time.

Mark's grandfather Nicola taught him to play cards as a youngster. The gambling side was never promoted, but Mark quickly became intrigued by the mystery and uncertainty of a poker deck. There was always a card game in progress at the Waikerie Italian Club, and on most occasions it was loud and jovial. Mark watched his father and grandfather play and enjoyed the games enormously.

He also learned about horses at an early age. The family of a Waikerie school friend owned a well-performed trotter, and occasionally Mark would travel down to Gawler or Globe Derby Park with them to watch it run. Sometimes, if he had a couple of spare dollars, he would place a bet on the horse through its owner and was understandably excited when he had his first win.

Having the occasional bet while living in Waikerie became a ritual within his close circle of friends. There was never much money involved during those early years, but by studying form and keeping tabs on which horses were running where, the lads enjoyed a bit of success. When Mark began playing football in Adelaide and was earning real money, his punting horizons expanded somewhat and it wasn't long before he began dabbling in syndicate-based horse ownership.

The first horse was a gelding called 'Arabian Storm', which ran second a couple of times in the city, but failed to live up to expectations and was soon moved on. (The owners even dressed up as Arabian sheikhs to attend the gelding's first few races, but when its form deteriorated, off came the Arab clothing and off went the horse!) The next was a filly named 'Amen Ruby', which won her first start in Melbourne and followed up with a strong second place in a Group Two race. When she suffered knee problems after just nine starts, she was sold off to stud to minimise any further expense. Mark was starting to learn that this business of racehorse ownership was both costly and frustrating, but by this stage it was in his blood and, as his income increased, so did his desire to own a top-class galloper.

In 2003, Mark formed a syndicate with some friends, as well as Crows team-mates Kane Johnson, Simon Goodwin and Wayne Carey, and high-profile Adelaide businessmen Rob Gerard and Alan Sheppard. After doing some homework, Mark went along to that year's Adelaide Magic Millions sale with well-known local trainer Leon MacDonald, intending to buy a particular yearling that had been highly recommended. However, Leon had his eye on another horse that would come up for auction a little earlier in the program and the pair decided to bid on that one first. If they were successful there, they would abandon their original plan and call it a day.

The bidding for this particular horse was spirited. Mark and Leon's agreed ceiling bid of $140,000 level came and went in the blink of an eye and, after a quick discussion, they decided to go as high as $160,000 before being forced to throw in the towel. The horse eventually sold for $190,000 and would go on to be named 'Undoubtedly'. Mark and Leon ultimately bought the yearling, 'Battle Boy', for $140,000.

A year later, while Mark was involved in a trial match against Geelong in Port Lincoln, 'Undoubtedly' won the Blue Diamond Stakes in Melbourne, a million dollar Group One sprint race. The horse, whose father had also won this event some years previously, immediately became a hot property. Its breeding potential went through the roof and in no time at all it was rumoured to be worth around $10 million.

'Battle Boy' went on to finish second in a couple of races, but then dropped quickly off the pace. The gelding was soon costing a lot more than he was bringing in, and he was eventually offloaded for $10,000 – another ill-fated investment that is typical of 'amateur' racehorse syndicates. The return on racehorse investment across the board is in the order of eight per cent, so most who outlay cash in order to become involved in the 'sport of kings' can expect never to see their money again. Mark carries on, undaunted, in the hope that one day that special horse will come along that is good enough to make him a Group One winner, where the glory often still outweighs the financial return. The wounds are still fresh from race-horse failures to date but, once they heal, Mark has no doubt he will be back with another syndicate to try again.

'Lady luck' operates the same way with greyhounds, though on a smaller, and generally less expensive, scale. Mark's most successful dog, 'Bogan Blue' (which he insists he didn't name), turned out to be well worth the time, money and effort spent. It showed plenty of promise by winning three races in a row, and when it was scheduled to compete at a meeting at Gawler, Mark and a few mates decided to make the trip to watch it run. Among the group were Jason Lehmann, Craig, Mark's Uncle Ralph and Tony Modra, Mark's Crows team-mate.

'Bogan Blue' won the race easily and, to celebrate the occasion, the boys decided to have a couple of beers on the way home. They stopped in at the Old Spot Hotel, where the publican recognised them and announced that their drinks would be on the house. Lehmann had a small problem, however: he was wearing thongs, which contravened the hotel's dress code. Mark ended up buying a pair of old sneakers, which were about three sizes too big for Jason, from a patron who was leaving the hotel.

The 'couple of drinks' turned into quite a few, and before the boys knew it, the night had got away from them. At around eleven o'clock, they decided to head for home, but they couldn't convince Tony to join them. To the delight of all in the bar, he was dancing on the tables and having the time of his life. Modra ended up hitching a ride back to Adelaide on the back of a Harley-Davidson the next morning, just in time to do his regular seven o'clock radio surf report in Hindley Street!

Thoroughbred racing is a huge industry in Hong Kong, and it was at the famous Sha Tin track in 1994 that the nineteen-year-old Mark had his first taste of the international scene. The Adelaide Crows had played the West Coast Eagles in a post-season exhibition match in London, after which they spent a week touring Spain. A Hong Kong stopover on the way home seemed a good way to round off what had been an enjoyable trip and, as the boys had all heard about Sha Tin and its high-rolling punters, they decided to investigate.

There are usually two meetings a week at this track, which attract crowds as big as AFL football matches, and there is often a strong Australian contingent in attendance. The Sha Tin events generally feature a nine-race program, and it seems the amount of money wagered on each race increases dramatically as the meeting progresses.

There are a lot of fanatical punters in Hong Kong, many of whom back horses for a living, and while they generally start off conservatively, they invariably come home with heavy bets on the final two races. Crows vice captain Tony McGuinness had a friend in Hong Kong who was a professional punter, so under his guidance the boys decided to join the crowd and have a flutter on a mob of horses they knew absolutely nothing about. Mark decided that his day out at Sha Tin would either pay for his overseas excursion or make it a really expensive one!

Their maiden Sha Tin race meeting started off reasonably well for Mark and his team-mates. They had backed a couple of winners, enjoyed great food and a few drinks, and generally soaked up the atmosphere of one of the world's most famous horse-racing venues. Mark was about HK$500 (approximately A$100 at that time) in front as the final race on the card was announced. The professional punter in their group liked two horses in the last, one of which was number two and would start at the odds of three to one. The other was a long shot wearing number four that would return around twenty to one.

As he had been accustomed to doing in Australia after a fair day with the bookies, Mark opted to invest all his winnings on the last race. He's by no means a conservative punter, preferring either to win big or break even rather than take things easy and come away just a couple of hundred bucks in front. He thought about his tactics for the last race for quite a while, then backed both number two and number four straight out. He also selected them in a quinella bet, so his whole day hinged on the advice of a man he had only just met and a pair of horses he had never heard of before.

Both jumped well, with the number two horse leading the field for much of the distance and number four well back in the pack. As they approached the home turn, the 50,000-strong crowd appeared to jump into the air as one, waving their arms frantically and shouting excitedly. Number two kicked well clear as the horses entered the main straight and the boys knew they had backed the winner. Now all they needed was number four to run second, which it did after sprinting four deep around the pack and charging home. Mark would collect nicely on number two for a win, but even better on his quinella bet, which covered most of the cost of his end-of-season trip to that date.

Six years later, after the Australians had toured Ireland to play the annual International Rules series, Mark would again find himself among 50,000 punting-crazy Asians at Sha Tin. On this occasion it was with his team-mate and business partner Simon Goodwin, who also enjoys a bet. The pair had been away for over three weeks and were looking a bit scruffy when they landed in Hong Kong. Before they could contemplate an afternoon spent at the races, haircuts, shaves and some new clothes were definitely in order.

Once again, the Aussies were looked after by a local punting professional who had organised a private room for them with betting facilities. The boys enjoyed a cold Crown Lager after every race and, as had been the case back in 1994, the best tip of the day was held over until the last event. They had collected on a few small wins during the course of the afternoon and, once again, Mark was in good shape to invest heavily on race nine.

Well-known Adelaide-born trainer David Hayes had a horse running in the last race at Sha Tin that day and, as he was quite friendly with Mark and Simon's professional punting friend, he advised them to back it for a win. As he had done previously, Mark threw all his winnings on the Hayes-trained horse, which got up to win at the odds of three to one and returned over $6000. Once again the Sha Tin racetrack had proven lucky for Mark, but the best part of the day was still to come.

It turned out to be David Hayes' birthday and, to their delight, Mark and Simon were invited to attend an exclusive party at the track after the meeting had concluded. Only 30 people were invited, and the Crows boys felt honoured to be among them. There were several high-profile trainers and jockeys at the party, including Corey Brown and Shane Dye. It was a night Mark says he will always remember.

Like Hong Kong's Sha Tin track, the Cairns racetrack in Queensland has been a happy hunting ground for Mark and some of his Adelaide team-mates. The Crows boys had been to Cairns on a couple of occasions on post-season football trips and thoroughly enjoyed themselves, particularly if their visit coincided with a race meeting. On their latest Cairns visit, Mark and about twenty others left their hotel at 10 am to ensure they didn't miss a race. Decked out in Crows Footy Trip shirts ($10 navy Bonds T-shirts with a ridiculous and unprintable slogan across the back), they were the first patrons into the track that day. They stood out like beacons when the racetrack began to fill, and created quite a bit of crowd interest when they all entered the betting ring together.

There was only one on-course bookmaker in attendance, who was taking bets on Sydney, Brisbane, Adelaide and Melbourne races, as well as the local ones. Mark and a couple of his more astute punting mates decided to take the bookie on that afternoon. They had done a bit of homework, especially on the other capital city race cards, and weren't all that interested in what was about to unfold on the local course, so there would be no real home-track advantage for the hapless bookmaker.

Through their own research, and with some tips from reliable sources around the country, Melbourne had emerged as the best place for an off-course bet, so Mark and the lads got stuck into the grog and into the punting. They had a syndicate organised, which, at $50 a head starting money, provided a base betting pool of over $1000. Mark likes syndicate betting, as it ensures everyone in the party stays interested and involved all day and they each get a turn to pick a winner.

They backed a five-to-one shot in race one in Melbourne, which kicked proceedings off nicely, then followed up with a second win in race two; all up, they had six Melbourne winners from a possible nine. By the end of the afternoon, the poor Cairns bookmaker was near to tearing his hair out. The Adelaide boys had gone to the track with the intention of going home with their pockets either empty or chock-a-block full, and it would most definitely be the latter.

Three times during that meeting the bookie left the track to get more money, and each time he climbed down from his stand to do so, the Crows boys gave him the Bronx cheer. There were several hundred Cairns locals at the meeting, and when they picked up on what was happening, they started betting on the Melbourne races as well. The bookie was forced to offer worse odds than Mark and company could have found on the TAB, but they continued placing bets relentlessly and eventually cleaned him right out.

The Cairns greyhound meeting followed at the same venue a couple of hours after the horse racing had finished, so the Adelaide boys elected to stay on and see how far they could push their lucky streak. By this stage, however, they had all had a bellyful of beer and were so overconfident, they managed to give a fair bit of their afternoon's winnings back to the same bookmaker.

After the greyhound meeting had concluded, a few of the boys decided to round off what had been a spectacular day by stripping down to their shorts and conducting their own sprint race down the home stretch of the dog track. This delighted the locals, and it's a safe bet that the Adelaide Crows picked up a few new out-of-town supporters by caning the local bookmaker and providing some post-meeting entertainment. They made the local paper and were immediately installed as Far North Queensland racing legends.

A little closer to home, but no less noteworthy, was a Saturday afternoon in October 2005 before a close mate's bucks party at the Alma Hotel in Norwood. As usual, Mark put himself in charge of organising a betting syndicate while the boys were sitting around enjoying a laugh and a few beers. Arrangements had been made for all those interested to meet in the front bar of the Alma at midday. Mark eventually seconded 40 people into his betting syndicate at $50 a head and, with a pool of $2000 with which to tackle the various afternoon race meetings being held around the country, the planning began. Once again, it was Melbourne that held most interest for tipsters in the know and, on the strength of some solid 'mail', the syndicate embarked on yet another fruitful afternoon.

As had been the case in Cairns, the Alma syndicate got off to a flying start. They bet big from the outset and backed several consecutive winners. So impressive were their results, in fact, that the TAB office phoned the hotel a couple of times to check that there wasn't something wrong with the betting machine! Practically all those in the hotel not involved in the syndicate were caught up in the excitement, and many started outlaying their own money on the same horses. Mark had never seen anything like it at the Alma Hotel before, nor has he seen anything like it since.

By the end of the Melbourne race meeting the Alma syndicate had turned its original $2000 cash pool into $16,000. Mark gave everyone in the syndicate $250 each – a return of 500 per cent on their money in just over three hours. He took his soon-to-be-married mate and twenty others to the Crazy Horse nightclub in Hindley Street with $6000 for a night none of them will ever forget! The nightclub management phoned Mark a couple of days later to inform him he was welcome back at any time – probably because the money they had spent had paid for a good part of the renovations being undertaken at the time.

Melbourne's Spring Racing Carnival has long been a favourite time with many AFL players from around the country. It falls during the post-season break, and attending the Carnival has become something of a tradition with Mark and several close friends. During the year a small syndicate of six or eight each put in $25 a week, which they take turns in betting on a Saturday race meeting. Usually they end up with a reasonable-sized pool to take to Melbourne on Derby Day.

On one such occasion, Mark and his syndicate friends got to Flemington fairly early to reserve some good seats in the marquee organised by Mark's management group, Elite Sports Properties. As had become the norm, they kicked off brilliantly with a good win in the first race and maintained good form throughout the afternoon. As well as his bets with the syndicate, Mark had been investing independently and by the time the final event came around, he had amassed a tidy sum.

A reliable source had passed on a tip for the last race that was predicted to return around ten to one, but due to track conditions that didn't really suit the horse, it drifted out to double those odds. One of the 'gun' punters who had been sitting close to Mark for much of the afternoon asked him which horse he was going to back in the final race. When Mark told him about this twenty-to-one shot, the other man laughed. The horse had never run a place on a slow track in its career. The 'gun' then asked how much Mark was planning to bet. When he told him he was going to invest $500 each way, the 'gun' said he would hold the bet, but reneged when he worked out he would have to fork out more than $10,000 if, by some twist of fate, the roughy got up to win.

The boys decided to stay inside the marquee to watch the last race. As it unfolded, they rose to their feet as one as 'Scenic Peak' blasted around the outside of the field in the straight and crossed the line to win by a half head. Mark, dressed in a dinner suit and wearing his hair in a blond mohawk style, ran around the marquee, punching the air and high-fiving anyone within range. He left Flemington with over $20,000 more than he had arrived with, and this remains one of his most successful punting days.

Sydney's Rosehill Racecourse has also proven to be a worthwhile punting venue for Mark and a few of his friends over the years. On one end-of-season trip they arrived at the track to find a special marquee area had been set aside for them. There was the usual gourmet food and plenty of drinks, which always makes an afternoon at the races an enjoyable experience. However, meeting the renowned trainer Gai Waterhouse turned out to be the day's true highlight. Mark had had a few beers by the time Gai arrived and he eventually summoned enough courage to walk over and ask if she would mind posing with the boys for a photograph. He had always admired her for her contribution to the racing industry and, once the ice had been broken, was cheeky enough to ask her for a few tips on the Sydney races. Always the consummate racing professional and about as polite and personable as any high-profile sporting identity could be, Gai provided her repertoire of best bets without hesitation.

A couple of these came in at quite good odds, which set the trend for yet another interstate victory. When Mark picked a boxed trifecta and collected nearly $7000, he could scarcely believe his luck.

It was in Sydney again, just a year later – this time with Waikerie mate Clinton 'Scratcher' Eustice – that Mark once more struck gold. The pair had decided to go on a trip around Australia by air, with Mark using his frequent flyer points to visit Perth, Darwin, Brisbane, Sydney and Melbourne before coming home to begin pre-season training. They visited Rottnest Island while in Western Australia, caught barramundi in the Territory, watched the Indy Car Race on the Gold Coast, and eventually lobbed in Sydney for a few days of leisurely sightseeing and relaxation. Naturally, as they were there over a weekend, a race meeting beckoned, but Mark opted to stay away from the track and instead placed his bets through the TAB.

On this occasion the punting 'mail' came from Dennis DeGilio from Port Lincoln, who had four strong tips in the one race meeting at Rosehill. Instead of simply backing these four horses straight out, as he would normally have done, Mark decided on a slightly different tack. He opted for a series of 'all up' bets: he would select the horse from his four tips most likely to win, and back it to win with the second tip, then again with the third tip, and once again with the fourth tip. The odds of a collect with this style of bet are huge, but so is the payout if you're lucky enough for all four horses to come in. In essence, Mark would lose everything if his most heavily favoured horse failed first up.

In fact, three of the four horses ended up winning, and for an initial outlay of $150 Mark collected just over $6000. This meant that he and 'Scratcher' could continue their trip in grand style, booking one of the most expensive rooms at the Crown Casino in Melbourne, eating in the best restaurants, and drinking only from the top shelf.

With River Murray houseboat holidays always a favourite way to relax in the off-season, hotel stopovers en route often provided Mark and his friends with the opportunity to have a counter lunch, a beer and, of course, the occasional bet. One afternoon, they pulled their boats up at Morgan and walked up to the local to stretch their legs. It was a Tuesday and there were only a few race meetings being held around the country in obscure locations, so picking winners on form was pretty much out of the question. Undeterred, however, Mark collected the obligatory $50 from each person and set up a syndicate that would ensure the remainder of the afternoon would be spent drinking beer, placing TAB bets and watching the hotel's television set. With no 'mail' from outside sources to guide them, the syndicate did its best to come up with the goods unassisted. This would be foreign territory for most, but with a few beers under the belt and unlimited optimism, they prepared to take on the TAB.

Remarkably, the syndicate was well in front for most of the afternoon, collecting on several horses none of them had heard of and on racetracks that were anything but household names. When it came to the final event of the afternoon, it was Brett Burton's turn to pick a winner and he came up with a long shot called 'No Excuse'. Its quoted starting price on the tote was $13.50, which, in a field of less than brilliant runners, was anything but inspiring. However, there was no way Mark or any of the others could talk Brett out of throwing all of the syndicate's winnings on 'No Excuse'. When it won, the lads nearly lifted the roof off Morgan's Commercial Hotel.

Mark can't recall exactly how much went on the 'Birdman's' last race selection, but it was enough to clean out the pub's TAB cash drawer. Their win ended up being the second highest in the long history of the Morgan Commercial, which caused jubilation all round. A collect of that magnitude is no skin off the publican's nose, of course, as the more money that is wagered, the more he picks up in commission from the TAB, and the more he makes in beer sales after correct weight is signalled and the big win is confirmed.

So as to share their winnings around and keep everyone in Morgan happy, the boys visited the town's other hotel after leaving the Commercial, where there were more celebrations, loud music and plenty of dancing. There were sore heads the next morning, but also indelible memories of cleaning out the TAB – something that doesn't happen all that often, anywhere in the country!

One day during the 1999 off-season, at the Port Broughton Hotel, one of Mark's old mates from the Riverland, Andy Lehmann, asked Mark to order lunch for him while he bought a round of drinks. He gave Mark five dollars and said he would have the lasagne, which was on special. When Andy's meal hadn't shown up some 40 minutes later and everyone else at the table had finished theirs, he began to grow restless and enquired as to where his lunch was. Sheepishly, Mark admitted that he had become sidetracked on the way to the counter to order Andy's lasagne and had instead put the five dollars on a horse. Unfortunately, there had been no collect and, of course, there was no lunch. The kitchen had now closed, so all Andy could do was join in the laughter around the table. At Mark's 30th birthday shortly afterwards, Mark did a very funny phantom race call and prominent among the fictitious nags was an outsider called 'Five Dollar Lasagne'.

When nine of the Adelaide Crows visited Las Vegas after the 2003 football season, things on the gambling side didn't go quite so smoothly. Mark was very excited at the prospect of doing a casino run and rubbing shoulders with some of the world's highest-profile punters. Of the Adelaide touring party, only Wayne Carey had been to Vegas before, and there were plenty of wide eyes once the lads had settled into their hotel and began checking out the myriad gambling houses.

It didn't take long for the Adelaide boys to realise it was very easy to get into casinos in Vegas, but quite difficult to get out again. There are no clocks on the walls and no windows to the outside world, so once you become 'zoned in', it's hard to distinguish day from night. There are no exit signs, the cashiers are deliberately hidden away and difficult to locate, and the gambling rooms are fed with pure oxygen to minimise patrons' drowsiness. The casino management rely on players spending as much time at the tables and machines as physically possible.

Of the touring party of nine, only one left Las Vegas a winner and that definitely wasn't Mark. All the rest lost as much as they had budgeted to lose, but they enjoyed themselves in the process. After spending countless hours at the gambling tables and managing on little or no sleep, they decided to book a scenic flight over the Grand Canyon before departing Nevada. They couldn't go to Vegas and not see one of the world's natural wonders, they figured. So tired were they all, however, most slept for the entire flight and didn't get a glimpse of the Canyon at all!

There are some who would argue that gambling and trading on the share market are one and the same. Both involve a degree of risk, but there are strategies used by knowledgeable investors that can mean the difference between a healthy, expanding share portfolio and one that keeps them awake at night. Good advice and the willingness to research the market are crucial to long-term investment success – and, fortunately for Mark, he has both.

He began dabbling in shares in 1997 with the purchase of stock in AFIC and Argo, both of which are considered low-risk, blue-chip investments. These are companies that buy a lot of stocks from various areas and, although the return is rarely spectacular, it's better than the All Ordinaries Index and about as secure as any newcomer to the game could hope for. From there he moved on to some banks such as NAB, CBA and ANZ, which are also blue chips with a low risk of failure.

In the decade since those initial purchases, Mark has built up a healthy portfolio of around twenty blue-chip stocks, but he has also enjoyed a bit of a punt on small or 'specky' stocks along the way. Most with a lot of experience in this field advise that a blend of 80 per cent blue chips and 20 per cent small stocks is the way to go, as it combines steady, low-risk growth with the opportunity to make some quick money if your research and advice are sound and your luck is in. Naturally, you've got to be prepared to take both hits and misses in the small stocks sector, but this is what keeps most serious investors on their toes and makes the game interesting.

The share market seems to work in cycles. When Mark first started to speculate on small stocks it was the 'dot.com' phase, followed by the 'bio-tech' phase and now it's the resources boom, with uranium leading the way. Shares in all three have proven volatile at times and, like most, Mark has had his quota of successes and failures. As is often the case with horse racing, it's the information you receive that generally determines the outcome of your share market investment. This information can often come from unlikely sources, such as taxi drivers, friends of friends and even far-flung family members, and it's the way you interpret and use it that really counts.

The comparison between 'specky' shares and horse racing is a valid one, but Mark says there is one major difference: in a horse race you know the fate of your investment within a few minutes of handing the bookmaker your money, and you have the opportunity for another shot half an hour later if you've lost. With small stocks, on the other hand, a bad investment can be like a slow, drawn-out death. You simply sit back and watch your money disappear by degrees.

Like many speculators, Mark sees uranium exploration and mining as an exciting, ongoing small shares opportunity. South Australia has 35 to 40 per cent of the world's uranium and, with the level of exploration constantly on the increase, it's something that holds a lot of interest for many small shares investors. It's always a lot easier to get accurate and up-to-date information on a commodity being mined in your own backyard, than to rely on advice from interstate or overseas. Mark's connections at the Adelaide Football Club and the network of reliable advisers he has built up through those connections provide him with a constant stream of tips in the resources area. Without such cutting-edge information, investing in small resources shares would be prohibitively risky.

While Mark has had some reasonable wins with small shares, he has also experienced some memorable losses with mining stocks. Matrix Oil was one resource share that definitely burned him. The tip to buy Matrix came from an associate in the mining industry who was usually very reliable, so Mark bought a heap of shares at 25 cents. The strong tip was that these shares would reach a dollar each very quickly, which would have made a tidy return. The trouble is, most shares are meant to 'make a dollar in no time', but not all do. Not only was Matrix supposed to have plenty of oil reserves, but also enough natural gas to push the share price to two dollars or more. It all sounded very promising and, as he believed his 'mail' to be spot on, Mark sat back and waited for a nice little profit to accumulate.

When the Matrix shares hit 30 cents in next to no time, there was plenty of excitement, but after a couple of unexpected poor results the price began to slide back. Mark watched his Matrix stock come back to the original purchase price, then slip to twenty cents, further still to fifteen cents and he eventually bailed out at ten cents before the company went into receivership and the stock became worthless.

Another stock with which Mark had an up-and-down ride was Lafayette, a resource company based in the Philippines. He knew that investing in overseas stocks, and particularly those from Southeast Asia, was fraught with risk, but again his tips appeared solid and the initial stock price was good. Silver, gold and copper were Lafayette's main mining resources and Mark bought 1.5 million shares at seven cents, more at eight cents, a third lot at nine cents and a final parcel at eleven cents. The stock had shown a steady increase in value all the way through and when it topped 26 cents in just a few weeks, it looked like Mark and a few friends were on a definite winner. At that stage his Lafayette holdings were worth about $400,000.

However, a chemical spill near one of Lafayette's mines caused production to cease for a couple of months and in that time the stock price began to slide back. Environmental groups applied pressure to shut the place down. No one was quite sure if the spill was caused accidentally or if the plant was sabotaged. Either way, shareholders had their wings clipped dramatically. Mark's stock had drifted back to around twelve cents by the time he eventually sold it.

For Mark, plenty of dollars may have changed hands in both directions over the years, but in his punting, camaraderie, mateship and fun have always been the bottom line.

19

TAKING CARE OF BUSINESS

All the while Mark had been building his career as a top-level AFL footballer, he had also been keeping an eye on another ball: business.

While playing football these days at the elite level is more time-consuming than it has ever been, many players involve themselves in other business interests for a variety of reasons. Naturally, the incentive to boost their income outside of football is always a strong one, and it's a fact that quite a few established players begin setting themselves up for later life long before their careers are over. Hotels, sports stores, car yards, media involvement and consultancy businesses traditionally have been popular with high-profile players, and Mark already has an involvement in some of these. Setting himself and his family up for a secure and comfortable future has been a high priority since the middle part of his career with the Crows, and there can be no doubt he has done it well.

He bought his first house in 1994 after just one full season with Adelaide. It was a neat place on the River Torrens at Lockleys, which not only reminded him of being near the river at home but also turned out to be a good investment. He paid it off very quickly, providing a great start in capital accumulation and the impetus to keep investing as much as he could in property.

His next step was to buy his grandfather's house, and an adjoining six hectares or so at Waikerie, the following year. But this would never be a property destined for resale. It has been in the family for over 70 years and had seen all manner of market gardening before Mark ultimately bulldozed the block and planted shiraz and cabernet wine grapes. The original Ricciuto house is old and run-down, but Mark has a passionate wish to restore and extend it, and ultimately to present it as a family 'estate' for his children and grandchildren. He regards it as an investment property for sure, but that investment will be in family heritage rather than in capital terms.

In 1999, Mark began to take notice of how successful his then club captain, Mark Bickley, was becoming with his AFL Stores. 'Bicks' was certainly a good operator, using his profile and his strong association with the media to promote his retail outlets. He provided the perfect role model for any enterprising young player with sufficient drive and financial reserves. Mark realised that the media were very good at using high-profile sporting identities for their own benefit in interviews, on television shows and in newspaper columns, and he saw no reason why the reverse couldn't apply. He put his thinking cap on and eventually decided to contact the well-known Adelaide-based hospitality entrepreneur Peter Hurley, to seek advice on possible future investments. Prominent footballers traditionally have done well in pubs, and Mark, having always enjoyed the hospitality industry, knew it was time to cash in on the fame he had achieved through football.

Hurley and his wife, Jenny, seemed like the ideal couple to talk to about the industry. The Hurleys were strong Crows supporters and player sponsors at the time. They are genuine, down-to-earth people with a reputation for being among the best in their field.

The Hurleys had got to know Mark through his long-standing friendship with Andrew Johnson, who was managing the Royal Hotel for them at Torrensville. It became obvious quite early in the piece that there was a great opportunity to combine the Hurleys' knowledge of the hotel game with Mark's high profile to form a very effective working partnership.

Mark had always admired the Hurleys. Peter had been a schoolteacher and Jenny a nurse, but they had both decided on career changes and ultimately found their way into hospitality. Through sheer hard work and good business sense, they gradually acquired businesses such as the Wudinna Hotel, the Spencer Hotel in Whyalla, the Marion Hotel, the Royal Hotel and, the big daddy of them all, the Arkaba. Like most who succeed in business, the Hurleys made huge sacrifices along the way to the top.

Peter Hurley recalls Mark's enthusiasm when the decision had been made to form a business partnership. His phone calls were many and generally went along the lines of: 'Mate, I've heard that Pub X is coming on the market. What do you think? How do we go about it?' They began searching for a hotel in the metropolitan area with long-term potential, and some twelve months later, in September 2000, they eventually settled on the Alma Tavern on Magill Road at Norwood. Instead of simply taking over the hotel lease, they bought the freehold as well – bricks, mortar, land and business – and then formulated a redevelopment plan for the entire complex.

The Alma was a bit run-down at that stage and it was obvious it would take considerable time, planning and capital outlay to bring it up to the standard the new consortium was looking for. Mark had the profile to attract new patrons to a well-appointed, conveniently located hotel, and Peter Hurley certainly had the business expertise to get it up and running efficiently, so they forged ahead.

On Mark's suggestion, his Crows team-mate Simon Goodwin was also brought into the partnership, albeit on a smaller level. Mark had been considering Simon's potential as a business partner for some time; despite being a few years younger, he had the right personality, plenty of drive, and the potential to inject some good ideas into the Alma project. 'Goody' had already established himself as a very good footballer and future leader of the club, and his profile would further benefit a business that was looking to improve its identity. His father was on the board of directors at real estate giant Brock Partners, so Simon had a good background in commercial enterprise and fitted quickly into the Alma consortium.

A few years and several renovation stages later, the Alma Tavern has become one of Adelaide's most successful suburban hotels. Mark doubts it would have been in the top 100 when they took over, but there are few establishments that can now boast such consistent patronage and turnover as the Alma enjoys. Both Mark and Simon try to put in as much time there as their frenetic football schedules allow; they know the value of pouring a few drinks or serving the odd meal for regular patrons and enjoy the hands-on side of hotel management. Both are warm, approachable people who appreciate that many keen football fans come to their hotel in the hope of meeting and chatting with them. It's a part of the job some high-profile sportsmen will avoid, if possible, but not so these two.

Peter Hurley says many people are under the impression that he and Jenny drive the business operationally, but nothing could be further from the truth. 'Roo has extraordinary pub savvy, combined with a strategic focus, and whilst everyone knows he's a Brownlow-standard footballer, many may be surprised to know he is also a Brownlow-level businessman,' says Peter.

It didn't take Mark a long time in the hotel game to work out that the same qualities that go into making a good sportsman also apply in business. To succeed at the top level you've got to have a good work ethic, be disciplined and be prepared to make sacrifices. You also have to know your own strengths and weaknesses, as well as those of the opposition. Mark understands the value of good personnel, and the need to be strict but fair with all managers, employees, security staff and, if necessary, patrons as well. Without having all of this under control, the chances of being able to run a profitable, hassle-free business in the long term are remote.

In 2003, with things ticking along nicely over on Magill Road, a second hotel opportunity arose. Peter Hurley owned the freehold of the Kensington Hotel and, as his tenant had decided to move on, Mark and Simon were invited to join him there as well. The Kensington is situated well away from a main thoroughfare and has always been a quiet, friendly pub with healthy local patronage and great character. Like the Alma, it needed sprucing up and a lift in profile, and once it had received both, it started to go ahead in leaps and bounds. The Kensington will never be in the same mould as the Alma, but it was never designed to be.

Mark's financial interests in both the Alma and Kensington hotels prior to his Brownlow Medal win that year meant a lot of promotional work outside of football, and the fact that he was playing at his peak made him feel confident about combining the two. In fact, both Mark and Simon Goodwin feel they have played their best football since taking on outside interests. Having something other than the game to concentrate on for much of the year has, they believe, enabled them to think more clearly and to remain sharp in all aspects of life.

Simon Goodwin feels another business partner could not have brought out in him all that Mark has. 'Roo's attention to detail, his head for figures and his ability to make good decisions has always inspired confidence with me,' he says. 'Like on the footy field, he knows how to be the boss and rarely has trouble letting those around him know it. We may not always agree on everything, but our relationship is such that we can talk through any issue and usually come up with a solution that suits us both.' Simon is confident the two have a long and healthy business partnership in front of them.

When Port Lincoln's most successful tuna fisherman, Sam Sarin, decided that his home-town needed an upmarket hotel to cater for growing business and tourism demands, the Ricciuto/Hurley/Goodwin consortium was offered the opportunity to become involved. Port Lincoln's resurgence as both a commercial fishing hub and tourist resort excited all three of them, and they were quick to register their interest when a broker approached them and explained Sarin's proposal.

The Port Lincoln development would be, by far, the biggest financial risk Mark or Simon had ever taken. It would be a totally different proposition from their involvement in the two Adelaide hotels, which were both renovation projects that were established and returning income prior to takeover. The deal between the Ricciuto/Hurley/Goodwin consortium and Sam Sarin would see them completely designing and fitting out the new hotel in return for being granted the lease. Starting from scratch in a development of this magnitude was always going to be a daunting experience, but with Peter Hurley on board and both Mark and Simon having learned plenty in their relatively short time in the hotel game, they grabbed the opportunity with both hands. Peter Hurley says the publicity that Mark and Simon Goodwin have attracted to the project is a massive leg up, but it pales into significance compared with their vision and input into the business model. He is very excited about the new complex, which he describes as 'undeniably the largest tourism infrastructure development in the history of regional South Australia'.

The Port Lincoln Hotel is designed with 111 accommodation rooms on seven levels, three bars, a gymnasium, gaming room, restaurant, 300-seat conference facility, swimming pool, beer garden and bottle shop. It is the sort of complex that works well in East Coast tourist centres and, given Port Lincoln's ever-growing profile and forward-thinking local government, there is no reason to think it won't do big business in the Tuna City.

Mark copped plenty of flak from mates when his head appeared on a giant illuminated sign overlooking a used-car yard at Blair Athol in 2005. Mark Ricciuto Car Sales is a venture undertaken with his brother, Craig, and is ticking over nicely. Main North Road is one of Adelaide's premier thoroughfares for the new and used-car business, and when the Blair Athol site became available, it was simply too good to pass up.

Craig Ricciuto has a lengthy history in the automotive game, having worked for the Adtrans Group for over ten years. The conglomerate owns several prominent automotive outlets around Adelaide, including the Stillwell, Graham Cornes and Adrian Brien dealerships, and provided Craig with plenty of managerial experience in the cut-throat business of selling cars. Craig had always wanted to run his own yard, and having a high-profile brother as his partner seemed the obvious way to go. Mark did quite a bit of research into all aspects of the venture and, when he was convinced the project could work, it was up and running in the blink of an eye.

As is the case with most newly established car outlets, Mark Ricciuto Car Sales experienced a few teething problems in the early days, but once these were sorted out and word got around that the 'Roo Brothers' were in the trade, business took off. Their long-term aim is to pick up a new car franchise – hopefully, a Toyota dealership if one becomes available – and to use Craig's experience and Mark's profile to make it competitive. Mark considers going from used to new cars is like receiving a promotion from assistant coach to head coach; the rewards are often greater, but so are the risks.

In 2005, Mark, Simon Goodwin and Simon's father-in-law, Mark Ambrose, acquired a small financial planning business and installed Mark's Waikerie buddy Danny McMahon as finance planner. Danny had always shown a keen interest and a lot of potential in this area and jumped at the opportunity to be involved. Ambrose, a financial planning consultant in Adelaide with over 25 years' experience, was instrumental in the new business. The idea was for him to take Danny under his wing and fast track his development with a long-term view that Danny might one day manage the business.

The new venture became viable very quickly, acquiring a couple of smaller businesses and growing at a rate that surprised all the partners. When it merged with Mark Ambrose's long-established company, its future became assured. Financial planning is a service that is rapidly gaining popularity, particularly among those with an increased disposable income and little time to manage it. 'Planning Forward', as the Ricciuto/Goodwin/Ambrose/McMahon venture will be known, offers cutting-edge advice to anyone keen to maximise return for investment and is an exciting new challenge, particularly for McMahon.

Combining business and football commitments has always been something of a juggling act for those at the sport's top level, and it certainly takes a lot of careful thought and planning. Tony McGuinness and Chris McDermott both ran successful businesses while leading the Crows, providing the perfect example of how to manage the two pursuits effectively. Mark spends about 70 per cent of his waking hours either at the Adelaide Football Club or involved in allied activities, with the remaining 30 per cent divided between business and family. Consequently, efficient time management is critical. Mark knows how quickly the media can jump on high-profile sportspeople whose on-field performance starts to dip as their off-field interests escalate. Fortunately, he and Simon Goodwin have won five of the last seven Best and Fairest awards at the AFC, so it's fair to assume there will be no debate about where their loyalties lie.

Football has always been Mark's top priority, and always will be until he calls it a day. If hotel or other business meetings clash with football commitments, they are put to the side without question. He considers himself lucky to have Peter and Jenny Hurley as partners, as they understand the complexities of his life and are prepared to pick up the slack whenever necessary for as long as it takes. As club captain, Mark knows the extent of his responsibilities, and most would agree there have been few more committed skippers in the game. He now prides himself on impeccable time management, which enables him to fit 100 hours into an 80-hour week and keep everyone happy. Private time is a scarce commodity these days, but he has been aware of this all along and intends to make it up to family and friends once the boots have been hung up and his life becomes his own again.

If there is one thing that Mark has learned from his various business ventures over the past decade and which stands out from all else, it is to seek the help and advice of experts when making important decisions. Learning from the best in a particular field has always been paramount in his thinking: Adtrans has always been a leader in automotive, the Hurleys are hospitality kings and, back in the Riverland, the DeVitos are among the best growers. Sometimes you have to pay for expert advice and sometimes it comes for free, but either way, he says, it should be treated like gold and used to full advantage.

Mark is looking forward to spending more time in his three hotels after his retirement from football. He loves the hospitality game and enjoys nothing more than hosting people who are having a good time. There are certain to be a lot of trips to Port Lincoln at the conclusion of the 2007 football season as the hotel construction project nears completion. Mark is also looking forward to spending a lot more time in his beloved Riverland, and says he would jump at the chance to be involved in the Waikerie Hotel if the lease ever became available.

He has often been asked about potential involvement in the media and coaching once he retires, and says he has a definite interest in both. The financial security he has worked hard to achieve throughout his football life will ensure there is no panic once his number 32 jumper is passed on to another Crows player. Mark will be able to sit back for a while and assess his options – a luxury most of us are rarely afforded when it comes time to change careers.

20

FAMILY AND THE FUTURE

If parents should be judged by the way their children turn out, then Murray and Carolyn Ricciuto deserve gold medals. They instilled in Lisa, Craig and Mark the values needed to make them hard-working, caring and generally successful people, who are aware of and grateful for the sacrifices their parents made for them. Lisa still lives in Waikerie, while Craig and Mark are based in Adelaide. The brothers return to the Riverland as often as their hectic schedules permit. The Ricciutos are about as close and tight as a family group can be, and it's a fair bet that will continue as Murray and Carolyn's bevy of grandchildren expands.

As he has grown and matured, Mark has learned to look inside himself from time to time to work out what he is happy with and what could be improved; it's something most people do, either consciously or subconsciously, as their list of life experiences grows. He says he now recognises there's a lot of his parents in him. There have been times in his football career, both on the training track and in matches, when he has managed to find reserves of strength, toughness and determination he didn't know he had. He believes that inner strength comes from the values that were instilled in him by his parents.

Murray Ricciuto had recognised his sons' talent for football when they were still in primary school. As they progressed through the junior grades at Waikerie, he was excited by what he saw. He suspected they would both be good enough to go on and play in the South Australian National Football League, and he did everything he could to help them develop their skills and dedication to training. The one thing he didn't do was become the type of parent who puts sporting success before all else and forgets that kids need space to develop in other areas as well.

It's unfortunate when kids with obvious sporting talent are pushed beyond normal limits by parents with unrealistic expectations. Many of these youngsters simply can't handle the pressure they're under from home and subsequently fail to achieve their full potential. Neither Murray nor Carolyn ever pushed their children to the edge; instead, they provided a home environment that encouraged them to push themselves. They insisted on hard work, but were always fair and provided ample rewards when any of the three kids achieved well at school or in sport.

Mark describes his father as being a 'bit of a softie, at times'. He could often con his dad into taking him fishing when all Murray really wanted to do was relax after a hard day's work on the fruit block. Mark regularly scored a lift home from school, even when he had ridden his bike there in the morning. Murray would often schedule the delivery of a bin of oranges to the packing shed to coincide with school letting out; he would be waiting outside the school in his ute, to save Mark having to ride his pushbike home. Invariably, it was Murray and Carolyn who would drive a mob of young footballers to Saturday morning matches, many of the other parents being too busy; and, of course, Murray spent countless hours coaching Waikerie's Juniors.

Mark hates to think how many kilometres the family Commodore clocked up while he was training and playing for West Adelaide. Murray would regularly drive the 400-kilometre return trip from Waikerie to Richmond Oval two and sometimes three times a week. If his father hadn't been willing to spend up to twelve hours on the highway each week, Mark concedes he may never have reached the heights he has in football.

Generosity is a family trait of the Ricciutos. It wasn't something Carolyn or Murray pushed down their children's throats; it was a part of everyday life as they grew up. Nicola Ricciuto had been a very generous man and it seemed to flow on down through the generations without ever needing to be taught. Mark enjoys nothing more than bringing back a load of fruit from Waikerie after a family visit and dropping it off at his mates' homes in Adelaide, exactly as his father and grandfather had done before him. He also likes to see others do well in business and has helped several friends to set themselves up in successful careers. If he gets a stock-market tip (reliable or otherwise), he's usually on the phone to friends to let them know about it before he gets around to investing himself. He has provided financial assistance to a couple of close mates in need, and set up business deals that he could have cashed in on himself, but opted to let others benefit from. Sarah says you can take the boy out of the country, but you can't take the country out of the boy, and there's no doubt that Mark's upbringing in Waikerie has had a lot to do with his generosity and loyalty to friends. It is this aspect of Mark's character that Sarah says she admires most of all.

The way in which Mark and Sarah bring up their children will be heavily influenced by the values they have inherited from their own families. Mark is determined his children grow up with the same strong work ethic that was passed on to him by Murray and Carolyn. He concedes this won't be quite as easy if they grow up living in the city, but it's something he'll make a conscious effort to instil in them. While his children won't have to worry about money, as he and his brother and sister had to when times were tough in the early years, he is determined to make them aware of its value and of how difficult it can be to earn. There will be no silver spoon for Sophie Jane or her future siblings.

One of the most important things Mark learned from his parents is to enjoy the successes that come in life. Murray and Carolyn always celebrated when things went right, and it's a custom commonly practised in Italian communities around the world. Like his parents, Mark can see little point in achieving success in sport, business or any other worthwhile aspect of life unless you're able to find the time to enjoy it. The Ricciutos will always celebrate. That's the sort of people they are.

These days, Mark, Sarah, Sophie and Nellie, the family dog, live in a high-rise complex south of the Adelaide CBD. It's a very fashionable address, with an incredible panoramic view of the city. Mark and Sarah find the apartment lifestyle suits their busy schedules – at least for now. Sarah says Mark has cleaned up his act of late and is far tidier than he used to be. He is quite a good cook, too, when he has the time. As most who know him would expect, he's a doting dad and helps out wherever and whenever he can to share the parenting load. There are usually very few 'upsides' to having suffered a broken nose while playing football, but Mark's impaired sense of smell due to the nasal break makes it a lot easier for him to change Sophie's less-than-fragrant nappies!

An annoying, but unavoidable, fact of life for both of them is Mark's mobile phone, which Sarah says is very much a constant part of their day. Although Mark screens his calls, there is scarcely a half-hour period any day of the week when he isn't talking to someone about football or his business commitments, or both. Mark is a very driven person whose head is always full of ideas, which he likes to act on immediately. As he spends a lot of his life on the road between home and AAMI Stadium, or between home and any of a dozen business commitments each day, the phone is also an important communication link between the two of them. Like most people who lead a hectic lifestyle, Sarah wonders what it would be like in a world without mobile telecommunication and concedes it would be both pleasant and more difficult.

There is one aspect of Mark's rural upbringing that took Sarah a little time to get used to. Like all the Ricciutos, Mark loves the company of others and is often at his happiest when surrounded by a dozen friends or relatives. Sarah struggled with this in the early days and craved time alone with him. However, she gradually realised that 'sharing' Mark with a group of close friends and family didn't necessarily mean she wasn't the most important person in his life. He is a man who shows his love in many ways, and Sarah has learned that Mark enjoys sharing his *whole* world with her and included in that world are the people who are nearest and dearest to him. Sarah knows their children will be brought up to have similar values, which she accepts is a positive thing.

Unlike a lot of elite sportsmen, Mark isn't superstitious about his pre-game routine – or about much at all, for that matter. He doesn't need to wear the same underwear each week, put on his left sock first, or wait until the last minute before tying his bootlaces, as some players do. About the only thing Sarah notices in the lead-up to a match is that Mark becomes quiet and more introspective. She knows to leave him to his thoughts at such times, as he prepares himself mentally for the next challenge. She is aware, like the partners of most top-level footballers, that playing before 45,000 fanatical fans in the stadium, and trying to preserve the hopes of hundreds of thousands more watching the match on television, is about as demanding as it gets in professional sport. She admires Mark for having done it so well, for so long.

Mark's emotional side, and particularly his willingness to wear his emotions where the outside world can see them, is something Sarah finds both unique and admirable. A lot of modern footballers would rather run a hundred metres on broken glass in bare feet than shed a tear in public, and Sarah is grateful that Mark is able to let things out if he needs to. Coping with the premature deaths of two very close friends certainly affected his emotional development and helped him to realise that tears are there for the moments our hearts and minds simply have no other outlet.

Although it's a very personal thing, Sarah can't help but share at least some of Mark's frustration when he misses extended periods of football through injury or illness. Like all AFL players, he has always hated sitting on the sidelines, but especially so since he was appointed team captain in 2001. She says Mark's competitive nature still pushes him harder than his body can handle after more than 300 games at the top level, and that slowing down is something he has difficulty in accepting. But he is slowly facing the fact that he can no longer be as physically competitive as he was in his younger days. His chronic back complaint in the first half of the 2007 season was one of the most frustrating injuries of all, as his doctors were unable to put a definite time frame on his recovery.

Sarah has a close relationship with Mark's parents. Murray is one of the most likeable characters she has encountered, she says, with a perpetual smile and a heart of gold. He is always the first to pitch in and help, and rarely, if ever, has a cross word to say about anyone or anything, except maybe umpires! Carolyn is extremely strong, supportive and very caring. Even when Mark and Sarah weren't seeing each other, she felt she could phone the Ricciutos for a chat. If she ran into them at the football, they always still treated her like one of the family. One of the few occasions when Mark can recall his father being upset with him was when Sarah and he broke up. It was the first time in years that Murray had really taken him to task about anything, and Mark was left with no doubts about how his parents felt about Sarah Delahunt.

Because of their commitments in Adelaide, Mark and Sarah don't get to spend as much time with his parents as either of them would like. They drive to Waikerie whenever they can grab a couple of days off, but such opportunities are rare these days. Fortunately, Murray and Carolyn drive down to see most of the Crows' home matches and stay with Mark and Sarah in the new apartment. This provides at least some catch-up time, as well as the chance to spoil their baby granddaughter.

Mark gets on equally well with Sarah's parents, Mick and Irene. Sarah says it was a little difficult for them when she and Mark first started going out seriously, as the Delahunts have always been Crows supporters and had to adjust to treating Mark as their daughter's boyfriend, rather than their football hero. However, Mark's unassuming, down-to-earth nature soon put them at ease and he became part of Sarah's family as quickly as she had become part of his.

One of Mark and Sarah's ambitions when he eventually hangs up his footy boots is to travel around Australia. Sarah says she can picture the family in a motor home, cruising along the coast with no particular plan or time frame, and doing the sorts of things they both love doing. They have quite a few friends in different parts of the country and would like nothing better than to call in on them and stay until the mood takes them to move on. An extended break from the high-pressure world that has long dominated their lives would totally recharge their batteries, they believe, and it's a fair bet they will be off as soon as the opportunity arises.

In the longer term, Sarah feels they may move back to Waikerie and a country lifestyle. Exactly when this might happen depends largely on Mark's business commitments, and on how they can be structured to enable the family to move away from the city. Mark is keen for his children to be brought up in the country and, if possible, go to school at Ramco, of which he still has very fond memories; so fond, in fact, he has often joked with Sarah that if Ramco Primary School had boarding facilities, he would send his kids there rather than somewhere in Adelaide. Mark insists that Ramco Primary is the best-maintained school in the state, with just 130 students, pristine grounds and a caring, nurturing staff.

It would be no surprise to those who know Mark and Sarah well if they had five or even six children. Family has always been very important to both of them, and it's obvious that a spacious country house and a heap of little ones running around is where they see their lives headed. Mark is very keen to restore, renovate and build on to the riverbank house his grandfather built and of which he is now the proud owner. He plans to make it into an estate that will perpetuate the Ricciuto name; somewhere his extended family can visit at any time and feel welcome.

Football has been the top priority in Mark's life for twenty-odd years. It is impossible to attain the sort of status he now enjoys, and to accumulate all the success and rewards that go with it, without giving everything to the game. There have been countless sacrifices during the journey, but once his AFL career has ended, the focus will shift. Family will become his number one priority and, with the grace of God, the Ricciutos will live happily ever after.

Sarah often thinks back to the day she sold Mark a pair of jeans when they were both teenagers. There has been a lot of water under the bridge since then, of course, but with the flow now starting to slow a little, she is looking forward to sharing whatever the next phase of her life with Mark Ricciuto may bring.

WHAT THE EXPERTS THINK

There are few people concerned with football who don't admire and respect Mark Ricciuto. Everyone seems to have an opinion, of course, about his abilities, his strengths and weaknesses, his ranking in the Crows' all-time list of great players, and even about his future. However, it's the opinions of high-profile media commentators and those who have played with and against Mark that are most credible. Unlike the average one-eyed Crows supporter, these are the people who know the game intimately and have the necessary credentials to be considered experts.

Several of these football identities and commentators, both past and present, were asked to respond to three questions. They were also given the opportunity to add any other comments they felt appropriate. For the most part, their responses were thoughtful and well considered.

The questions were:

How do you rate Mark Ricciuto as a player?

How do you rate Mark Ricciuto as a leader?
How do you rate Mark Ricciuto as a person?

Given Mark's accessibility and close association with the media, particularly in Adelaide, most commentators know him well enough to be able to respond to all three questions. The same applies to surveyed opposition players, most of whom are mortal combatants out on the field, but, away from the game, are happy to enjoy a chat and a beer with Mark when the opportunity arises. The respondents are listed in alphabetical order.

Bruce Abernethy – Port Adelaide, Collingwood and Crows player, Channel Seven Adelaide sports reporter

Roo is the classic old-style centreman – skilled, hard, tough, enjoys the physical side of the game as much as anyone, but this aspect should never overshadow his skills.

Just from watching, he has total respect from his team-mates and opponents and that is not only rare, but speaks volumes for his leadership ability.

As a person, he seems very comfortable with who he is, where he's come from and where he's going. Off-field he is almost a model for what young footballers should aim for in setting up their lives around football. And on top of that, a genuine, level-headed, good bloke with a rational grip on what can sometimes be a very artificial world that surrounds him.

Malcolm Blight – Magarey and Brownlow Medallist, Crows coach 1997–99

Roo has been a stand-out player since he began as a kid in 1993. He has all the skills, as well as a great footy physique and a totally committed attitude. He was an excellent track worker when I was coach and actually learned to push himself harder than he thought he could. Of the younger guys at the club when I was there, he definitely had the best work ethic.

I'd like to have had him busting through and putting the ball on my chest, lace out, when I was playing. He would certainly have fitted well in any era of football.

His inner drive was extraordinary. It wasn't something he showed much of on the outside, but you just knew he was always trying to improve himself and didn't mind how hard he had to work to do it.

It was pretty obvious Mark was going to be Crows captain at some stage and probably as soon as Mark Bickley gave it away. He had all the attributes needed to be a good leader and that has since proven correct. You've got to lead by example in today's footy and Mark certainly does that.

Off the field, he's a great guy. Living in Queensland, I don't get to see him much these days, but it's always nice to catch up when the chance arises. I always enjoyed having a beer with him when I was coach.

James Brayshaw – host of Channel Nine's *The Footy Show*

Mark is the sort of player I would have been if I had played AFL football – hard ... tough ... uncompromising ... courageous ... skilful ... brave ... unselfish ... inspiring. In fact, as I read those words back, I realise not one of them actually describes anything I have ever done! This man is a champion. I only ever put one filter over footballers. Would I like to see them wearing a North Melbourne jumper? And in Roo's case the answer is – every day of the week!

And as a leader ... well, the only place Roo has ever led me is into trouble after-hours – and he was bloody good at that!

As a person, he is a ripper. I first met Mark as a teenager, fresh from the Riverland, and I loved him then because he was unaffected, loyal and honest. Nearly fifteen years later, after all the success he's had, he is exactly the same bloke and that says plenty, I reckon!

Nathan Buckley – Collingwood captain

As a player, I rate Roo as just about perfect for the modern era. His sheer size, strength and hardness are stand-out attributes. He's got a bit of a mean streak to him, which he uses at times to his advantage. Sometimes players like that can be a bit in and out, but Roo's also very consistent. He would definitely have fitted into the Collingwood team nicely and would have made a great team-mate.

I doubt there is a better leader in the game at present than Roo. He's the sort of captain who gives 110 per cent every time he takes the field and expects all those around him to do the same. Leading by example is really what it's all about, and I compare Roo with James Hird in this department. You give until you can't give any more; and if you do that often enough, it's got to rub off on your team-mates.

Although we don't get to mix with opposition players as much these days as we used to, I've had a couple of opportunities to have a chat with Roo off the field. He's a down-to-earth sort of bloke who obviously enjoys what he does. I enjoyed his company when we toured Ireland together in 1998 and I also enjoyed playing with him. The Irish were a bit intimidated by him, which was good for all of us!

I remember when I was playing in the early days at Port Adelaide and hearing about this kid from Waikerie who was going to be the next 'gun' full forward. With Tony Modra starting at about the same time, I guess Roo had to change his game a bit and look to playing another position, which he has done with aplomb.

Sharing the Brownlow with Roo was something I enjoyed. A lot of people have asked if the three-way tie detracted from the honour of winning, but I look at it differently. I reckon being up there with Roo and Adam Goodes added to the honour. These guys are champions and I was certainly humbled to share the Medal with them.

Wayne Carey – Kangaroos champion, Crows team-mate, radio and television commentator
When I played against Roo, things were always tough. I didn't think I actually ever stood him, but Glenn Archer, whom most regard as one of the hardest men in footy, would always say how tough it had been to play

on Roo. He was one of those on-ballers who would always hit the ball or the pack going flat out. He could read the play so well, like from a ball-up or boundary throw-in, that he was always at top pace when he got to the ball. This made him difficult to tackle because of the momentum he'd build up. That's a skill not many players have.

It was great for me when I came to the Crows to have an on-baller like Roo. We quickly developed an understanding, and he'd nearly always look for me when he was running into attack. I wasn't as quick as I used to be at that stage, and he had the knack of pinpointing a pass to my lead. As a forward this is invaluable, and he really inspired a lot of confidence. He could read my movement better than most I've played with and this always makes life a lot easier.

There's no doubt Roo is one of the great captains. When I came to play at Adelaide, Roo was in his third year as captain and he had the total respect of everyone at the club. He has the sort of demeanour that really makes you want to play for him. He never really said too much on the field, but his presence was always obvious and he could lift you with the things he did and the way he did them.

We became pretty good mates when I was at Adelaide. We knew each other from the 1998 tour of Ireland, which helped break the ice when I transferred to the Crows. We share a lot of interests, like a punt on the horses, fishing and the outdoor life, and that helped to cement our friendship.

Mark's a ripping sort of bloke. In fact, he's one of the best blokes you could ever meet. The Crows have never had a better captain and, for that matter, a better footballer than Roo.

Josh Carr – former Port Adelaide and current Fremantle player

In the early part of my career at Port I was given tagging roles each week, which usually meant I came up against the best opposition players. I always found Roo difficult to play on. You don't get eight All-Australian jumpers unless you're pretty good at the game. I always knew it was going *to be tough when I had to tag Roo. He plays as hard as anyone around.*

I remember the first Showdown I played in. I'd been into him all day, which he wasn't all that happy about, and when a bit of a scuffle broke out, he got me in one of his headlocks. I simply couldn't move and remember having to stop everything to get him to let go. One more second and I reckon I would have choked! That was a memorable day.

I rate Roo with the best leaders. He's obviously totally committed and is happy to put his body on the line if that's what it takes to win a contest. He's not only respected by his team-mates, but by most of the opposition as well. That's the sort of guy any club would want as captain.

There's no doubt our off-field relationship was strained a bit, especially when I first started playing and was tagging him each Showdown. The Ramsgate fight didn't help that much, of course. But these days that's all history and we get on pretty well. We can sit down for a beer and a talk, and enjoy each other's company.

Roo's a good bloke and definitely Adelaide's best player ever.

Graham Cornes – Adelaide Football Club's inaugural coach

Mark was always destined to be a great player. His work ethic, both at training and during matches, was about as good as I've seen. He came to the Crows as a youngster from the Riverland, but he was already well developed, both physically and in the skills of the game. His inner determination always impressed me. It came as no surprise that he became a top-quality AFL player so quickly.

Mark had good leaders in Chris McDermott and Mark Bickley to model his captaincy on, and he's gone on to become a very strong leader himself. He's certainly very well respected by everyone associated with Adelaide.

He's the typical country lad made good. His success as a footballer has never gone to his head, and I doubt it ever will. He likes all the typical country things and gets back home whenever he can.

Appendix 1

Robert DiPierdomenico – former Brownlow Medallist and media commentator

Roo has always been my type of footballer. Like me, he obviously enjoys the physical side of the game, but is also highly skilled. Unlike some of the players of today, Roo could have fitted into any side, anywhere, at any time. He would have been a regular in our Hawthorn Premiership sides of the 1980s. It's a pity injuries have caught up with him late in his career, but I guess this happens to the best of us!

There's no doubt he's a great captain, probably the best the Crows have had. He busts a gut on the field, which inspires his team-mates, and this is the best way for any skipper to lead his troops. Again, he would have made a top-class captain in any era.

I doubt I've met a better bloke in football. We had a ball together when we toured Ireland in 1998, especially when having a bet, playing cards and harassing Irish hoteliers. We still keep in contact today and he's still as friendly and down-to-earth as the first time I met him. I guess being a country boy means he'll always be this way.

Chris Dittmar – Channel Seven Adelaide sports reporter

As a player, it's been said before, but I wish he played for the Power. His uncle is the great Bruce Light. Couldn't we get him in some uncle/nephew rule? He is outstanding, fearless, a great kick for goal and, as tough as he is, I don't think I've ever seen him doing anything questionable on a football field.

I heard Simon Goodwin say recently that Mark helped turn the club around in recent years. He was the obvious leader, as the new, young list was being knocked into shape and needed direction. Among the captains in the AFL, it's fair to say he gets more respect from his players than any other.

I've heard his mum and dad are absolute rippers, and I reckon they must be because for everything Mark has achieved, he is so unaffected and is a good, genuine bloke. He'll talk fishing to you, or golf. It's never about him.

Rex Hunt – former VFL player and 3AW football commentator
Mark Ricciuto can stand among the greats of the game. Although riddled with injury late in his career, the Roo has been a star for many years. As a footy lover and a commentator, he is one of the reasons I go to watch the game. The Roo's games tally, his Premiership, and his inspirational play elevate him to star status.

The Roo is inspirational. I can recall many games at crunch time with Ricciuto displaying something out of the norm and leading his side to victory. He is admired and respected by his team-mates and opposition alike. If I wanted a leader in my team, the Roo would be it for sure.

What I like about Mark Ricciuto is his common touch. In other words, the Roo has never forgotten where he came from, nor got ahead of himself. This was highlighted to me recently at Telstra Dome in Melbourne when I went down to the boundary line prior to the game to have a closer look at a couple of young guys who were making their debuts for the Crows. The Roo could not have been more helpful. We even chatted about the fishing. That gets me in every time.

Paul Kelly – former Sydney Swans captain and Brownlow Medallist
Although we didn't actually play one-on-one against each other often, Roo was always a tough nut on the field. I can only remember a couple of times when we were direct opponents and I reckon I came out on top once and he beat me the second time. The Crows used to tag me, and we would always tag Roo. He was always very strong overhead and could kick a goal from a long way out, which made him dangerous when they played him up forward.

The one day I kicked four goals on him at the SCG – he was playing half back and I was at half forward – it was just one of those games when everything went right for me and not much for him. It didn't matter where I went, the ball fell in my lap. It was funny after a while and I felt like apologising at one stage. I was still happy when he was moved off me, though. It always seemed he was out there having a good time, which is pretty much the same way I always looked at my footy.

Roo seems to lead the Crows pretty much the same way I always tried to lead the Swans. There's only one real way to get and hold the respect of your team-mates and that's to do everything at 100 per cent. He didn't seem to say too much out on the field, but all the Adelaide boys knew what he expected of them. He always seemed to bob up with an important goal when the Crows needed one to get back into the game or stay in front. That's the sort of stuff a good leader can do.

Roo is a country boy, like me. Just a knockabout sort of bloke. I don't know him all that well, but on the few occasions we've spoken he's seemed pretty laid-back. He obviously likes to get away to go fishing or camping, which I can relate to, so we've probably got a fair bit in common.

Bruce McAvaney – Channel Seven sports commentator

It's difficult to imagine what else Mark could achieve as a footballer. I'm not sure what he was dreaming about when he was playing against men as a youngster in the Riverland, but you would think all his dreams have come true: a Premiership, club captain, 300-plus games, eight times All-Australian, multiple Best and Fairest awards, leading goal kicker and the Brownlow Medal.

There's so much to admire about the way Mark has played the game and the reputation he has been able to forge since his debut in 1993. He typifies the modern-day footballer – a great athlete who can play in a number of different positions.

One of the impressive things about the Roo is that, like all great sportsmen, he has overcome adversity; the disappointment of missing Adelaide's first Premiership in 1997 through injury, and the more recent late-season injuries, suspension and illness that have prevented him from playing a major part in Adelaide's quest for a flag.

Wherever I travel in Australia, the Roo is admired and is up there with Voss, Hird and Buckley. They are all contemporaries and great leaders in their own right.

AAMI Stadium can be an exciting place to be, and for Crows fans there is nothing more exhilarating than when their team is making a charge with their captain about to launch another attack and that 'Roo' roar engulfs the stadium.

Mark is a great bloke, a great player and a great leader. But perhaps the ultimate compliment I can pay him is to say that, if my team were three points down in a Grand Final and the siren had sounded and you could ask for anybody to kick the goal from 45 metres out, on a 45-degree angle, he'd be my choice.

Michelangelo Rucci – *The Advertiser*'s chief football writer
It seems far too bland to say Mark Ricciuto is one of the game's greatest players. 'Champion' doesn't do enough to tell of his ability or achievements. Thankfully, there will always be video to show just how influential and inspirational Mark has been as a player. Once you see him play, you realise why his team-mates are inspired by his ability and character. And why his rivals respect him.

Some time ago a man walking through the very false world of business and politics summed up leadership in this way: the first duty of a leader is to make himself be loved without courting love; to be loved without playing up to anyone, even himself. That's Mark as a leader. He does it. Not for what it will give him, but for what it will give everyone. There have been times in Mark's captaincy that from the outside it has been obvious the Crows were not far from fracturing. How Mark kept it together – and without any public moment – says he has been a magnificent leader. One the Adelaide Football Club should always regard itself as fortunate to have.

As a person he's humble, successful, motivated, honest and true. All those attributes came to mind at the same time. If only there was one word that captured all those strengths.

Robert Shaw – Crows coach, 1995–96, currently Fremantle Football Club operations manager

I came to the club a distant twelve years ago. Mark was obviously very young and we had basically gone and got a lot of young kids to put in the side. Vardy, Edwards, McLeod, Goodwin and Johnson. In hindsight it proved to be the core of future teams, and Mark was the standout and apparent leader of this young group. Thumping kick, ability to play off the half back flank, mid-field and forward ... committed physically. I felt we lacked presence in physical contests and I erred by pushing Mark up as that physical leader, for one so young. I take the blame, no problems with that, as it distracted Mark from his natural instincts as being a hunter of the football. He had power and explosive pace. It was apparent he was going to be so important to the future of the club.

It was written in his makeup even so long ago that he would be a leader. I guess that's why I had such a high opinion and expectations of him. My opinions were right, but [it was] too early to push him up. He never complained, did what was asked of him. He always had an aura about him, which is the sign of a commanding person and player. In my time back at Essendon, and now at Fremantle, I have enjoyed watching him grow into the role, represent his club really well as a leader and, of course, influence games with his willpower and skill. His physical stature also immediately commands respect ... and his performances over the years have been top-shelf.

In two years I didn't get to know Mark that well, obviously. He was very young. One story sums up Roo, in my opinion. My mum is in her eighties and was at the airport in the last couple of years, when she went up and introduced herself to Mark. 'I'm Robert's mum' ... that sort of thing. Mark addressed her as 'Mrs Shaw' and was polite and patient and took the time to talk. Good country values, or just a good bloke ... both. You don't forget people who take the time.

John Worsfold – former player and current coach of the West Coast Eagles

I didn't really know him as a person. I've met him a few times and he's always been good to talk to, very polite. I've always enjoyed talking to him, even though it was only for short periods.

As an opponent, playing against him, that's where I had the most contact with him. He was a very tough opponent and he had all the attributes that you'd be looking for: endurance, speed, strength, skills, mental toughness and all those sort of things. I played on him a couple of times when he was up in the forward line and I had to pick him up; he was pretty tough to play on. Obviously, we also saw him running around the mid-field a fair bit, creating havoc.

One of the biggest hits I saw in footy was Ricciuto bumping Dean Kemp, when he was chasing a bloke. It was just a massive hit, a fair hit, but a player like Ricciuto weighing in at 90 kilos plus hitting Dean Kemp at about 80, it took the wind out of his sails. He's obviously a very talented player.

In relation to his leadership, again it's hard to judge when I've only really seen him on the field. But he certainly had a presence and I always felt he showed very good leadership on the field. He seemed to be able to lead by his performance; when Adelaide needed someone to stand up, he always came through and played well. He also seemed to have good influence with his voice out on the field. As I said, I don't know much about him behind the scenes and off-field, so it's hard to comment on that.

MARK'S 'PICK OF THE CROWS'

In its sixteen-year history the Adelaide Football Club has bred many class players – players who would have fitted into most top sides in any era of the game. Mark Ricciuto has played alongside most of them in his time at AFL level and when asked to select his best ever Crows side, he had to think long and hard. It was a task that proved much more difficult than he'd first imagined.

In order to fit his best 25 players into one 'super team', some would need to be selected out of position, which is essentially what happens at State of Origin level. He made several amendments along the way, and still isn't certain of his selections. Being a selector is never an easy job, and nominating one team from a talent pool of this size was never going to be a walk in the park.

Mark's 'Pick of the Crows' is as follows:

Forward pocket: Tony McGuinness
Tony McGuinness had a fantastic record at Footscray before coming home to become the Crows' inaugural vice captain. There have been few more skilled players to pull on the red, blue and

yellow, and even fewer who could boast McGuinness's work rate. His leadership at the club was vital during the early years, with much of this stemming from his time playing for the Bulldogs.

McGuinness's dedication to training was outstanding, and he demanded the same from all those around him. Mark really appreciated his honest, forthright approach and rates him as one of the club's truly great leaders. The fact that he also ran a high-pressure business like Rowe and Jarman while playing AFL football speaks volumes for his dedication and work ethic.

Full forward: Tony Modra

Tony Modra was always a freakishly talented footballer, from the time Mark first watched him play in the Riverland competition to his last game at Fremantle. He quickly became a cult figure at the Crows, and Mark will be surprised if any other player achieves the sort of god-like status Modra did with Adelaide fans. When he was on fire, it was like The Beatles were in town. The girls loved him; in fact, everyone associated with the Crows loved him, and he drew a lot of spectators to each game in the hope of seeing 'Mods' grab one of his trademark 'screamers'.

Despite the fact he hated the hard, physically punishing side of training and wasn't the most disciplined player away from football, Modra became one of the game's truly great full forwards. Mark enjoyed his casual nature, which enabled him to play uninhibited, spectacular football and also to cope with the adulation constantly heaped on him by adoring fans. He was the perfect full forward for any mid-fielder to kick to, as his lead was lightning-fast and he was superlative overhead. Mark considers Modra's sacking in 1999 as one of Adelaide Football Club's biggest ever blunders.

Forward pocket: Darren Jarman

Mark considers grabbing Darren Jarman back from Hawthorn to be one of the club's greatest coups. He was already a brilliant footballer before becoming a Crow and undoubtedly the most highly skilled ever on the Adelaide list. His efforts in the 1997 and 1998 Grand Finals were unbelievable, kicking big bags of goals to propel the Crows to victory.

Always tagged heavily by the opposition, Mark reckons Jarman had another gear to change into whenever the situation arose. Unlike his brother Andrew, Darren wasn't a talkative character, nor was he a natural leader, but he certainly led by the way he played. For a guy who was probably never super-fit, Darren Jarman often played the game at a level above most of those around him and regularly left both the opposition and his team-mates in awe.

Half forward flank: Andrew Jarman

Mark has never met two brothers who are so different in personality, yet played football with near identical skill. Andrew was an important leader at the Crows in the early years, both on the field and at training. His flamboyant and extraverted nature, his willingness to speak out, and his occasional outlandish behaviour were legendary during his time at Adelaide, but he was also noted for his lightning-fast hands and incredibly accurate disposal.

Like Tony Modra, Andrew Jarman brought a lot of people to the football each weekend – especially those who liked a bit of entertainment as well as a good match. He was just a great bloke to be around and a good friend when Mark was new to the city and to AFL football.

Centre half forward: Matthew Robran

Mark reckons Matty Robran was in the same mould as his father, and one of the most skilful players of his era. He could kick a mile with either foot and really stood up in big games, such as against St Kilda and North Melbourne in the 1997 and 1998 Grand Finals. Robran's height and agility made him one of the most versatile forwards Adelaide has ever produced, with the ability to help out in ruck if the need arose.

Like Darren Jarman, he was reclaimed from Hawthorn, where he learned a lot about playing at the top level. Serious injury, most notably a leg fracture, robbed Matty of playing more games, but he remains the Crows' stand-out centre half forward.

Half forward flank: Brett Burton

The 'Birdman' has been one of Mark's closest mates since he came to the Crows from Woodville-West Torrens. The pair shared a house for some time. Burton's freakish ability to take spectacular marks, and his apparently endless stamina and endurance, combine to make him one of the most damaging forwards the club has bred.

Because his body has never been as durable as many of his team-mates', he has had to limit training in some areas, but he still blitzes the squad in time trials and can run at high speed for longer than anyone Mark has ever known. Mark considers Burton to be the Crows' 'X Factor', with the ability to turn a game in the blink of an eye with a couple of huge grabs and subsequent goals. Like Tony Modra, he drags spectators through the turnstiles with his spectacular playing style.

Wing: Tyson Edwards

With 250-odd games now under his belt, Mark feels that Edwards is one of the most versatile players Adelaide has ever had. Despite being a tad under 180 centimetres, he can play in many positions, from half back to centre to ruck roving and even up forward, and rarely loses out in a one-on-one situation. His skills on both sides of the body are silky smooth and he's just about as cool under pressure as anyone in the competition.

Mark is sure that Edwards was underrated outside of Adelaide by opposition coaches for a long time, but that's definitely no longer the case.

Centre: Simon Goodwin

Mark and 'Goody' are best mates and business partners away from football, but his selection here has nothing to do with his constantly asking Mark to be included. Goodwin began his career with South Adelaide, but when he arrived at the Crows, he made an immediate impact and became a top-line player. A serious quad' muscle injury robbed him of much of his first season in the AFL, but he certainly made up for that by playing as a youngster in both the 1997 and 1998 Premierships.

With three Club Champion jackets and four All-Australian selections already under his belt, Goodwin is one of the Crows' elite. Like several others in this bracket, injury has seriously interfered with his football career, but he is the obvious choice to play in the game's most pivotal position. Mark considers 'Goody' to be his perfect deputy when it comes to leading the club, as he communicates well with team-mates and is more professional in his attitude and preparation than anyone at West Lakes. In fact, there are few people Mark feels would make a better role model than Simon Goodwin.

Wing: Kane Johnson

Recruited from Victoria as a youngster, Kane Johnson was a member of the back-to-back Premiership sides and made an immediate impact with his quality possession style of football. Despite his body not coping all that well with heavy training and being prone to soft tissue injuries, Johnson was always hard at the football and showed enormous courage throughout his time in Adelaide. He probably pushed himself too hard too early in his career, which impacted on his body and caused him to miss more games through injury than he would have liked. He hated losing as much as anyone Mark has seen.

Johnson was never going to call Adelaide home, and Mark feels that returning to Melbourne and being appointed captain of Richmond must have been like a dream come true for him. His football has risen to a new level since returning home, and it's certainly not his fault the Tigers haven't been able to put more wins on the board. Mark often wonders how he's feeling, playing for a side that's unlikely to contest finals football in the foreseeable future. Losing Johnson was as much a blow to the Crows as it was a boost for Richmond.

Half back flank (and captain): Chris McDermott
'Bone' was another established player who took young Mark under his wing when he first moved down from Waikerie. Always the consummate captain and football professional, he taught Mark a lot about leadership and total dedication to the cause. As was the case with Tony McGuinness, McDermott did an amazing amount of work in the Crows' formative years – work that essentially stood the club in good stead for the future.

Chris McDermott was one of those tough-as-nails footballers who was always at the bottom of the pack and won more than his share of the hard ball. He commanded respect from all those around him, and Mark still uses a lot of what McDermott taught him in his current leadership role.

Centre half back: Peter Caven
A good bloke both on and off the field, Peter Caven fitted into the Adelaide lineup perfectly after coming across from Sydney. His

work ethic was second to none and, having already played a lot of top-line football for Fitzroy and the Swans, Mark considers he was one of the Crows' best ever pick-ups. His efforts in the 1997 and 1998 Premiership games were superb.

Caven's arrival allowed Malcolm Blight to use Nigel Smart in several different roles and essentially strengthened up a backline that was already one of the best in the competition. His penetrating left foot kick and strong overhead game certainly set up many Crows' attacks from half back, and Caven was sorely missed when he eventually hung up the boots.

Half back flank: Nigel Smart

One of the club's most revered players, Nigel won multiple All-Australian selections. Because of a lack of bigger, bulkier defenders at the Crows for much of his career, he was often forced to play in key positions against players like Tony Lockett and Saverio Rocca, who were much taller and heavier. Mark reckons he got by with courage, skill and dogged determination, and he won consistent accolades from the media, even in Victoria.

Smart loved to run with the football, then kick long into the forward lines, which he did whenever the opportunity arose. Always a thinker, he had strategies planned for different opponents, most of which proved spot-on and definitely assisted in the Premiership years of 1997 and 1998. It was probably Nigel's versatility that made him one of the Crows' most valuable players of all time.

Back pocket: Ben Hart

The first Crow to play 300 games, Ben Hart came to the club as a teenager and quickly established himself as a skilful and reliable defender. He was thrown around in different positions at times, but played his best football at half back or in the back pocket. Dual Club Champion and three times All-Australian, Benny's consistency was his strongest suit, as well as the ability to match up well on both small and taller forwards. Weighing in at just over 80 kilograms, he was often asked to take on opponents who were more than 20 kilograms heavier.

Rarely beaten for a contested mark or when the ball was on the ground, he was close to the ultimate competitor and did great jobs on some legendary opposition players. It was a pity that persistent hamstring and Achilles injuries prevented Hart from playing out his career on his own terms. Mark feels that he will make a great backline coach some time in the future.

Full back: Ben Rutten

Although he has only played four seasons at top level, Mark considers 'Truck' to be one of the most exciting players unearthed by the Crows in many years. Despite his relative youth, he has already achieved All-Australian selection and is one of the strongest footballers Mark has ever come across. He has taken on some of the game's biggest name full forwards and beaten them consistently, and Mark looks forward to watching his future development. Ben Rutten is definitely a potential club captain.

Back pocket: Mark Bickley

What 'Bicks' lacked in skills, he more than made up for with pure courage. In fact, Mark considers Bickley to be the most courageous footballer he has ever met. Putting his body on the line was what Bickley's game was all about, and he commanded absolute respect from all around him. Mark recalls him copping a knee in the head prior to half time in one match and requiring more than 30 stitches to close the cut. He played the following week, despite serious concern from the club doctor.

He was the natural choice for club captain when Chris McDermott departed, and held up the Premiership Cup on the MCG in September 1997 and 1998 with absolute pride and elation. In Mark's opinion, Bickley is the ultimate role model for any aspiring youngster, both on and off the field.

Ruckman: Shaun Rehn

Despite three knee reconstructions during his career, Mark rates Shaun Rehn as the best big man ever to play for Adelaide. Always a super-determined competitor with an angry on-field attitude, Rehn took on and beat most of the game's premier ruckmen. He was instrumental in the club's dual Premiership years, particularly in his role of dropping back across half back to repel opposition attacks. This made life a lot easier for mid-fielders to run and receive to set up forward thrusts.

Mark really enjoyed ruck roving under Rehn, as he won a lot more aerial contests than he lost and was a terrific tap ruckman. Mark, along with most at the Adelaide Football Club, was very disappointed that Rehn finished his career with Hawthorn.

Ruck rover: Mark Ricciuto

Modesty naturally prevents Mark from expanding on his selection in the Crows' best 25. Suffice to say a Brownlow Medal, multiple Club Champion awards and All-Australian captaincy dictate that he's an automatic inclusion. However, Mark says you should feel free to fill in this section yourself!

Rover: Andrew McLeod

Few, if any, players to have worn the Crows' guernsey can match it for skill and pace with 'Bungee'. His career credits include dual Club Champion awards, dual Norm Smith Medals, four All-Australian selections and a list of media awards too long to contemplate. Mark still scratches his head at some of the things McLeod does on the playing arena and concedes he's probably the best footballer of the modern era not to have won a Brownlow Medal.

Interchange: David Pittman

Although he usually played second fiddle to Shaun Rehn, Mark considers 'Pitto' to have been a great ruckman in his own right. Whenever he came off the interchange bench to replace Rehn, he would run out like a big lion from a cage and regularly crash into the opposition ruckman at full pace. Another string to David's bow was his ability to play in a key position if required, and Malcolm Blight used this to the team's advantage on several occasions.

Interchange: Graham Johncock

Mark considers 'Stiffy' to be very similar to Andrew McLeod in his skill level, with pace and the ability to side-step opponents very important. Johncock has fitted nicely into the back pocket in recent times, beating several highly credentialled forwards and setting up many Adelaide attacks from defence.

With a higher level of fitness and endurance, Mark feels Johncock could elevate his game to another level and follow closely in McLeod's footsteps to be one of the best at the club. He needs to expand his 'engine', so that he can move into the mid-field and realise his true potential.

Interchange: Nathan Bassett

Mark regards Nathan Bassett as the real lieutenant of the Crows' backline, especially since the departure of Ben Hart. He's never frightened to speak up when things need to be said, and invariably leads by example out on the field. His fearless approach to the game has often seen the wind knocked out of him while backing into a pack. Any young player looking for a courageous role model need look no further.

Appendix 2

Interchange: Tyson Stenglein

As was the case with Kane Johnson, the Crows knew they wouldn't be able to hang on to 'Stinger' forever, but they managed to get a hundred quality games from him before he returned to Perth. His courage always amazed Mark, and he quickly became the Crows' most effective tagger. Now having Stenglein playing for the West Coast Eagles and the tagging roles reversed makes life difficult whenever the Crows play against them.

Mark wouldn't be at all surprised to see him captain the West Coast in the not-too-distant future.

Emergency: Rod Jameson

Mark classes Rod Jameson as a highly skilled player who showed versatility by playing good football in both attack and defence. He won the Crows' goal kicking one season, then found himself at the opposite end of the ground trading blows with Scott Cummings the next. Jameson was a terrific team man, who always gave his all for the Adelaide Football Club. Versatility and great skills on either side of the body were 'Jammo's' strong suits.

Emergency: Matthew Liptak

Playing AFL football and studying medicine full time is a juggling act Matthew Liptak managed for most of his career, and Mark wonders when he ever found time to sleep. His work ethic at training and on match days was unbelievable and it's little wonder he won a Club Champion blazer during a stellar career. It was Liptak's blistering pace and ability to rack up possessions that really set him apart at the peak of his playing days.

Emergency: Simon Tregenza

'Trigger' took Mark under his wing to some degree when he arrived at the club as a youngster, and the two became great mates. Already a top performer at SANFL level before joining the Crows, his efforts from the wing regularly created strong attacking moves. Tregenza was incredibly quick, but he wasn't the best kick in the business, which let his game down at times. However, through sheer weight of possessions his contribution was enormous in the club's early years.

'Trigger's' consistency was one of his strong suits, but recurring hamstring problems throughout his whole career made life difficult and ultimately forced him out of the game before his time.

Coach: Malcolm Blight

Mark couldn't go past Malcolm Blight for taking the Crows to back-to-back flags in 1997 and 1998. No one had a greater impact on all Adelaide Football Club personnel than Blight. He taught the game like few others before him and, although he was tough on his squad, he also enjoyed a laugh and a beer with them. More significantly than anything else, Blight allowed Mark and his team-mates to play with flair, and the club certainly reaped the benefits.

THE CREAM OF THE OPPOSITION

When you have played at the top level for fifteen years, chances are you've come up against most of modern football's truly elite players. Although many would argue that the 1980s was the 'golden decade' of VFL/AFL, producing some of the game's biggest-ever names and greatest matches, there were plenty in the 1990s who also attained 'legend' status and a few more in the new millennium.

As with his best ever Crows team, Mark has had to select several topnotch opposition players in positions they may not necessarily have played on a regular basis. It's simply a case of too much talent and not enough spots on the footy field! There are few coaches, past or present, who wouldn't give their right arm to be in charge of this team.

Forward pocket: Jason Dunstall
An absolutely freakish forward with one of the most imposing records in the competition, he kicked 1254 goals in 269 games when Hawthorn was at its greatest. Not only was Dunstall very

strong overhead, he was lightning fast on the lead and an extremely accurate kick.

Full forward: Tony Lockett
'Plugger' was one of Mark's undisputed heroes when he started with St Kilda. He loved his physical game, and particularly the way he could intimidate opposition defenders. Mark remembers tackling Tony quite early in his career and feeling pretty good to have got him to the ground. He then ran off before Lockett could work out who had brought him down!

As the VFL/AFL all-time record goal kicker, Tony Lockett was the obvious choice to play in the key forward position. Mark feels it's unfortunate that big, classic full forwards like Lockett have disappeared from the game, as it was players like this who really drew people to the footy.

Forward pocket: Jason Akermanis
Pretty much the 'human headline' these days, Mark says that 'Aker' is lucky that his on-field performances back up most of what comes from his mouth. Although he has become one of the most heavily tagged players in the game, his skill level, enormous work rate and ability to kick freakish goals have elevated him to the football elite. There are few players whose skills on either side of the body have ever been as good. (Mark hopes 'Aker' doesn't read this, because he feels his ego doesn't need the boost.)

Half forward flank: Gary Ablett
Mark always admired Ablett's unique combination of skill and toughness. He could take spectacular overhead marks, kick with uncanny accuracy, and put you on your back if you gave him half a chance. Ablett was also very strong and hard to match up

on, which often presented problems for the Crows, especially at Geelong's Kardinia Park.

Centre half forward: Wayne Carey
Mark can't recall another player who beat the Crows virtually on his own as regularly as 'Duck'. For a guy his size, Carey's work rate and stamina level were amazing. He was fast, intimidating and one of the strongest overhead pack marks in the game. Carey played with a calculated arrogance, which often upset opposition supporters and caused a few defenders to think twice about taking him on. He is Mark's choice as the best centre half forward ever to play the game and maybe the number one player of all time.

Half forward flank: James Hird
Tough, courageous, skilled and totally dedicated, is how Mark describes Essendon's James Hird. Although restricted severely by injury over much of his career, Hird has the ability to play just about any position. Scrupulously fair, but prepared to dish out a solid hip and shoulder when it's warranted, he really is a coach's dream come true. Few players, if any, push themselves as hard as James Hird. His work ethic is undoubtedly second to none.

Centre wing: Craig Bradley
His longevity in the game was truly remarkable. Few other players have been able to maintain such a high standard throughout their entire career, due mainly to an incredible fitness level. Mark had the pleasure of playing alongside Bradley in several State of Origin games for South Australia, but by far the most memorable occasion was when Bradley absolutely tore the Crows to pieces in the 1993 Second Semi-final while playing for Carlton. He was unstoppable that day and effectively ended Adelaide's finals campaign off his own boot.

Centre: Greg Williams

Although his stature and physique may have seen him overlooked in today's draft camps, Greg Williams is one of the best players Mark has ever seen. Mark compares him with Andrew Jarman, who may not have been the fittest or fastest player in the team, but was so accurate by hand or foot and found the ball so often, his contributions were invaluable.

No one wins two Brownlow Medals and comes close to winning a third unless they are an exceptional footballer, and Williams was certainly that.

Centre wing: Peter Matera

Mark never really liked Matera, but he admired him for his lightning pace and silky skills. Mark was reported, and subsequently suspended for one match, after trying to knock Matera out in a Crows/Eagles match in 1995. A five-time All-Australian and a member of the West Coast Eagles' 1992 and 1994 Premiership teams, he was definitely one of the finest footballers ever to come out of Western Australia. Matera loved to carry the ball and was almost impossible to catch when screaming into the forward line at Subiaco at top pace.

Half back flank: Nathan Buckley

Although he started in the AFL a bit later than most, 'Bucks' established himself as a class player before moving to Collingwood from Brisbane. He has been one of the longest-serving Collingwood captains, six times Best and Fairest winner, and certainly one of the club's most skilful players. Mark considers him one of the best kicks he has ever seen and, despite copping heavy tags most games, he still manages to get plenty of the ball. The two have had many enthralling head-to-head tussles.

Centre half back: Glen Jackovich

A four-time Best and Fairest winner with West Coast during that club's 'golden era' in the early 1990s, Jakovich was always like a rock in defence. He was an intimidating guy to play against, as he liked the game tough and was always happy to inflict some pain if the opportunity presented itself. Mark regards Jakovich as one of modern football's toughest men. His duels with Wayne Carey when both were at the peak of their careers were memorable.

Half back flank: Michael Voss

Mark played on Voss as his direct opponent many times. Built similarly to Mark, he became a real general at Brisbane and was one of the reasons the Lions were so successful over a long period. Three times Premiership Captain, 1996 Brownlow Medallist and five-time All-Australian, there have been few more decorated players in the modern era than Voss. Mark also considers Voss to be one of the nicest guys he has played against.

Back pocket: Gavin Wanganeen

Mark considers true versatility to be Gavin Wanganeen's strongest point. He could play virtually anywhere, but became an absolute back pocket specialist for both Essendon and Port Adelaide. He was very difficult to match up on, as he was lightning fast and had the uncanny ability to extricate himself from tackles like no one Mark has ever played on. Courage was another of Wanganeen's strong points and he would always back into a pack, regardless of the consequences.

Fullback: Stephen Silvagni

'SOS' was the ultimate fullback who played for Carlton through the era of big, tough full forwards such as Lockett and Dunstall.

He had the ability to play an attacking style of game from the last line of defence and could take a big overhead mark when required. Like his father, Stephen quickly became a legend at Carlton and is considered by some as the best fullback of all time.

Back pocket: Paul Roos

Roos's career was winding down as Mark's was taking off, but he was impossible to leave out of this team. He played 356 games over a distinguished career for Fitzroy and Sydney, picking up four All-Australian jumpers along the way. They played against each other a few times, and Mark recalls Roos taking some fantastic overhead grabs and clearing from defence with his trademark long drop punt. Since retiring, he has gone on to become a top-line AFL coach.

Ruckman: Paul Salmon

A huge man, 'Fish' was one of the most daunting opponents Mark can ever remember. Apart from being a first-class knock ruckman, Salmon could also kick goals and there are few modern big men who can boast a career tally of over 500. When he went forward, Salmon was always difficult to match up because of his height and strong overhead marking capability.

Follower: Robert Harvey

Mark has played on Harvey many times and considers him a 'running machine'. Despite undergoing a knee reconstruction and suffering a lot of debilitating injuries, he has played for an incredible twenty years at the highest level, which puts him in truly elite company. Harvey's greatest weapon on the football field is his incredible endurance, which he relied on constantly to run opposition taggers ragged. Mark finds it hard to believe he is still playing high-possession football for St Kilda at age 35 and rates him as one of the all-time greats.

Rover: Chris Judd

Mark considers Judd as the best mid-fielder he has ever seen. Despite copping heavier tagging pressure than any footballer in the competition, he still manages to rack up consistent best-on-ground performances. His speed and agility through heavy traffic set him apart from the rest, and Mark feels his 2004 Brownlow Medal win could be the first of several. No one carries the ball as far or as well as Judd, which is why Mark selected him as a 'tallish' rover in this team.

Interchange: Stephen Kernahan

One of the best leaders Mark has ever come across, Kernahan became an instant superstar after crossing from Glenelg to Carlton. Mark considers himself fortunate to have played State of Origin football with Kernahan, who was one of his idols as a young lad in the Riverland. Kernahan captained Carlton for a record 226 games, was a five-time All-Australian, and kicked over 1000 goals for Carlton and Glenelg. He was also captain of Carlton's Team of the Century.

Interchange: Adam Goodes

One of the best players of the new millennium and a significant part of Sydney's rise to the top, Adam shared the 2003 Brownlow Medal with Nathan Buckley and Mark. He is incredibly fast and agile for his height, which makes him very difficult to match up. One of Mark's most vivid memories from the 2006 Grand Final was Goodes playing on Chris Judd – a contest between two stars of the game that was worth travelling to Melbourne to see.

Interchange: Paul Kelly

Mark considers Kelly to be one of his most difficult direct opponents ever. Despite a wiry frame, he was tough, hard and very fast.

In fact, Kelly is the only opponent Mark felt he simply couldn't keep up with. One day at the SCG, Kelly ran him absolutely ragged, kicking four goals in a half from the half forward flank. Mark had to look for someone else to take over. Injuries interfered with Kelly's career towards the end, but he was still one of the Swans' greatest.

Interchange: Scott West
With 300-plus games under his belt and an incredible seven Best and Fairest awards with the Bulldogs, West is a truly great player and one of Mark's most testing opponents, despite playing in a team that has struggled for many years. Mark rates him as one of the best at stoppages in the current era, setting up countless clearances with lightning-fast handballs. The two played International Rules together. Mark says West is a great bloke, as well as a terrific footballer.

Emergency: Ben Cousins
Mark considers Cousins unlucky not to make the starting 22 in this team after winning four Best and Fairest awards at West Coast, six All-Australian jumpers and the 2005 Brownlow Medal. Like team-mate Chris Judd, Cousins has an enormous 'engine' and is capable of running taggers off their feet while they try to shut him out of the game. He is one of the reasons the West Coast Eagles have re-established themselves as an AFL powerhouse.

Emergency: John Platten
Although the 'Rat' was winding down as Mark was gearing up, their paths crossed a few times as opponents and they also played State of Origin together for South Australia. One of an elite group to have won both a Brownlow and a Magarey Medal, Platten became an idol of Hawthorn supporters. His skills were silky smooth and his work rate was second to none.

Emergency: Anthony Koutoufides

At his best, 'Kouta' was a sensational footballer who could change the course of a game with his size and strength. Built like a Greek god, with a six-foot-three frame, he could play anywhere. Unfortunately, Koutoufides copped more than his fair share of injuries, which essentially prevented him from achieving true superstar status. Mark recalls him dominating in a couple of games for Carlton against the Crows, who always found him difficult to match up on.

Coach: Leigh Matthews

Mark found it difficult to go past 'Lethal' after three consecutive Premierships with Brisbane and one earlier with Collingwood. Matthews coached Mark in a series of International Rules matches against the Irish and, like all good coaches, hated losing with a passion. Transforming the Brisbane Lions from an ordinary outfit to one of the truly powerful clubs of the modern era was undoubtedly Matthews' greatest achievement.

Mark Ricciuto's Career Achievements

D.O.B.: 8/6/75
Club: Adelaide Football Club
Position: Midfield, Utility
Debut: 1993
Games: 309 (current as of 1 Aug 2007)
Goals: 289 (current as of 1 Aug 2007)
Honours:
Australian Football League Life Member
Adelaide Football Club Life Member
Member of Adelaide Football Club Team of the Decade 1991–2001
Adelaide Football Club Player of the Decade 1991–2001
AFL Premiership Side 1998
Wizard Home Loans Cup Premiership Side 2003
Adelaide Football Club Captain 2001–2007
Adelaide Football Club Vice-Captain 1997–2000
AFLPA Best Captain 2005, 2006
Adelaide Football Club Best and Fairest 1998, 2003, 2004
Adelaide Football Club 3rd Best and Fairest 1994, 1997, 2000
Best Team Man 1994, 2003
All-Australian 1994, 1997, 1998, 2000, 2002, 2003, 2004, 2005
All-Australian Captain 2004, 2005

International Series 1998, 2000

Brownlow Medal Winner 2003

Brownlow Medal 2nd 2004

Brownlow Medal equal 4th 1997

Brownlow Medal 5th 1998

Career Brownlow Votes (144, equal 13th overall in the most votes won)

Second Youngest Player to reach 300 Games – 31 years and 43 days old, R16, 2006

Quickest Player to reach 300 AFL Premiership Games – 13 years and 83 days

Adelaide Football Club Rising Star Nominee 1993

Adelaide Football Club Leading Goal Kicker 2006 (44 goals)

VFL/AFL Italian Team Of The Century – Captain 2007

ACKNOWLEDGMENTS

I am lucky enough to have a really tight, close-knit family. We have always worked hard for what we have got. We respect each other greatly, and share a love for spending time with family and friends and we do this as often as possible. What I have achieved would never have been possible without your support. Special thanks to Dad, Mum, Lisa, Craig and families.

And, Sarah, it took me a while to realise how good a catch you are but, luckily for me, I finally woke up. Since becoming engaged to you and having Sophie, I have never been happier. Thank you for everything.

To Max Stevens, Justin Reid and everyone at Elite Sports Properties, thank you for your advice and management. To my personal sponsors, Foster's Group, Channel Seven, Nike and Austereo, thank you for the opportunity to work with you.

Sincere thanks to the Waikerie Football Club and all the players, coaches and staff I was involved with, from Under 10s in 1981 through to the A Grade in 1991. I could not have wished for a better football club to play for in my early years. Maintaining the connection with Waikerie has been very important to me. I am also extremely grateful for the support I have received from the entire Riverland.

To the West Adelaide Football Club, thank you for not only giving me my start in league football, but also for allowing me the flexibility of living in Waikerie and travelling to train and play. Special thanks to Neil Kerley and Doug Thomas.

And the Adelaide Football Club, where I have spent over half of my life – thank you to all the players, both past and present. It has been a privilege to play with you all.

To all the coaches and assistant coaches, thank you for everything you have taught me along the way.

To Bill Sanders, Steven Trigg and all the board members, thanks for running the club in such a professional manner.

To all the doctors, physios, chiros and trainers, I couldn't have played this many games without your help.

And to all the other staff who have worked at the Adelaide Football Club throughout my career, thanks for your efforts.

A big thank you to all the club sponsors, headed by the AFL's longest serving major sponsor, Toyota. Your support has been invaluable.

Also, I would like to thank the members and supporters from all over Australia. No matter where we play, you are there in numbers. Your dedication is inspiring.

And, finally, I'd like to thank Shane Mensforth for putting together a sensational book.

Mark Ricciuto, July 2007